Early Childhood Education

In an accessible and meaningful way, *Early Childhood Education* examines foundational topics that encourage early childhood education students to think, reflect, and develop opinions, theories, and philosophies about their field. This interactive book invites the reader to develop a personal philosophy of early childhood education and an identity as an early educator, in order to build a sufficient foundation for continual growth as a teacher.

Divided into three sections that deal with the past, present, and future, *Early Childhood Education* asks the reader to think about important ideas underlying and encompassing today's early childhood education. First providing historical and philosophical perspectives of the field, authors Krogh and Slentz then look at careers in early education and what it's like to be a teacher or caregiver today, compare and contrast contemporary models of early childhood education, and examine cultural and individual differences that confront and challenge teachers. Finally, the book looks to the future of the field and discusses debates of current issues. This newly updated edition includes the most contemporary issues in the field since the first edition and integrates further discussion of diversity and children with special needs throughout the entire book.

Special Features:

- End of chapter questions invite readers to develop an ongoing philosophy of teaching and learning.
- "Extending Your Learning" activities provide opportunities for further discussion and debate.
- Glossary and Internet Resources offer important tools for the early childhood education student.

Suzanne L. Krogh is Professor of Elementary and Early Childhood Education at Western Washington University.

Kristine L. Slentz is Professor of Special Education at Western Washington University.

WITHDRAWN

Early Childhood Education

Yesterday, Today, and Tomorrow

Second Edition

SUZANNE L. KROGH
AND
KRISTINE L. SLENTZ

 Routledge
Taylor & Francis Group

NEW YORK AND LONDON

KH

First edition published 2001
by Lawrence Erlbaum Associates, Inc.

This edition first published 2011
by Routledge
270 Madison Avenue, New York, NY 10016

Simultaneously published in the UK
by Routledge
2 Park Square, Milton Park, Abingdon, Oxon OX14 4RN

Routledge is an imprint of the Taylor & Francis Group, an informa business

© 2001 Lawrence Erlbaum Associates, Inc.
© 2011 Taylor & Francis

The right of Suzanne L. Krogh and Kristine L. Slentz to be identified as authors of this work has been asserted by them in accordance with sections 77 and 78 of the Copyright, Designs and Patents Act 1988.

Typeset in Sabon and Neue Helvetica by Book Now Ltd, London
Printed and bound in the United States of America on acid-free paper by Edwards Brothers, Inc.

Trademark Notice: Product or corporate names may be trademarks or registered trademarks, and are used only for identification and explanation without intent to infringe.

Library of Congress Cataloging-in-Publication Data
Krogh, Suzanne.
Early childhood education : yesterday, today, and tomorrow / Suzanne L. Krogh and Kristine L. Slentz.
—2nd ed.
    p. cm.
1. Early childhood education—Curricula—United States. 2. Curriculum planning—United States.
I. Slentz, Kristine. II. Title.
LB1139.4.K736 2011
372.210973—dc22   2010029513

ISBN13: 978–0–415–87826–5 (hbk)
ISBN13: 978–0–415–87825–8 (pbk)
ISBN13: 978–0–203–84201–0 (ebk)

3/23/11

Contents

Preface

The book you are about to begin asks you to think about the important ideas underlying and encompassing today's early childhood education. It contains chapters on topics that are typically and traditionally regarded as foundational to other, later learning. Foundational topics ask us to think, reflect, and develop opinions, theories, and philosophies. Rarely do they directly answer that basic question of survival, "What will I do Monday morning?!"

Topics that cause us to reflect, however, have a long-term utility that supports us far beyond next Monday. They help us understand why we think the way we do about our methods of teaching, the materials we select, and our expectations for children. So, when we have run out of activities in all our practical activity books, we aren't left high and dry wondering what to do next. Because we have developed a solid philosophy and understand *why* we do what we do, we can begin to create plans that support children's growth in all the best ways. And, when we explore more of those activity books, we know how to choose the very best experiences.

Divided into three sections that deal sequentially with the past, present, and future, this book offers sections at the end of each chapter to guide you into the kind of thinking that will get you beyond next Monday. For example, starting in Chapter One and continuing to the end of the book, there are two alternate ways to develop your personal philosophy over time, and your identity as an early educator (see 🖊 and 🔍 under "Extending Your Learning"). In addition, there are opportunities provided for discussion and debate at the end of each chapter, culminating in an entire chapter (Chapter Five) devoted to such activities. Other features of note include a glossary and helpful internet sites for each chapter.

One important goal in publishing a second edition of this text was to update the information in each chapter in order to provide readers with the most contemporary preparation possible. It was also our intention to integrate substantive content related to diversity and children with special needs. Toward this end we have used "People First" language throughout the book. "People First" language means writing and/or speaking in a way that describes children using people (boy, girl, child, children) words first, and then identifies problems or delays. For example, we write "Children with special needs …" rather than "Special needs children …" and "The boy with Down Syndrome" rather than "The Downs boy …". People First language acknowledges that children with special needs are first children, with disabilities or developmental delays that are not their most important characteristics. In Chapter One we may quote historical figures using their own words, but for the most part we use People First language, and encourage you to do the same. It may seem awkward at first, but after becoming accustomed to People First terminology you will notice a harshness and insensitivity to other ways of speaking and writing.

In Chapter One we meet the most influential leaders in the history of early childhood education. Although each was the product of his or her nationality, culture, and time period, the influence of their work and lives is still felt today in many of our classrooms and centers. This chapter shows clearly that the opinions we sometimes take for granted as the best ones often have their roots in the thinking of someone who died decades, even centuries, ago. It is true, too, that conflicts between differing viewpoints are generally based on thinking that evolved many years ago. Readers who believe that the best learning is structured, well planned, and goal focused will be interested to read about John Locke, a 17th-century Englishman. Those who are more drawn to a hands-off approach, in which young children run free and unencumbered by teachers' demands, will find their philosophical forefather in the 18th-century Jean Jacques Rousseau. Some of the other important figures described in this chapter will, themselves, have been influenced by either Locke or Rousseau or, perhaps, both.

Chapter Two introduces an array of careers available to those who take coursework in early childhood education. It deals with such issues as remuneration (often not good), required training for different responsibilities, and good and bad reasons to choose careers in the field. Because early education is still in the midst of a longtime struggle for recognition as a true profession, Chapter Two also discusses this issue. There is a national need for teachers and caregivers who regard what they do with full respect—and expect others to do the same. Professional teaching standards as delineated by the foremost professional organizations are discussed in full. The chapter ends with an invitation to the reader to begin thinking philosophically, and the primary theories of early education are introduced.

Applying theoretical perspectives in actual early education sites is the subject of Chapter Three. Several schools and centers are described in some detail, and their links to theory and philosophy are explained. The reader should begin to see that successful teaching requires a foundation of thought rather than a simplistic presentation of apparently appealing activities. Each school or center is different in some ways from all the others, but each one also is committed to excellent experiences for children and was chosen for this book because of its success.

The United States has always been a nation of immigrants (even the pre-nation "native" Americans came from someplace else). In recent decades, however, the mix of nationalities and cultures providing new residents and citizens has become increasingly complex. With this new complexity has come the need to redefine what it means to be an American. In addition, the last half of the 20th century put into focus the inequality of education that had separated Blacks and Whites for centuries. Schools were forcibly desegregated, but inequalities remained. The second half of the century also brought a nationwide discussion of the best way to educate children with various disabilities. Experience and observation led many to believe that including these children in regular classrooms was the most advantageous for everyone. Laws were enacted to ensure just such a result. With momentous societal changes such as these, issues relating to the diversity of children, families, and professionals in early childhood education now provide one of the most important chapters in any foundational textbook. Chapter Four first discusses the changing face of America, and then provides opportunity for readers to reflect on what all the changes mean to them as teachers. Finally, we provide a historical context for several cultural groups found commonly in centers and schools today. For each group, suggestions for interacting with families are given. We struggled with the tension between providing historical information that many readers may find valuable, while at the same time avoiding stereotypes and acknowledging that there is great variability within every culture. We remind readers continually throughout the chapter of the latter point, and that these descriptions help beginning teachers to think about their client families' beliefs, values, and needs before interacting with them.

Armed with the information provided by Chapters One through Four, you should be ready to debate some of today's most complex issues, particularly as they pertain to the future practices in early childhood education settings. Several of these issues are described in Chapter Five, with documented arguments on opposing sides of each one. From the hard-to-face reality of this culture's violence, to the television that we love to hate, you should find some debates worth having. You might argue the issues with your family, your roommates, your classmates, and even (or especially) within yourself. In any case, spend some time thinking through the various viewpoints, and challenge yourself to see things the way others do; you might even find your own opinions altering a bit.

Because you are invited to develop your own philosophy of early education throughout this book, we hope that the ideas provided in it give you sufficient foundation to make some major progress toward doing so. Consider keeping your ongoing statement of philosophy, and plan to look back on it in a year and then again a few years after that. Doing so can be an important step away from stagnation and toward your continual growth as a teacher.

part one
Yesterday

The first section of this textbook is just one chapter long, but covers a long history of over 2,500 years related to the early childhood profession. In addition, we introduce a wide variety of educational philosophies that originated and have evolved across a two-century plus time span. The history of our profession provides the background for the remainder of the book, and you will see many of the concepts and philosophies reflected in subsequent chapters. This first chapter also asks you to consider which philosophies and which historical figures most appeal to you, as a first step in developing your own identity as an early educator. As you identify those ideas and people you are most drawn to, ask yourself what it is about each that appeals to you. Then, take your conclusions with you into the following chapters and build upon them to begin constructing a knowledge base and a metaphor for your own practice in early childhood education.

one
Perspectives on History and Theory

Always and everywhere children take an active role in the construction and acquisition of learning and understanding. ... So it is that in many situations, especially when one sets up challenges, children show us they know how to walk along the path to understanding.

Loris Malaguzzi (1920–1994)

Chapter Objectives

After reading this chapter, you should be able to:

- Identify significant leaders in early childhood education.
- Understand and apply the major ideas and contributions to early childhood education of history's most important figures.

As you think about and apply chapter content on your own, you should be able to:

- Begin to formulate your own philosophy of early childhood education, with awareness of the original sources of your thinking.
- Observe elements of historical influence in various early childhood settings.

When you look at a young child, what do you see? Surely your interest in pursuing a career in early childhood education means that you see beyond outward appearances: an open smile, an adorable outfit, a charmingly awkward pose. If you think of yourself as a teacher of this child, do you see a small being waiting eagerly for you to share the knowledge that you have gained over the years? Or do you see someone who will learn best if allowed to remain independent, with you as an occasional guide? Do you see this child as innately good but in danger of losing that goodness within a hostile environment? Or do you see a child born neutral, ready to soak up the social environment as a sponge might?

All these views, and many more, have been held by large groups of adults at different times in history, with many remaining today, in whole or in part. A primary purpose of this chapter is to help you better understand your own attitudes toward young children by seeking out the roots of these attitudes. To do this, we must look back at key figures in history because what and how we think today is part of an intellectual tradition that dates from antiquity.

Some Ancient History

The centuries of prehistory are, of course, unknown to us, but we can safely assume that the education of young children during this period was directly related to survival issues and was nearly always the responsibility of the same-sex parent. Teaching techniques were probably quite simple and direct. We can relate to this method, for example, when we take a child out for her first walk in the woods. Since there may be poisonous plants and dangerous areas to avoid, we depend on simple instructions rather than hands-on discovery learning. Thus, in survival situations, we still retain a close kinship to our ancient ancestors.

Once beyond the survival level of instruction, however, we can begin thinking about what else children might need or want to learn and how we might best teach them. To look at the oldest recorded thoughts on early education, we turn first to the ideas of the Greek philosopher Plato and then move on to the Romans and the early Christians. At this point, you may wonder why we appear to ignore philosophies from other parts of the world. Our reason, quite simply, is that the cultures we discuss are those that still influence the way we view and teach children here in the United States.

The Early Greeks

So, let us begin with Plato (427?–347 B.C.), who, in the fourth century B.C., could look at and respond to a fairly well-developed educational system and comment on the status of childhood itself. Although the Greek view of infants and young children varied from state to state, it is fair to say that young children were not generally cherished. Infanticide was a universal practice, particularly in regard to girls and infants with birth defects. At best, an unwanted infant might be "potted," that is, put in a pot or basket and left at a temple gate in hopes that someone who needed a servant might adopt it. As Lloyd deMause (1974) noted, "The further back in history one goes, the lower the level of child care, and the more likely children are to be killed, abandoned, beaten, terrorized, and sexually abused" (p. 1).

It was to the city-state of Athens that Plato wrote his philosophical views, at a time when its government was in some disarray. In the context of describing the ideal state, Plato suggested a design for early childhood education. From birth to age 6, learning should be informal, for "knowledge which is acquired under compulsion obtains no hold on the mind. So do not use compulsion, but let early education be a sort of amusement" (Gwynne-Thomas, 1981, p. 14). Good health and good social habits were to be inculcated by attentive parents who would provide plenty of close supervision; freedom was only to be earned over time.

For boys old enough to start school (at about age 6), Plato argued that the racier stories about the gods should be cleaned up and presented in a more ideal fashion to impressionable young minds. His enthusiasm for musical training also came with reservations, and he suggested that music be chosen that would promote the right attitudes, particularly toward the state.

It should be pointed out that Plato's ideas about education were tied to an ideal republic that could only function successfully with a large slave class. In fact, the word pedagogue is almost identical to the Greek word for slave–teacher: an educated person, enslaved by victors of a battle, assigned as a child's tutor and companion.

Aristotle (384–322 B.C.), like his teacher and mentor Plato, believed that early education was important. He argued that children have varying talents and skills, and that these should be enhanced. Thus he may be the first writer to recognize the educational importance of individual differences (Osborn, 1980).

The Early Romans

The inability of the Greek states to stop warring among themselves eventually led to their downfall, as Roman armies conquered them one by one. Once again, many educated Greeks found themselves in the role of teacher–slave, this time to the eager-to-learn Romans. Until their rise to power, Roman thought was considerably less sensitive, inventive, and curious than the Greeks'. Roman education was restricted to the basic necessities of life: fighting, farming, swimming, and riding, for example. There was little to read except for the rules of the state gathered in "The Laws of the Twelve Tables," published in 450 B.C. Greek influence changed all that.

Perhaps the best known and most influential Greco-Roman thinker was Quintilian (A.D. 35–97). Born in Spain but educated in Rome, Quintilian felt that in order to produce young adults of good character, education must begin at the age of 1. Responsible parents and tutors, as well as carefully chosen companions, were important because they set examples for impressionable youngsters. And examples were important in the development of character and speech patterns. According to Quintilian, what the child learned while young and still at home would have lifelong implications.

Quintilian recommended making lessons as interesting as possible. Encouragement should come from the use of praise and never from corporal punishment. Academics should be balanced with gymnastic training, Quintilian said, in order to promote health.

Rome's overexpansion eventually made it impossible for it to keep all its territories fortified and under control. As new groups of less educated outsiders began to conquer Roman territories, education began to decline, until much of the learning of the past centuries was all but lost.

The Early Christians

By the middle of the fifth century A.D., the Roman Empire had officially collapsed, and new struggles for control took place. Most notable was the Christian church's rise to power. Earlier this had worked in favor of young children, since the newborn was deemed the owner of a soul, and infanticide was considered murder and punishable. In 313, the emperor Constantine decreed Christianity the official religion of the Roman Empire, and Christian schools spread throughout much of Europe.

With the fall of the Roman Empire, the influence of the Christian church began to be increasingly anti-intellectual. Fewer and fewer lay people were educated, and the newly emerging monasteries became the principal repositories of knowledge. Even there, however, intellectual freedom was highly constrained. For example, one monk who tried to translate all of Plato and Aristotle from the Greek to Latin was sentenced to die for his "crime." Over the next five centuries, few children received an education: only those who planned to enter the monastery and those who belonged to wealthy families. As convents arose, girls were occasionally educated, particularly in what is now Germany.

The prevailing view of young children and their upbringing changed gradually from the Greek, Roman, and early Christian attitudes. As the concept of original sin took hold in religious thought, children came to be seen as inherently evil and subject to punishments that today we would define as child abuse. Furthermore, the concept of childhood itself changed. As soon as children had outgrown the most helpless stages of infancy, they joined in the general adult life, both for work and play.

It was for later generations to term these centuries (from the Fall of Rome to the rebirth of Greek and Roman ideas) the Middle or Dark Ages. The people who lived through this period knew little, if anything, about better times. But better times did come, and with them new interpretations of the ancient ideas that provide the foundation for today's views of early education.

The onset of the Renaissance (from the Latin meaning *rebirth*) was very good news for young children. During the Middle Ages physical and sexual abuse had been widespread, even condoned by some of the great philosophers and religious thinkers. The beginning of the Renaissance produced an increasing number of child instruction manuals, demonstrating a new view of children that could only be an improvement on that of the previous centuries. These manuals and other writings show a new understanding of children's needs and identities as being separate from those of adults.

To some extent, Greek and Roman views of child development and learning have been revisited and revised over the centuries, as we shall see. First, we shall delve into the biographies of, and the history surrounding, some especially influential men and women. Following that, the theories that have evolved based on their philosophies will be explained.

The Roots of Today's Views on Early Childhood Education

Whereas the Middle Ages gave us no educational leaders in the field of early childhood education, later centuries did. Like ancient Greek and Roman philosophers, influential thinkers wrote about their ideas so that today we can look back and evaluate them. The Moravian John Amos Comenius was the first to posit a complete system of education in the style of Plato.

John Comenius

John Amos Comenius (Jan Amos Komensky in the original Czech, 1592–1670) was a bishop in the persecuted Moravian church who spent most of his adult life in exile. Nevertheless, his educational ideas were widely received throughout Europe, his books were translated into more than a dozen languages, and he was invited by several European governments to reconstruct their educational systems. In succeeding centuries he was sometimes forgotten, and that is surely now the case. Yet if any thinker was responsible for pulling education, including early childhood education, out of the Middle Ages, it was Comenius. Below are some of the things he posited in his book *School of Infancy* (1633/1896), which dealt with children to age 6. Note how closely his ideas fit with our own. For example, a major issue in early education today is developmental appropriateness in children's learning. This concept comes directly from Comenius. He believed that younger children are best able to grasp knowledge that relates to their own lives and that learning must be concrete before it can be abstract.

Today the study of history typically begins with the here and now and, as children grow older, adds on previous centuries. It was Comenius who first observed that young children need help in simply understanding yesterday and tomorrow and that they need to do this before trying to comprehend last year and beyond. Geography is another of the social studies influenced by Comenius. He realized that just as children first understand time in terms of today, they first understand space in relation to what they can see around themselves and that geography should begin with the study of familiar places. Science study also begins with what is nearest and dearest to young children: nature, another idea that originated with Comenius. His views on arithmetic appear in today's textbooks and lesson plans, too. He suggested that young children should begin by learning such basic concepts as a *lot* or a *little*, and that rote counting is a different and much simpler skill than the understanding of numbers necessary for addition and subtraction. In this, as in so many other instances, Comenius was far ahead of his time. Perhaps that is one reason that at a practical level his educational ideas were not as widespread as his popularity might indicate. But it is his ideas that affected later educational thinkers, some of whom we discuss in this chapter.

John Locke

An English philosopher of the following century, John Locke (1632–1704) was brought up in a Puritan family, but his adult thinking was more influenced by the scientific revolution than by Reformation Protestant thinking. At Oxford he studied and later taught Greek, rhetoric, and moral philosophy. In his mid-30s Locke's more practical and scientific nature eventually led him back to the university to study medicine. He only practiced medicine a short while, but the balance between the scientific and the philosophical in Locke's thinking and learning is evident in his later writing on education. While working as the personal secretary to the earl of Shaftesbury and tutoring the earl's son, he began to formulate his views on education, which, along with his anti-authoritarian political ideas, were revolutionary for their time. A cousin and her husband asked Locke to write some letters giving advice on the upbringing of their son, and these were eventually published in book form as *Some Thoughts Concerning Education*. All Locke's philosophical and medical thinking, as well as his past experiences, went into these letters. So did his views on social class. His cousin's son was to be raised as a gentleman, and Locke differentiated the education of a future gentleman from that of a commoner's child. Thus, despite his increasing involvement in the politics of the Enlightenment, Locke did not propose the kind of universal education that Comenius had.

Nonetheless, Locke's ideas on early education represented new ways of looking at children and formed the basis for much of what we think and do today. His view of infants was that they are born with great potential for learning. Their minds, he said, might be viewed as white paper or an empty cabinet or a blank tablet. What they become as adults is then defined by their total education: "I think I may say that of all the men we meet with, nine parts of ten are what they are, good or evil, useful or not, by their education" (Locke, 1692/1964, p. 9).

Another idea that set Locke apart from the educational thinkers of his day was his belief that in educating children we need to be aware of individual differences: "There is a difference of degree in men's understandings, apprehensions, and reasonings to so great a latitude … that there is a greater distance between some men and others in this respect, than between some men and some beasts" (Cleverley & Phillips, 1986, p. 18).

This concept is in contrast to the prevailing idea that there was a general mass of knowledge out there to be learned, and everyone in a group or class should move along together in conquering it. For Locke, our minds might all begin as blank slates, but some slates are higher quality than others. In other words, Locke did not completely dismiss heredity and even said: "God has stamped certain characters upon men's minds, which, like their shapes, may perhaps be a little mended, but can hardly be totally altered and transformed into the contrary" (1692/1964, p. 43).

To keep children from getting too spoiled, as well as to promote rugged health, he suggested cold footbaths, open air, loose fitting clothing and not much of it, a simple diet, and a hard bed. He may be the first educational philosopher to discuss toilet training, and on this subject he maintained his stern view, recommending regular visits with enforced sitting. For Locke, "A sound mind in a sound body is a short, but full description of a happy state in the world" (1692/1964, p. 9).

FIGURE 1.1a John Locke

Locke and Rousseau proposed different views of early education based on different views of human learning. Locke saw children's minds as blank slates or empty buckets to be filled by the teachings of knowledgeable adults.

As will be seen in the upcoming sections on theory, much of Locke's thinking pervades early childhood education today, although the form it takes in practice may be much altered.

Jean Jacques Rousseau

Jean Jacques Rousseau (1712–1778), born in Switzerland not long after Locke died, combined philosophical and educational thought in his writings as Locke had done. Like Locke, he was an influential force for egalitarianism and democracy in his society, but the conclusions he reached were different enough from those of Locke to inspire a very different form of early education.

In some ways it is difficult to believe that someone of Rousseau's background could affect both politics and education in the intense ways that he did. His mother died while giving birth to him, and his father first spoiled and then deserted him. He was passed around among relatives and received little education, although by age 10 he had read countless novels. Apprenticed to an engraver, Rousseau tired of the cruel treatment he received and ran away. He began the life of a wanderer, trying various occupations (clerk, secretary, music copyist, even priest) and usually failing. At age 27 Rousseau was

FIGURE 1.1b Jean Jacques Rousseau

Rousseau, however, saw children's minds as naturally programmed to unfold in their own way and at their own pace if given a secure environment by nurturing adults.

hired as a tutor to two young boys. He lasted just about a year, failing miserably at disciplining them in any way. But by now the wanderer was in France, where he became involved in society and numerous love affairs, in particular with one woman from the lower class. She became his lifelong companion (he eventually married her when in his 60s) and bore Rousseau five children, all of whom he abandoned to a foundling home.

How, then, did Rousseau manage to influence his own and future generations in two major fields, politics and child development? As one author (Wodehouse, 1924) explained it almost a century ago, the enlightened gentlemen of the age of Locke were ready for new influences, something of a more "natural" condition and:

> about 1760, a few books connected with this subject struck the general imagination with extraordinary force. They came from a somewhat lower cosmopolitan level, being the work of a rather disreputable Swiss from Geneva, living in France, who happened to have genius.
>
> (p. 101)

In *Emile*, his major work on education published in 1762, Rousseau seemed to idealize the details of his own life in the fictional biography of a "perfectly" brought up and educated boy. Was Rousseau abandoned as a child, and did he abandon his own children? He could turn that into a positive experience for Emile, who would be given freedom to roam, play, and follow his spontaneous impulses. About this Rousseau wrote, "What is to be thought of that cruel education ... that burdens a child with all sorts of restrictions and begins by making him miserable, in order to prepare him for some far-off happiness which he may never enjoy?" (Weber, 1984, p. 27).

Rousseau argued that early childhood education should come from all the senses, and that reading should not be pushed. In fact, he felt that it would be better for a child not to read at all until about age 12. The teacher or tutor should not use direct instruction but should act as a guide, being aware of the child's interests and letting him follow those interests rather than prescribing a curriculum. Discipline should be primarily through the natural consequences of the child's actions. Much of the child's education should take place outdoors, and emphasis should be placed on healthful development. One of Rousseau's views of the child set him apart from the traditional religious thinkers: Where they saw infants as inherently evil, Rousseau saw them as basically good. "God makes all things good; man meddles with them and they become evil" (Weber, 1984, p. 27). Thus, the general approach in the education of young children was to tuck them safely away from the world in a protected environment where the only influences were those of good.

We should note that Rousseau's ideal education was reserved for children of the middle and upper classes. Like Locke, he believed that little education was needed for the lower classes. In Rousseau's case, this could be justified by his idea of naturalism, in which children are educated by their surroundings. The poor, he decided, could take care of what little education they needed right where they were.

Rousseau's ideas on education were complemented by his thoughts on politics. Much of what he wrote influenced anti-royalist thinkers and helped bring on the French Revolution, which he did not live to see. Occasionally, some progressive fathers of his century and the next actually tried Rousseau's ideas on their own little Emiles, often creating ill-mannered, self-centered, illiterate adolescents. He did not live to see this either, as his ideas on both politics and education had more effect after his death. Still, his ideas offered inspiration for more practical interpreters. In Rousseau's native Switzerland, a man of the next generation molded his ideas into a more useful form and succeeded in educating children in a more natural way than ever before.

Johann Pestalozzi

Johann Heinrich Pestalozzi (1746–1827), like Rousseau, had an unhappy childhood. Born into a comfortably affluent family, his whole life changed at the age of 5, when his father died. He was subsequently brought up by his mother and a family servant. Pestalozzi had a delicate constitution, and his apparently odd appearance and personality made him the object of other children's jokes. Even in his later years, commentators referred to his peculiar personality.

His motives in life were tied from his early years to the fate of the downtrodden. Like Locke and Rousseau before him, he was politically attuned to the need for some democratization in his country. Unlike them, he was sympathetic to the needs and deprivations of the poorer classes. As a young man he married and settled on a farm, having been inspired by his readings of Rousseau to seek the "natural" life. Soon he was providing a home for some 20 orphans and poor children. His unskilled business management ensured that he would eventually fail at the effort, but within a short time Pestalozzi published a successful novel, *Leonard and Gertrude* (1781), which made him famous

FIGURE 1.2 Johann Pestalozzi

Among the enduring contributions of Pestalozzi were his insistence on universal education for both the rich and the poor of both sexes and for early learning that moves from the concrete to the abstract through the use of manipulative materials.

and gave him some income. It contained his views on education, which were influenced by his earlier reading of Rousseau's *Emile*. In one important respect, however, he took issue with Rousseau. To Pestalozzi, unlimited freedom would not bring children to the desired educational level. In Pestalozzi's view, "liberty is a good thing, obedience is equally so" (Gwynne-Thomas, 1981, p. 235).

In 1799, Napoleon invaded Switzerland and, after sacking the town of Stanz, left hundreds of children destitute. An orphanage was established with Pestalozzi in charge. There he was able to put into practice the domestic love, emotional stability, and sensory education he had been writing about. Although the French eventually returned and commandeered the orphanage for a military hospital, Pestalozzi's life career had begun. By 1805 he had established a school in the town of Yverdon, which, for 20 years, was an internationally known model of the latest in education.

In his school, Pestalozzi took Rousseau's basic ideas about natural education, freedom, and sensory learning and made them work. Rousseau had escaped his own life by writing about a fictional ideal; Pestalozzi chose not to deny his own experience but to use it to empathize with and help others. Although his writings were well known, it was his ability to put his ideas into practice that gave Pestalozzi his lasting fame.

Much of what Pestalozzi did and recommended still influences what we do with young children today. He believed then, as most of us do today, that poor children have as much right to education as their wealthier counterparts. In fact, it was Pestalozzi's intention to attempt a real elevation of their lives. Additionally, he matter-of-factly included girls in his educational plans, a radical departure from tradition. Although he believed in equal access to education for everyone, he also valued diversity, saying, "Idiosyncrasies of the individual are the greatest blessings of nature and must be respected to the highest degree" (Weber, 1984, p. 29).

In the classroom, Pestalozzi geared experiences so that they went from the concrete to the abstract, a major innovation for his time. For the younger children there were "object lessons," what we might call manipulative materials, that gave children their first understanding of form, language, and number.

Today we describe Pestalozzi's choice of natural, concrete materials as developmentally appropriate for young children. He also saw these materials as a way to interest young children in school. In his best-known book, *How Gertrude Teaches Her Children*, Pestalozzi remarked at length on the wonderful freedom of preschool children and decried what traditionally happened to them once they attended school:

> Suddenly, after five years of blissful sensuous life, we banish all Nature from their eyes ... we herd them together like sheep in an evil-smelling room; for hours, days, weeks, months, and years, we chain them unmercifully to the contemplation of miserable and monotonously unexciting alphabets, and condemn them to an existence which, in comparison with their former life, is repulsive in the extreme.
>
> (Pestalozzi, 1912, p. 89)

To counteract such "misery," Pestalozzi developed activities and materials that encouraged children to learn from the concrete to the abstract. If you observe first in a preschool and then in a third grade you will, no doubt, see this developmental sequence in action. Four-year-olds, who gain an intuitive understanding of division when they share crackers equally among the group, can later transmit that understanding to pencil-and-paper problems, as long as they have something concrete to help them understand.

Another enduring contribution was Pestalozzi's insistence on universal education. He believed that both rich and poor, boys and girls deserved to learn. The increasing democratization of Western thought made such a concept more acceptable than it had been in previous generations.

It was the observations of his school at Yverdon that made Pestalozzi famous throughout the world. For early childhood education, it was the visit of the German educator Friedrich Froebel to the school that was most important. His experience there transformed Froebel from a rural schoolmaster into a theorist and philosopher.

Friedrich Froebel

Yet again, we have an example of an influential educator shaped by his own unhappy childhood. Friedrich Froebel's (1782–1852) mother died early in his life, and Froebel later wrote, "This loss, a hard blow to me, influenced the whole environment and development of my being: I consider that my mother's death decided more or less the external circumstances of my whole life" (Shapiro, 1983, p. 19). At the age of 15 he was apprenticed to a forester and began a lifelong attachment to nature. Perhaps it was this experience that contributed to his inability to stick with university studies and sent him off to work as a land surveyor, estate manager, forest department official, museum assistant, tutor, and, finally, rural school teacher.

Between 1808 and 1810, Froebel attended the training institute run by Pestalozzi at Yverdon. Although he came away accepting the basic principles of Pestalozzi's theories, Froebel felt that something critically important was missing: the "spiritual mechanism" that is the foundation of early learning. "Pestalozzi takes man existing only in his appearance on earth," he said, "but I take man in his eternal being, in his eternal existence" (Shapiro, 1983, p. 20).

Eventually, Froebel's concern for children's moral, spiritual, physical, and intellectual growth led him to focus on their needs just prior to entering school. He shared Pestalozzi's horror of what happened to 5-year-olds whose uninhibited, happy lives were so radically changed by their entrance into school. What Froebel envisioned was a sort of halfway house between home and school, infancy and childhood that would be attended by 4- to 6-year-olds. Because it would be a place where children were nurtured and protected from outside influences, much as plants might be in a garden, Froebel decided to call his school a *kinder* (children) *garten* (garden).

To make his kindergarten successful, Froebel knew that special teacher training would be necessary. He also decided that new concrete materials must be developed. They must be age appropriate for children's interests and have an underlying spiritual message. To meet the first need, Froebel began a training institute alongside his first school. For the second, he developed a series of play objects as well as singing games that seemed appropriate to the interests and education of young children and had a spiritual message as well.

The educational materials were divided into two groups: *gifts* and *occupations*. The first two gifts were designed to be introduced in infancy by the mother, and Froebel fully expected babies to have a beginning understanding of what they were about. For example, the first gift was a yarn ball connected to a string, which was to be played with under the mother's supervision in such a way that the baby's senses and muscles would be stimulated. But Froebel also believed that the ball would "awaken spirit and individuality" while helping the infant intuit "unity" (from the shape of the ball) and "freedom" (from its swinging motion). Three more gifts introduced to children in kindergarten were small building blocks that would fit together in prescribed ways under the teacher's instructions.

It is important to note here that Froebel considered these directed exercises with their specific goals a form of play. Compared to what most children in those days dealt with in their daily lives, it probably would have felt like very liberating play. Today, however, we would no doubt quibble that close-ended, prescribed, teacher-directed activities might be enjoyable but could not be described as play.

The occupations allowed children more freedom and included such things as weaving, bead stringing, sewing, and stick-laying activities, as well as gardening. But even these held underlying spiritual messages that could be learned in such simple steps as the required and careful cleanup. This last step in every activity was considered "a final, concrete reminder to the child of God's plan for moral and social order" (Shapiro, 1983, p. 24). The essential harmony of the gifts and occupations had its counterpart in the songs and games that focused on social harmony. Break up a circle of children and you have an understanding of individuality; put it back together again and there is group unity. Teachers were to point out these symbolic acts to the children, and it was expected that the children would understand.

Froebel did not have the strong political inclinations of Locke, Rousseau, and Pestalozzi and, indeed, rejected political action as a way to achieve more rights for women, although it was a cause he championed. His definition of emancipation was that women would be permitted out of the home to teach. This may explain why one of his missions was to train women throughout the world in childrearing and teaching. Despite his rejection of politics, however, the Prussian government considered Froebel's ideas dangerous and ordered his schools closed in 1848. Despairing, he died four years later, not knowing that his educational ideas were about to take hold in the United States.

The same Prussian repression and political rebellions that closed Froebel's kindergartens also sent numerous educated citizens out of the country, many of them to the United States. Among these were a number of women trained in the Froebel system of early education, and it was they who were responsible for introducing the kindergarten to this country. The very first kindergarten was established in Wisconsin for German immigrant children, who were taught in German. Word of this new way of teaching eventually made its way to St. Louis, where the first public kindergartens were opened. Although those responsible for establishing the schools were native-born Americans, they coupled Froebel's ideas with those of the German philosopher Hegel. Just as today there are people who worry about foreign influences altering the "American way," so there were concerns held by parents and educators then that early education in the United States was being taken over by German ideals. Despite this setback, Froebel's ideas provided the major direction that kindergartens followed during the last half of the 19th century. However, in a country that was beginning to look toward scientific theories rather than metaphysics and religion as a way to understand children, his ideas were gradually replaced by those of more scientific thinkers.

However, one remaining influence that is unlike any other in our historical review is that the Froebel kindergarten actually left its mark on the art and architecture of the 20th century. The brilliant architect Frank Lloyd Wright once claimed that playing with the Froebel gifts as a child provided the foundation for his designs. And, one author has traced the styles of a number of well-known 20th-century artists and architects to their early kindergarten experiences (Brosterman, 1997).

To a large degree, Froebel remains forgotten today except in his role as the developer of the kindergarten. His belief that young children can understand the spiritual symbolism behind the games they play has been discarded. The rigidly structured use of play materials has been abandoned in most quarters. The finely detailed, perfectly measured and produced learning materials have been replaced by mass produced toys. Some things remain, however: the concept that children of preprimary years learn best through some form of play, the sense that group games help children feel a part of the whole, the idea that playing and working outdoors can lead to creativity and good health. Froebel's influence at the beginning of the 20th century was strong, however, and it took an exceptional intellectual force to move things forward. That force came from our next historical figure.

John Dewey

One of those responsible for the demise of Froebel's kindergarten movement was John Dewey (1859–1952). Born, raised, and educated in Vermont, Dewey graduated from the University of Vermont at the age of 20. He then spent three anxious months looking for work and more or less fell into teaching when a cousin offered him a job at the high school where he was principal. Dewey taught Latin, algebra, and science, but his reading and thinking leaned toward philosophy. One of his former philosophy professors encouraged him to publish, and he had immediate success with three articles. This encouraged him to pursue a doctorate in philosophy from Johns Hopkins University. He moved quickly up the academic ladder, going from professorships at the universities of Minnesota and Michigan to one at the University of Chicago in 1894. It was at Chicago that Dewey first gained national notice and respect for the application of his philosophical ideas to the education of children.

As a young man, Dewey read the German philosopher Hegel and came to reject his ideas. This was important for his own later theories on early childhood education, because much of the symbolism in the activities, songs, and games of Froebel's kindergarten could be traced, in part, to Hegel's philosophy. It was important, too, that Dewey went to the University of Chicago when he did, because both it and other institutions nearby were in the midst of exploring new ideas in education. Even Froebel kindergarten teachers in the area were interested in innovation and were considered far too radical by their more orthodox counterparts.

University laboratory schools were a recent innovation, and Dewey was instrumental in beginning one at Chicago. It included a kindergarten as well as the elementary grades. In putting his theories of early education into action, Dewey found himself caught between two popular but antagonistic philosophies: that of Froebel, which he considered outdated and rigid, and that of the more recent Child Study Movement, which he believed had gone overboard in attempting to be scientific. In the mid-1890s, the followers of Froebel were a force to be reckoned with, so rather than striking out completely on his own, Dewey chose to reinterpret Froebel. As one example, he took

Froebel's concept of unity (which we have seen expressed in children's circle games and in building blocks) and focused instead on unifying such concepts as *learning and doing*, and *child and society*. Learning and doing can be united if we consider that young children are constantly active and are enthusiastic about learning, leading us to conclude that perhaps children can and should learn by doing. Child and society are also two dissimilar concepts that can be united. The individual child can learn to be a part of society if the school itself becomes a small society.

In addition to his different interpretation of unity, Dewey's view on play was unlike that of Froebel's. Children at the experimental university school used the Froebel blocks but could play with them freely; no emphasis was put on observing the unity of the whole and the individuality of the separate pieces. No longer did children play with pretend or symbolic brooms and such as they would have in a Froebel kindergarten. Instead, they really took care of their own classrooms, structuring them as mini-societies.

Furthermore, Dewey believed that social development could best take place in classrooms with mixed ages. For him, the artificial divisions between grades were unnecessary and worked against children's social growth. In the laboratory school, the sub-primary classroom covered two years. To help the youngest children learn about society, teachers began with the already familiar home and the people in it. Bit by bit the outside world was then introduced. During the winter the children worked with Froebel building materials and arranged furniture and living spaces; in the spring they played outdoor games, studied nature, and took walks in the city. All the while, they played and worked with far more independence than children did in a Froebel kindergarten. Fostering democracy in the classroom was a major goal for Dewey and one of his most enduring contributions to education.

Dewey's influence on early education has been lasting, although sometimes misinterpreted or unpopular. Misinterpretation was probably inevitable as Dewey's philosophical views were simplified and watered down in their widespread application. His ideas in the wrong hands and directed by teachers who read little, if any, of his philosophy led to the kind of classroom anarchy that Rousseau's early followers experienced. By the late 1940s, Dewey-inspired education was coming under widespread attack. By the late 1950s, when the weak nature of American education seemed exemplified in the Soviets' jumpstart into the space race, Dewey's philosophy was blamed. The backlash led to a greater focus on academics and eventually to a back-to-basics movement. Of course, Dewey was never against academic learning. He believed, however, that children need to be actively involved in it and that academics should be meaningful to them.

A bit younger than Dewey and on the other side of the Atlantic, Italy's first woman doctor was, at about the same time, developing an educational philosophy that might be placed somewhere between those of Froebel and Dewey.

Maria Montessori

Maria Montessori (1870–1952) was born in a small town on the Adriatic Sea in the same year that Italy succeeded in unifying its various independent states into one nation. The spirit of optimism in the new country gave hope to women and the poor, both traditionally downtrodden.

When she was 5 years old, the family moved to Rome. Her mother expected her to take an active interest in helping those less fortunate, so she knitted for the poor and

FIGURE 1.3 Maria Montessori

befriended a neighborhood girl with a physical deformity. As a young child in school, she performed only adequately, but in time she grew interested in math and technical subjects. With the help of her mother, she overcame her father's objections, and at age 13 entered the kind of technical school few Italian girls of her time dared enter. For a time she considered going on to study engineering, but she decided on medicine instead. This was totally unheard of for a woman, and when her father finally gave in, he insisted on accompanying her to class each day. As might be imagined, there was much prejudice against her presence, but she matched her courage with enthusiasm and brilliance and eventually graduated with high marks.

When she was a new doctor, some of Montessori's research took her to the University of Rome's psychiatric clinic. There, amid insane adults, she saw large numbers of children with learning disabilities, placed there for lack of other options. The inhumane treatment of these children touched her, and she began to read everything she could find on the education of children with such disabilities. Although she disagreed with Rousseau's idea of unstructured education in the wilds of nature, she liked his idea of developing the senses before abstract learning takes place. She also studied the work of Pestalozzi and Froebel and adapted them to her own use.

Because Montessori wanted to help those who were termed "idiot" children, she also studied the writings of two French men who had pioneered work in that area, Jean Itard and Edouard Seguin. Itard, a doctor born a century before her, had gained international fame when he attempted to educate a young boy found running wild in the woods, "The Wild Child of Aveyron."

Seguin, who studied with Itard, founded schools for those with severe learning difficulties both in France and in the United States. The unique methods he developed for educating children historically thought uneducable seemed to Montessori to hold promise for the children she observed locked up in insane asylums. She was convinced that it was education, not medicine, that would improve their lives. Soon she was speaking at conferences about the need to educate children with learning disabilities, and she proposed a school along Froebel's lines. Before long she found herself appointed director of a teacher-training institute that was a pioneer in the field of special education in Italy. Pulling her ideas from Froebel and others, Montessori experimented with teaching materials and activities, succeeding so well that her 8-year-old so-called "defectives" eventually did as well as or better than those labeled "normal" in state examinations for reading and writing.

For the next several years, Montessori moved back and forth between medicine and special education. During this time she developed a close relationship with one of her colleagues, gave birth to their son, and sent him off to the country to be raised by others. Only in his teens did she raise him herself, usually claiming that he was adopted or belonged to someone else (Kramer, 1976).

Meanwhile, Montessori was given the opportunity to test her educational ideas with children of normal intelligence when she was asked to start a day-care center in a new public housing project. Success came quickly as she experimented with methods and materials, and international fame followed. Some of the school's approaches were born of necessity, but remained because of their effectiveness with children. Aspects of the so-called Children's House (Casa dei Bambini) that were new in that time and place were insufficient materials to go around (to foster sharing), mixed ages (to promote positive interrelationships), freedom of movement and child-choice of materials (to enhance self-direction and democracy), structured activities for the youngest and newest (to provide a sense of stability and confidence), and real tools for real work (to demonstrate respect for the children's abilities and to help them adjust to the real world).

Just as Pestalozzi's and Froebel's teacher-training institutes had attracted enthusiastic students from afar, so did Montessori's. Several Americans learned Italian for the purpose of attending, and in the early years of the 20th century Montessori schools began to bloom in this country. Soon, however, they were denounced by influential scholars and for a time almost disappeared. You have, no doubt, noticed that there are Montessori schools today, however, and this is due to their rebirth in the late 1950s, when our society became newly concerned about academic learning for young children. The Montessori method, which encourages children to go as far as they can in their cognitive development, seemed to many an effective alternative for early childhood education.

Maria Montessori did not live to see this resurgence of popularity in the United States. Her last years were spent largely in exile from Italy and its fascist dictator, Benito Mussolini. Her travels gave rise to her belief that if people, beginning in their early childhood, could have more learning and experience with democratic processes, they would be less likely to follow a Mussolini or a Hitler. It was a sentiment that no doubt would have been shared by John Dewey.

B. F. Skinner

At the beginning of the 20th century, psychology (along with many other fields) was moving toward a more scientific orientation. Carefully controlled experiments on animals were used as inspiration for the study of humans, including very young children. As one important illustration, John Locke's 17th-century views of environmental influences on children's learning and behavior were echoed by the emergent theory of behaviorism. The person most associated with behaviorism, in relation to early learning applications, has been B. F. Skinner (1904–1990).

Born Burrhus Frederic, but generally known as Fred, Skinner spent his early years in the railroad town of Susquehanna, Pennsylvania. Both Skinner and his biographers have described the physical aspects of the family home, yard, and neighborhood as messy, even "chaotic," a situation which the young boy found inspirational for tinkering, building, and exploration. His boyhood inventions were many and varied, and well known around the neighborhood (Bjork, 1997). In part, Skinner said, the unreliability of play materials led to "making do" with whatever was available, just as his storybook heroes such as Robinson Crusoe would have done. Making do, according to Skinner, "has always been a favorite theme of mine" (quoted in Bjork, p. 4). Such early experiences can lead to lifelong preferences in work. Bjork writes that:

> From the beginning Fred viewed invention as he would science: a matter of improvisation and accidental discovery rather than a premeditated process of ordering the environment. When the desk in his study was clean, he remarked, he had difficulty discovering what he wanted to say.
>
> (p. 4)

Young Fred's ambitions eventually outgrew Susquehanna. Seeing his lawyer father fail at becoming a judge, his music loving mother fail at being a musician, and his local high school fail at providing him a high level of education, made such a strong impression on him that a need to leave his birthplace began to emerge. As Fred spent his growing up years feeling increasingly marginalized, his younger brother Ebbie (Edward) proved popular, athletic, and happy to fit in wherever he might be. Tragically, Ebbie suffered a fatal cerebral hemorrhage at age 16 during Fred's spring break from Hamilton College in Clinton, New York.

Skinner's college experience proved disappointing to him. There he discovered that his assumption of an atmosphere of intellectualism and scholarliness was a mistaken one, and he spent his undergraduate years working on his own and with a few others to make the experience more productive.

Returning home after graduation to try his hand at professional writing, Skinner constructed a boxlike work area within a small space under the attic. It was his second such creation, the first having been built at age 10 when he created a writing space from a packing box. After a year and a half of writing struggles, Skinner realized his calling lay elsewhere, perhaps in the behavioral sciences. Harvard graduate school was his next stop, where he joined other students and faculty in experiments with small animals. Ever the inventor, Skinner spent much of his effort in creating new apparatus for his experiments with squirrels, rats, and pigeons. Most notable was his "operant conditioning chamber" or, more popularly today perhaps, the "Skinner Box." His discoveries about animal behavior, using his box, led to a research pathway that ultimately influenced much of behavioral psychology and education. Skinner's intelligence, strong work ethic, and inventiveness led to research positions at Harvard, teaching positions at the University of Minnesota and Indiana University, and finally many years at Harvard again.

A more personal Skinner invention that deserves mention was designed to make parenting easier for his wife Yvonne. For their two infant daughters, the "air crib" provided a clean, warm, and safely closed environment for sleep and play. Several attempts at making a commercial venture of this invention didn't succeed, although a great many parents created similar cribs of their own. The idea of a "baby in a box" offended any number of critics, but Skinner's daughters have, in their adulthood, repudiated the criticisms.

Whether it was creating apparatus to affect animal behavior or the right space for his own work or the most beneficial setting for his wife and children, Skinner's emphasis on environmental influences was an ongoing theme. Coming from a completely opposite viewpoint about developmental influence was Skinner's contemporary, Arnold Gesell.

Arnold Gesell

Arnold Gesell (1880–1961), the eldest of five children, was born in Alma, Wisconsin to a photographer father and a teacher mother. Observation of his younger siblings seemed to instill in him an interest in teaching and, to that end, he attended the Stevens Point Normal School. Although he did spend time as a teacher and a high school principal, Gesell's ambitions eventually led him to earn an MD from Yale after completing a PhD in psychology at Clark University. As a faculty member at Clark, Gesell was instrumental in founding the Yale Clinic of Child Development and for 30 years he conducted research there. The findings of the clinic's research had strong influences on childhood education, particularly for the early years.

The roots of Gesell's thinking went back to Froebel, Pestalozzi, and Rousseau. His view of the child was related to that of a growing plant or tree or even an accreting coral. He believed that the seeds of adulthood are present from birth, and what is most needed for proper growth is simply care and nurturing. Gesell's thinking put the most emphasis on the idea of the unfolding, predetermined plant, but it also left room for the influence of the (less important) environment.

The psychological term that Gesell gave to this automatic unfolding was *maturation*. Related to it was the educational term *readiness*. Observational research in the Yale laboratory suggested to Gesell that there were ages and stages to all aspects of growth: physical, emotional, mental, and school skills. Throughout his lifetime, even after retirement, he applied scientific methodology to what had, in Rousseau's time, been simply a philosophical viewpoint.

Jean Piaget

Jean Piaget (1896–1980), like Rousseau and Pestalozzi before him, was born in Switzerland. And, like theirs, his childhood was a difficult one, if perhaps not as radically so. In writing about it many years later, he explained that his mother, although "intelligent, energetic, and fundamentally a very kind person," also had a "rather neurotic temperament" that "made our family life somewhat troublesome" (Piaget, 1953, p. 237). To shut off this difficult part of his life, Piaget chose at a very early age to follow an interest in science, modeling himself after his father, "a man of painstaking and critical mind, who dislikes hastily improvised generalizations. ... Among other things he taught me the value of systematic work, even in small matters" (p. 237).

Turning aside childish play for serious study, Piaget published his first scientific observation (of an albino sparrow) when he was 10 years old. Later he apprenticed himself to a local natural history museum director and developed a lifelong interest in the study of mollusks. Although they were the subject of his doctoral dissertation, mollusks were not the focus of any further study until the last few years of his life. Instead, Piaget took a position in Paris analyzing responses to items on standardized intelligence tests. Soon, he noticed that similar wrong answers were given by children of similar ages, and this led to interviews with the children to satisfy his curiosity as to why this was so. From this initial experience grew a lifelong dedication to the study of the genesis or origins of human knowledge: genetic epistemology.

Piaget returned to Geneva, Switzerland, where he did research at the Institut Jean Jacques Rousseau, observing and interviewing children in the modified Montessori school there, marrying one of his graduate students, then publishing observations of his own children in their early years. Most of his observations of and interviews with children were devoted to cognitive development, but he also published one major study of children's moral development. Although his studies were published in the 1920s and 1930s, it was decades before they were translated into English and thus influential in the United States. Like Montessori, Piaget discovered that eager American educators wanted to use his ideas as a means to push children beyond their developmental capabilities.

Piaget's ideas had elements in common with those of earlier philosophers and scientists, yet the way in which he fitted those elements into a new view was the work of a revolutionary genius. Piaget rejected the path of those who followed Rousseau in believing that children, like plants, simply needed good tending to grow to their genetically determined fullness. He also chose not to take the path begun by Locke in which children, with their blank-slate minds, simply waited to be written on by a nurturing environment. Both nature and nurture, he said, affect how humans develop, so that we need not choose one path but must travel both. In Piaget's view, children are born with certain genetic traits and, as they develop, interact with the environment to construct their own intelligence. Piaget's view has been called *interactionism* or *constructivism*, the latter being the more popular term at this time.

Early critics of Piaget faulted him for basing his worldview of children on studies done in his own home. Subsequent research by others, however, seemed to indicate that his creative genius made it possible for him to do successfully what others would frown on.

Lev Vygotsky

Vygotsky is, like Piaget, of recent enough influence that research based on his ideas still goes on. If anything, his sphere of influence continues to grow, as Piaget's remains stable or even begins to diminish. Like Piaget, Lev Vygotsky (1896–1934) can be understood and discussed as a constructivist, but his life experiences and political inclinations led him to different conclusions as to how constructions are made.

Probably the word most often used by biographers to describe Vygotsky's short and difficult life is "tragic." Born into a Jewish family in czarist Russia, when an array of laws ensured that Jews could rarely rise to positions of influence or even live where they chose, the young Lev soon became known as a budding intellectual. His love for art, literature, history, and philosophy developed during his adolescence and continued to influence his ideas even years later when his academic interests became more focused on psychology and education (Berk & Winsler, 1995).

By the time Vygotsky was ready to enter university, the government had decreed that a lottery system would be used to determine which Jews would be chosen to fill the allotted 3% of the college population. Miraculously, Vygotsky's name was drawn, and he was permitted to enroll at Moscow University but not to study the fields he had come to love. Because his preferred studies could only lead to a teaching career and Jews weren't allowed to teach, Vygotsky studied medicine for a while, then settled on law. Still restless to learn more, he co-enrolled at Shaniavsky People's University, an intellectual home for professors who had left or been expelled from other institutions for their anti-czarist stands. There, Vygotsky studied the subjects he had loved for so long and graduated from both universities in 1917.

As it turned out, 1917 was not only an important year for Vygotsky but for all of Russia, as anti-czarist sentiment led to the government's downfall, revolutionary conflict, and civil war, and the eventual creation of the Soviet Union with its foundations in Marxist socialism. Vygotsky, now able to teach the subjects he most cared about, did so, adding to them pedagogy as he became more and more committed to the integration of psychology and education.

In his mid-20s, Vygotsky joined a growing number of Russians who succumbed to tuberculosis, a disease from which he never fully recovered and which eventually cut short his remarkably productive life. During this same period he married, fathered two daughters, and impressed others sufficiently with his thoughts on psychology that he was invited to join the faculty of the Psychological Institute in Moscow.

As Vygotsky developed his theories of human development, he was influenced strongly by the political changes swirling about him. No fan of the repressive czarist regime, he adopted wholeheartedly the promising future that seemed to loom ahead in the Marxist Soviet Union. Thus, whereas Piaget, in the same years, envisioned a theory that dubbed children the creators of their own intelligence, Vygotsky focused on developing a more sociocultural or sociohistorical approach. In Piaget's case, the influences for his more individualistic view might be traced back to the renaissance of Greek and Roman thought and the rise of democracy; in Vygotsky's theory construction, the new social views pertaining to Marxism held sway. Vygotsky put so much emphasis on social interaction, in fact, that he believed it the most important element in the successful development of children with psychological or physical disabilities.

In the 12 years following his first bout with tuberculosis, Vygotsky wrote or collaborated on nearly 200 papers, striving to complete his best known manuscript, *Thought and Language* (1934/1962), while on his deathbed. Despite this prodigious output, his work remained unknown outside his circle of colleagues and friends for many years. It was during these years that the dictator Joseph Stalin came to power, creating a repressive regime that squelched creativity and intellectual endeavors. This unfortunate period and beyond became the cold war years, in which little intellectual exchange between the United States and Soviet Russia took place. By the time *Thought and Language* was translated into English in 1962, Piagetian thought was uppermost in the minds of American educators and educational psychologists. It took another two decades before Vygotsky was truly discovered.

Erik Erikson

Born in Frankfurt, Germany to Danish parents, Erik Erikson (1902–1994) never met his biological father. His mother, at the time Erik was conceived, was married to someone else, was soon divorced, and then separated from Erik's father as well. Within two years she was married to a German pediatrician, but the circumstances of his birth kept him feeling marginalized throughout his growing up years.

Once he had graduated high school, Erikson spent several years traveling Europe and occasionally studying art, finally winding up in Vienna, Austria where he worked in a small school. Some of the children's parents were either psychoanalysts or were being analyzed themselves, and soon Erikson became interested enough that he underwent analysis by Sigmund Freud's daughter Anna. Although he was far from possessing the usual university and medical degrees, Erikson studied psychoanalysis and eventually became accepted and respected in the field. Nevertheless, throughout his life he felt constrained by his lack of education and this added to his feelings of being an outsider.

During the six years he spent in Vienna, Erikson not only taught school and studied psychoanalysis, but also studied Montessori education, painted, and married a Canadian who was in Europe to study dance. By the time he and his wife Joan had two children, Hitler was having Freud's books burned in Germany and had set his sights on Austria. Erikson's mother and stepfather were Jewish, thus putting him in double danger, and so the young family emigrated to the United States.

Subsequent years found Erikson at the University of California at Berkeley, at Harvard, and finally back in California again. Finding himself in a new country, learning a new language, brought Erikson to an understanding of development that included cultural and social, as well as psychological, influences. His studies of anthropology, particularly among the Sioux and the Yurok Indians, coupled with his background in Freudian thought and practice, led to Erikson's own theory of psychosocial development. As one biographer has said, "His approach is characterized by a healthy respect for the richness and complexity of human life" (Stevens, 1983, p. 2).

Erikson's first and best-known book, *Childhood and Society* was published in 1950 (later expanded in a 1963 edition). In it, he laid out what he viewed as the eight stages of human development, starting with birth and ending with maturity. Reflecting his background and interests, each psychological stage was also assigned a related social institution. (After his death, his widow Joan expanded the theory to include old age.) Details of the stages are given later in this chapter.

Although Erikson's stage theory was, of course, firmly grounded in Freudian thought and, to an extent, anthropology, it is possible to see traces too of Montessorian and Piagetian influence. Although Montessori was profoundly uncomfortable with Freudian sexuality, her views of children's development regarding social experiences and learning closely tracked with Erikson's. Additionally, Erikson had occasion to communicate personally with Piaget and remarked at one point, when describing his own observations of a child's block play, "I am reminded here of something Piaget said: 'In order for a child to understand something, he must construct it himself, he must re-invent it'" (Erikson, 1977, p. 34).

Howard Gardner

Although he is still very much alive, Howard Gardner (1943–) rates a place in our review of history due to his wide acceptance by and influence on the educational community. His ongoing work has been, from the start, controversial but important, particularly as applied in the schools.

Born to middle-class Jews who had escaped Germany for Pennsylvania just prior to what would become the Holocaust, Gardner understood from an early age the high expectations placed upon him by his parents. Fortunately, perhaps, the young Howard demonstrated a high level of precociousness and, when his parents had him tested, they were told that he was, indeed, highly gifted. His early capability in piano performance has led to a lifelong interest in the arts, particularly music. And learning at age 10 that he'd had an older brother who died while Howard was still in the womb, contributed to pressures, as a "replacement child" to succeed in school and in life (Berube, 2000).

As an undergraduate at Harvard, Gardner studied with Erik Erikson whom he credited with leading him "away from a life of legal or historical studies toward the investigation of psychology" (1989, p. 55). Philosophically, however, he began to lean more toward the ideas of Piaget, introduced to him right after graduation by another well-known professor, Jerome Bruner:

> Bruner's interests in cognition, development, and education have become my interests; his willingness to tackle broad issues and draw on evidence from a range of disciplines, his deep interest in literature and the arts, and his special penchant for cross-cultural studies have all had an abiding impact on me.
>
> (pp. 55–56)

After a year of immersion in the culture of England and Scotland, Gardner returned to Harvard as a graduate student. There, he joined the newly formed educational research team known as Project Zero, a project focused on the cognitive aspects of the arts. Applying a "Piagetian lens" to art development, Gardner learned much about children's increasing understanding and age-related views of visual art. Eventually, Gardner spent a number of years as the project's co-director and he continues to engage in its research.

As applied to early childhood education, Project Zero's collaborative work with the Reggio Emilia schools in Italy has provided Gardner with not only a view of education that suits his philosophy and theory, but a means of documentation as assessment (Giudici, Rinaldi, & Krechevsky, 2001). You will read about the Reggio Emilia schools in Chapter Three.

Other Contributors

The people we have just discussed are arguably some of the most important figures in the history of early education, but there are many others who are worthy of our attention. Perhaps you have read about them, or soon will, in other contexts. They may also be of interest as you engage in further research and writing.

Socrates (470–399 B.C.): Greek philosopher and Plato's teacher who discussed the education of children under the age of 6.

Martin Luther (1483–1546): A German leader of the Protestant Reformation who introduced the idea of music as a school study. Luther believed girls should be educated, too.

Margarethe Schurz (1832–1876): Founded the first U.S. kindergarten in Watertown, Wisconsin, in 1855. Classes were conducted in German.

Elizabeth Peabody (1804–1894): Founded the first English-speaking U.S. kindergarten in Boston in 1860.

Susan Blow (1843–1916): Opened the first public kindergarten in the United States in 1873, with the backing and sponsorship of *William T. Harris*, superintendent of schools, St. Louis, Missouri.

Margaret McMillan (1860–1931): With the help of her sister *Rachel*, founded the first nursery school dedicated to improving the health and general well-being of preschool children in England. The building was in the style of a lean-to and open to the elements. The curriculum included both cognitive and social focii.

Patty Smith Hill (1868–1946): A leader in the movement away from strict Froebelianism to more progressive education. She was influenced by Dewey as well as the psychologist G. *Stanley Hall*, both of whose philosophies were incompatible with much of Froebel's thought.

John B. Watson (1878–1958): A psychologist who affected childrearing during the 1920s and 1930s. Sometimes referred to as the father of behaviorism, he recommended little affection between parent and child, suggesting instead that children be treated as adults and given handshakes rather than hugs.

Albert Bandura (1923–): Originally from Alberta, Canada and a Stanford University professor since 1953, Bandura created a social cognitive theory that moved beyond behaviorism to include self-efficacy as a shaper of human functioning and development. His early work in early childhood development focused on the causes of aggression.

Lawrence Kohlberg (1927–1987): Creator of a theory of moral reasoning based on Piaget's early work in which the creation of logic and morality were observed to develop simultaneously and in coordination. Kohlberg focused on older students and adults, but researchers such as *Robert Selman* and *William Damon* expanded his studies to include younger children.

David Weikart (1931–2003): Founder of the Perry Preschool Project, which conducts research with disadvantaged children before and during the Head Start years. Follow-up studies have shown that the benefits of preschool are lasting, even into adulthood.

Kieran Egan (1942–): Founder and director of the Imaginative Education Research Group at Simon Fraser University in Vancouver, Canada. Rejecting much of Piaget's theory, Egan opts instead for Vygotsky's idea of the accumulation of "cognitive tools" in development. These include the ability of children to think abstractly long before Piaget would argue that they do.

From History to Theories: Applications for Today

When Plato and Quintilian anciently expressed their opinions about early development and education, they had little, if any, concrete evidence that their ideas would or could be successful, and it was centuries before their philosophical positions would be tested in any way. Eventually, over the centuries, the differing views of thinkers such as Comenius, Locke, and Rousseau came to be more developed and tested in child care centers and classrooms. Although there are overlapping characteristics between theories of development and their application to education, these theories can generally be organized into three major categories. Table 1.1 demonstrates how the historical figures you have been reading about can each be placed into a category that shows their primary point of view:

- that internal processes and factors inherent in children are responsible for their development;
- or that external factors are more important;
- or that interactions between children and their environment enable children to construct their own development.

TABLE 1.1 Developmental Theories: An Organizational Framework

Emphasis in explaining development	External factors in the child's life	Internal processes inherent in the child	Interactions between child and environment
Representative theories	Behavioral theory Social Learning theory	Maturational theory Psychoanalytic theory	Constructivist theory Ecological theory
Associated names	Locke, Watson, Skinner, Bandura	Rousseau, Gesell, Freud, Erikson	Comenius, Piaget, Vygotsky, Dewey, Gardner, Weikart, Egan, Kohlberg, Montessori

In the following sections, you will read more about the philosophies and theories that have emerged over time and about their influence on early education.

External Factors in the Child's Life

Theories that primarily take into account the influences of the many facets of the environment are important for teachers to consider. After all, the center or classroom contributes external influences that include not only the physical environment, but social situations and teacher attitudes. In recent decades, the behaviorism espoused by B. F. Skinner has provided a theoretical framework for this view and it has been influential in both psychology and education. The following concepts that come from Skinner can be applied to early education.

Behavior. There are two types of behavior: reflexive, such as a knee jerk or eye blink, and operant, or learned. Operant behaviors, which are the focus of education, are controlled by their consequences, that is, by the positive events that a behavior produces. Behaviorists carefully design and structure the physical and social environment to teach desired social and cognitive behaviors in children.

Positive Reinforcement. The frequency of desired behaviors can be increased by giving special food, toys, praise, hugs, or anything else the child sees as positive. For example, extra time on the playground is a positive reinforcer for most children and can be used as a reward for completing academic work.

Negative Reinforcement. Instead of adding a rewarding consequence, as in positive reinforcement, something aversive is taken away. For example, a child who is being disruptive during circle time may be required to sit next to an adult, whose hand stays on his shoulder during the ensuing activities. When the adult perceives that the child has calmed down, the hand is removed, and the child is once again permitted to participate freely. (This only works, of course, if the child does not consider sitting next to the adult a special treat.)

Punishment. Skinner (like Locke before him) objected to punishment because of its undesirable side effects: anger, dislike of school, and the return of the undesired behavior. Researchers have found that punishment can change behavior, but it must be quite negative and administered very soon after the undesired behavior takes place.

Extinction. In this case, the teacher simply ignores a behavior, either good or bad. A reason to ignore good behavior might be that it is time to wean a child from an expectation of continual rewards. In the case of bad behavior, non-reinforcement can often cause a child to stop the behavior because there is no reward in it, for example, ignoring attention-getting behaviors.

Behavior Modification. A child's behavior may be modified, or changed, through the use of any of the methods just listed. Teachers who subscribe to the behaviorist orientation must have very clear, observable, and measurable goals, and these must be stated behaviorally.

Learning is generally sequenced, moving from the simple to the more complex, from the concrete to the abstract. Usually, larger bodies of knowledge are broken down into more manageable pieces. In today's early childhood classrooms, the goals of learning are often defined by the teacher but with input from the children.

Most teachers occasionally use some aspects of behaviorist theory, even if only informally, but it is in special education that behaviorist techniques are most pervasive. The clear-cut, straightforward approach, with learning broken down into specific skill sequences, has had much appeal for those who use specialized instructional strategies to teach specific academic and social skills.

Going Back to the Theories' Roots. The roots of 20th- and 21st-century behaviorist theory go back all the way to John Locke in the 17th century. You have read about his life and some of his views. Now, here is more about his philosophical thinking that relates quite closely to today.

When Locke said that the environment would create the child, he referred to his or her entire intellectual, social, and physical entity. Full learning experiences should involve input from all these aspects of the environment and include the child's use of all the senses: When you see a classroom with much opportunity for learning through acting on sensory materials, you may well be observing a classroom whose roots go back to Locke's 17th-century views. For the materials to be truly Lockean, however, they must have a learning goal connected to them. Locke believed that the environment should be controlled so that children learn what they should know. Some examples of what you might observe today would be math games using concrete materials, cardboard cut-out letters used in creating simple words, or perhaps wooden puzzles; all of these are sensory and all have specific learning goals.

Today's behavioral psychology also owes some portion of its basic thinking to Locke. One of Locke's views was that children should be reinforced for their good behavior and intellectual successes. Little is accomplished, he argued, by approaching a child with a negative attitude or physical punishment. These should be saved for emergency cases. At the same time, Locke believed that too much reinforcement could have the wrong effect, making a child more demanding and spoiled, refusing to do schoolwork unless rewarded. Today's behaviorists have created classroom approaches to discipline that are much like those that Locke would have recommended. Reinforcements are positive, focus on negative behavior is avoided, and rewards are gradually withdrawn as behavior or performance improves. Since teacher behavior is usually more subtle to observe than learning materials, you may have to look longer and more carefully to see these influences from Locke. It may be nothing more than a carefully timed, "You worked hard at that, didn't you?" or the old standby, "I like the way Emily and Al are sitting," but these and other similar statements have a direct effect on children's attitudes and behaviors. Watch for them.

Internal Processes and Factors in the Child's Life

The emphasis on external factors in the previous section did not include a denial of the influence of internal processes, and the emphasis on internal processes that we will discuss next does not include a denial in reverse. Differences are to be found in emphasis and in the roles that processes and factors play. In the 20th century, maturational and psychoanalytic theories were both important to the fields of early development and education and continue, although less noticeably, today. Arnold Gesell and Erik Erikson, both of whom you read about earlier, provided research and theory that can be useful to early childhood educators.

Arnold Gesell's research led him to a norm-referenced assessment that included sequences of many behaviors within these areas. For example, he observed that children were biologically ready to read when they had attained a mental age of 6½ years. The school skill of reading, therefore, has the following developmental norms:

15 months	Pats identified picture in book.
18 months	Points to an identified picture in book.
2 years	Names three pictures in book.
3 years	Identifies four printed geometric forms.
4 years	Recognizes salient capital letters.
5–6 years	Recognizes salient printed words.

(Weber, 1984, p. 57)

To Gesell's way of thinking, a child who attains specific behaviors according to a maturational schedule is not amenable to pushing. His hands-off attitude was reminiscent of Rousseau's, as he argued the importance of waiting until a child demonstrates the appropriate "readiness." Gesell's arguments were widely heard, and readiness became an important byword for many people in early education. Eventually he was taken to task by other psychological researchers, who noted that he had done his studies at the Yale Clinic of Child Development, where the children's parents were students and professors. In this privileged atmosphere, norms were established that were probably not representative of the population as a whole. Gesell's detractors saw this lack of broad-based research and regard for environmental influences as the fatal flaw of his life's work. Furthermore, many have argued that the developmental schedules he established were too rigid and detailed to have universal application. Nevertheless, Gesell's legacy lives on, and work continues at the Gesell Institute in Connecticut.

Although the idea of readiness is no longer as popular as it once was, there are still educators and school systems that make use of the Gesell philosophy. The transitional kindergarten is one manifestation of the philosophy in action. The argument for it is that although everyone in a graduating kindergarten class may be close to 6 years old, it is likely that some children lack the cognitive and social maturity that will make it comfortable for them to succeed in first grade. It would be better to put the unready children into a class of their own to learn at their own speed.

Letting children learn at their own speed while developing, flowerlike, in an expected sequence, is a Gesell idea that dates back to Rousseau. And whereas it may be argued that this vision of children is a limiting one, the strength of the philosophy—in these days of pushing children too far too soon—is its reluctance to do so.

A stage theory was also created by Erik Erikson, but it grew from his work with other Freudians, thus being most applicable to the field of psychology. Each of the stages Erikson posited relates to the establishment of an age-appropriate ego identity with the possibility of success or failure; Erikson coined the term *identity crisis* to explain this struggle. Each of these psychological stages was also assigned a related social institution. The four psychological stages that apply to early childhood development (and, in parentheses, their accompanying institutions) are:

I. Basic trust vs. *mistrust (religion).* If this stage goes well, "The infant's first social achievement … is his willingness to let the mother out of sight without undue anxiety or rage" (1963, p. 247).

II. Autonomy vs. *shame and doubt (law and order).* The toddler desires to control his or her world, including toilet training, while still possessing the earlier need for parental support and constancy.

III. Initiative vs. *guilt (economic ethos).* The 4- or 5-year-old's "initiative adds to autonomy the quality of undertaking, planning and 'attacking' a task for the sake of being active and on the move, where before self-will, more often than not, inspired acts of defiance or, at any rate, protested independence" (p. 255).

IV. Industry vs. *inferiority (technological ethos).* As the child goes off to school, he "must forget past hopes and wishes, while his exuberant imagination is tamed and harnessed to the laws of impersonal things – even the three R's" (p. 258).

As you observe young children, see for yourself the ways in which, despite their individual differences, they share age-related developmental similarities such as those defined by Gesell and Erikson.

Going Back to the Theories' Roots. Today, you are as likely to see Rousseau's influences in the classroom as you are Locke's. Again, you can observe children interacting actively with materials that appeal to all their senses. But, in keeping with the concept of natural development, the materials are more open-ended and their use determined by the children. Math materials might be sticks brought inside by the children. These could be played with in a free-form way, while the teacher makes informal comments to inspire learning. Books might or might not be available, and the teacher could well choose to tell a story rather than read it. Giving children materials for costumes and props so that they might invent little plays would take preference over providing structured reading. Time spent outdoors would focus on learning about nature in an informal way.

A basic difference between Locke and Rousseau affects what you see in the classroom today. Along with others of his time, Locke assumed that there is a discreet body of knowledge that people of the upper classes should learn and that the function of education is to make knowledge accessible and interesting. Rousseau, on the other hand, was more interested in process, or learning how to learn. You can observe this difference in outlook when you see children playing with materials that have right solutions (Locke's view) or when you see them playing with open-ended materials, creating their own learning (Rousseau's view). In most classrooms you will find some of each kind of learning, living testament to our inability to decide which is the better course to take. Many teachers argue that a combination of the two views provides the best learning, although many of them aren't aware that their argument is based on a conflict in ideology that has been around for more than two centuries.

Interactions Between the Child and the Environment

The roots of the theories in this section evolved from those in the previous two sections and also emerged from other developments in psychology and education. For example, as the sterility of the back-to-basics approach became apparent, John Dewey's ideas began to return. Today, as you see young children learn how to run town meetings in their classrooms, or observe a teacher who focuses on all aspects of children's growth, or learn to plan and teach a theme unit, you come in contact with education that has its roots in Dewey's thinking. Underlying all these Deweyan elements is the idea of educating children to live in a democracy by providing them a democratic environment to learn in.

The more structured, though philosophically similar, Montessori approach to early education has survived to this decade relatively intact. Although there are various approaches to training, with some purists wanting to keep the schools as they were in Montessori's day and others arguing for updating them, a common element is found in all the schools: a carefully prepared environment. If possible, you should try to observe at least one Montessori classroom. There, you will find a selection of materials designed to enhance learning through the senses, concrete math activities that help preschoolers intuit complex principles, and children moving independently and at will. It is likely that you will see little play in the free-form sense, and in this way, Montessori schools have a strong relationship to those of Froebel. In most Montessori schools there is some mixing of ages. The intent is to help the older children take responsibility for the younger while reinforcing their own learning, and for the younger children to learn to depend on and trust their older peers. Furthermore, the mixing of ages is designed to foster the creation of a predemocratic society, or "society in embryo," as Montessori referred to it.

While Dewey and Maria Montessori focused their primary attention on education, Jean Piaget studied children's development, focusing primarily on the cognitive. Concepts and terms associated with Piaget include the following:

Equilibration is fundamental to school learning and refers to the child's continual process of cognitive self-correction, whose goal is a better sense of equilibrium. There are two subcategories of equilibration:

Assimilation. When children learn something new that they can just add on to their existing store of logic (cognitive structure), they are said to assimilate it. For example, a baby who can crawl and who has seen a ball but never one that is rolling, can put these two bits of knowledge together to crawl after a ball the first time she sees one roll by her. Piaget said that assimilation has a close identification with play, thus making play important to adequate cognitive development.

Accommodation, on the other hand, might be termed more serious learning. In this case, some part of a child's cognitive structure has to be modified to take in the new learning. Suppose our crawling child has never seen a ball and suddenly one rolls by. The spherical shape, the rolling movement, perhaps the color are all new, and the child must adapt her thinking to take all this in. Of course, she may still take off after it, but the learning is deeper. As you might guess, both assimilation and accommodation go on continually and in combination with each other.

Despite his reluctance to give much advice to educators, Piaget did have some general ideas as to what should happen in the classroom. From the constructivist view, if children create their own intellects, then they should be given the freedom to do so. This argues for play, experimentation, and guided learning activities as opposed to direct instruction and lectures.

Speaking of math, for example, Piaget (1972) argued that it is better to let children spend more time on a few problems, really working through them, than to cover a lot of territory: "It is in learning to master the truth by oneself at the risk of losing a lot of time and of going through all the roundabout ways that are inherent in real activity" (p. 104).

Today, early education is strongly influenced by Piaget, particularly when we put down the structured worksheets in favor of less directive hands-on learning.

Although he was Piaget's contemporary, Lev Vygotsky was, for a long time, little known in the United States, as we saw earlier. What Americans found when they belatedly discovered Vygotsky from the 1970s onward was a set of theoretical proposals that complemented Piaget's, perhaps answering questions that Piaget's research had raised. Other ideas were more directly in conflict with Piaget's, based as they were on socialist ideals rather than on those of a more individualistic society. Some of the major Vygotskian ideas to know about are:

The importance of language to development. Of all the symbol systems created by humans, language is the most important in Vygotsky's theory. In infancy, budding language capabilities are used for the sole purpose of social interaction; it is only later, in the preschool years, that language becomes a way of communicating with or influencing the behavior of the self. Because language is so important to early social development, and vice versa, Vygotsky had special concerns for deaf children. They would need extra coaching in their communication skills (primarily focused on lip reading in a time when sign language was not yet respected), and the intensity of the required training would lead to social isolation, a situation opposed to his general philosophy of effective development. Unfortunately, Vygotsky died before his views could be resolved and well before the prejudice against sign language was dispelled.

Instruction leads and influences development. Although Piaget agreed that education's role in child development was important, he also argued that teachers should avoid being too intrusive and intervene primarily for the purpose of facilitating the child's own self-construction. Vygotsky viewed the teacher—formal schoolteacher, parent, more knowledgeable peer, perhaps—as more directly important to development. His ideas were based, after all, on the importance of social interaction, and when applied to development, social interaction between teacher and learner would naturally hold importance.

The zone of proximal development. This zone is that space between what the child already knows or has mastered and the knowledge that is currently beyond his or her capabilities. It is the space where learning is challenging but not overly frustrating; where, with some help from a teacher, parent, or peer a child can develop new knowledge. Vygotsky created the concept of the *zone of proximal development* (ZPD) in response to his own arguments against intelligence and other tests that determine what a child already knows and has accomplished. To explain his position, he used the analogy of a gardener who must test not only the mature fruit in his orchard, but the developing fruit as well, if he wishes to know how healthy the orchard really is. "If he is to fully evaluate the state of the child's development, the psychologist must consider not only the actual level of development but the *zone of proximal development*" (cited in Newman & Holzman, 1993, p. 56).

Scaffolding. Vygotsky was certainly concerned about the teaching and learning that occurred within the ZPD, but it was for those who came after him to name and fully develop the idea of scaffolding. As in Piaget's theory of development, children are seen as self-builders. In Vygotsky's view, however, the role of the supportive social environment is of greater importance. The *scaffolding* provided by those in the child's social world helps him or her to develop to the fullest extent. It thus becomes a primary responsibility of the classroom teacher to identify, where possible, each child's ZPD and to provide just the right amount of guidance, direction, and encouragement to ensure optimum intellectual, social, and physical development.

Our final contributor to this set of theories is Howard Gardner. Perhaps it was inevitable that Gardner's wide-ranging interests, talents, and studies would lead to a dispute with the traditional narrow views of intelligence. The general acceptance of verbal and quantitative abilities as the only two measures of human capability began to appear as insufficient to Gardner, eventually leading to a totally new concept of "multiple intelligences." These Gardner laid out in his book *Frames of mind: The theory of multiple intelligences* (1983). Suddenly, fame came to this researcher and prolific writer, particularly from the education field. Here, in brief, are the seven intelligences proposed in Gardner's original book. The definitions come from his first book for educators, *Multiple intelligences: The theory in practice* (1993, pp. 8–9):

- *Linguistic Intelligence*: "the kind of ability exhibited in its fullest form, perhaps, by poets."
- *Logical-mathematical Intelligence*: "logical and mathematical ability, as well as scientific ability."
- *Spatial Intelligence*: "the ability to form a mental model of a spatial world and to be able to maneuver and operate using that model."
- *Musical Intelligence*: "Leonard Bernstein had lots of it; Mozart, presumably, had even more."
- *Bodily-kinesthetic Intelligence*: "the ability to solve problems or to fashion products using one's whole body, or parts of the body."
- *Interpersonal Intelligence*: "the ability to understand other people: what motivates them, how they work, how to work cooperatively with them."
- *Intrapersonal Intelligence*: "a capacity to form an accurate, veridical model of oneself and to be able to use that model to operate effectively in life."

Over time, Gardner has considered other possible intelligences, with the *Naturalistic Intelligence* being the one that seems most acceptable to the theory: "those with extensive knowledge of the living world" (1999, p. 48).

In Closing. We ask you now to return to the quote by Loris Malaguzzi that opened this chapter. Which philosophy or theory does it most closely match? Do you agree with it? Can you revise it to match any of the other viewpoints in this chapter? When you have completed this brief reflection, you will be prepared to explore the ideas in the next chapters which, incidentally, include more about Malaguzzi himself.

EXTENDING YOUR LEARNING

Suggestions 1 and 2 are the first steps in a sequence that starts here and continues through Chapter Five. In each chapter, Suggestion 1 presents ideas for ongoing development of your teaching philosophy. Suggestion 2 takes a metaphorical approach toward the same goal. You may choose one Suggestion, or both separately, or create a way to combine the two.

 1 Write a beginning statement of your philosophy of education. Base it on the historic figures you have just read about. Consider the positive and negative responses you had to their ideas. Some ideas for you to write down:

 a) Choose one historic figure with whom you would like to study. What would you most like to learn?

b) Choose one historic figure with whom you would like to take issue. What are the major points you would like to make? What do you think this person might answer?

c) Select the ideas you like best and suggest ways you might be able to apply them in your own teaching life.

d) Select the ideas you like least and explain why you would be reluctant to use them with young children.

2 Choose a historic figure you particularly like, or particularly dislike. Can you describe him or her in a metaphor? In other words, use word phrase that typically means one thing and apply it to someone from this chapter. For example, Pestalozzi's warm approach to caring for and educating children might make you think of him as a mother hen. (You might have a totally different view of Pestalozzi and choose to use it. There are no "right" answers.)

3 See if you can observe influences from centuries ago here in 21st-century America. Make a list of characteristics associated with education inspired by Locke and another list for Rousseau. Observe at least two classrooms, noting materials, teacher's style, children's learning behaviors and movement patterns, and teacher–child interaction. Compare your findings with the rest of your class.

4 Is there one best way to approach early education? Discuss the historical philosophies and theories and their most positive contributions. Would it be possible to combine the best of each to create the perfect early education? Why or why not?

Internet Resources

Web sites provide much useful information for educators and we list some here that pertain to the topics covered in this chapter. (Because this chapter is focused on history, you will find more selections in upcoming chapters.) The addresses of Web sites can also change, however, and new ones are continually added. Thus, this list should be considered as a first step in your acquisition of a larger and ever-changing collection.

Imaginative Education Research Group
www.ierg.net

Montessori (American)
www.amshq.org

Montessori (International)
www.Montessori.edu

Project Zero
http://pzweb.harvard.edu

Vocabulary

Back to Basics. Educational emphasis on reading, writing, and arithmetic with little or no emphasis on the arts or other electives. Most recently given this name during the 1980s.

Casa dei Bambini. Italian for Children's House. The first school for young children established by Maria Montessori.

Child Study Movement. Founded primarily by G. Stanley Hall in the late 19th and early 20th centuries to study children scientifically using observation and questionnaires. This approach broke with earlier, more philosophical and religious views of child development.

Cognitive. Pertaining to knowledge, information, and intellectual skills.

Egocentric. In early infancy, being able to differentiate between what is and is not the self. Later, understanding the world only as it relates to the self.

Gifts and Occupations. Materials developed by Froebel for use with infants and young children.

Pedagogue. An early word for teacher. Now, sometimes used to describe a dull, pedantic teacher or a curriculum specialist.

Self-correcting. Pertains to learning materials that have a control of user error built into the material itself.

Stage Theory. Posits the position that humans (or other organisms) develop through successive stages in a specific order, with later stages retaining characteristics of the earlier ones. While some people may develop more quickly than others, individual stages cannot be skipped.

Tabula Rasa. A blank slate; a term used by John Locke to represent the inexperienced mind of the child.

References

Berk, L., & Winsler, A. (1995). *Scaffolding children's learning: Vygotsky and early childhood education*. Washington, DC: National Association for the Education of Young Children.

Berube, M. (2000). *Eminent educators: Studies in intellectual influence*. Westport, CT: Greenwood Press.

Bjork, D. (1997). *B. F. Skinner: A life*. Washington, DC: American Psychological Association.

Brosterman, N. (1997). *Inventing kindergarten*. New York: Abrams.

Cleverley, J., & Phillips, D. (1986). *Visions of childhood*. New York: Teachers College Press.

Comenius, J. A. (1896). *School of infancy*. Boston: Heath. (Original work published 1633.)

deMause, L. (1974). *The history of childhood*. New York: Psychohistory Press.

Erikson, E. (1963). *Childhood and society* (2nd ed.). New York: W. W. Norton.

Erikson, E. (1977). *Toys and reasons*. New York: W. W. Norton.

Gardner, H. (1983). *Frames of mind: The theory of multiple intelligences*. New York: Basic Books.

Gardner, H. (1989). *To open minds: Chinese clues to the dilemma of contemporary education*. New York: Basic Books.

Gardner, H. (1993). *Multiple intelligences: The theory in practice*. New York: Basic Books.

Gardner, H. (1999). *Intelligence reframed*. New York: Basic Books.

Giudici, C., Rinaldi, C., & Krechevsky, M. (Eds.) (2001). *Making learning visible: Children as individual and group learners*. Reggio Emilia, Italy: Reggio Children.

Gwynne-Thomas, E. H. (1981). *A concise history of education to 1900 A.D.* Washington, DC: University Press of America.

Kramer, R. (1976). *Maria Montessori*. Chicago: University of Chicago Press.

Locke, J. (1692/1964). *John Locke on education*. New York: Teachers College Press.

Newman, F., & Holzman, L. (1993). *Lev Vygotsky: Revolutionary scientist*. New York: Routledge.

Osborn, D. K. (1980). *Early childhood education in historical perspective*. Athens, GA: Education Associates.

Pestalozzi, J. (1912). *Pestalozzi's educational writings*. London: Arnold.

Piaget, J. (1953). Autobiographie, Jean Piaget. In *A history of psychology in autobiography* (Vol. 4). Worcester, MA: Clark University Press.

Piaget, J. (1972). *The principles of genetic epistemology*. New York: Basic Books.

Shapiro, M. (1983). *Child's garden*. University Park, PA: Penn State University Press.

Stevens, R. (1983). *Erik Erikson*. New York: St. Martin's Press.

Weber, E. (1984). *Ideas influencing early childhood education*. New York: Teachers College Press.

Wodehouse, H. (1924). *A survey of the history of education*. New York: Longmans Green.

part two
Today

The next three chapters are designed to provide a framework that addresses essential elements of early childhood education for students entering the field. Your ideas and attitudes about early childhood education will have been shaped, to some extent, by your own history and that of the field. Thus, we ask that you not simply move on from the previous *Yesterday* section, but continue to keep it in mind as you read the three chapters that constitute *Today*:

Chapter Two provides information that serves as a point of departure for you to begin identifying a career path in early education. We ask you to look at the early childhood education profession as a whole, as well as at many specific roles and potential career choices, any of which might be appropriate for your own professional goals.

Chapter Three introduces the many models of early education available to families seeking early care and education for children from birth to age 8. It is our opinion that there are strengths and advantages to be found in all the models presented. You will no doubt find yourself more interested in some types of programs than in others, another important aspect of assembling your own future role as an early childhood educator.

Chapter Four addresses the diversity of the children and families with whom you will interact on a daily basis as an early educator, raises current and historical issues, and outlines successful strategies for creating inclusive and welcoming environments. Our goal is to make it evident that early education requires careful attention to both similarities and differences among children and their families. And your primary task as an early educator is to insure that each and every child and family is recognized, valued, and empowered to participate fully in early care education experiences. This chapter identifies diversity in broad terms and seeks to eliminate an "us" and "them" perspective in areas of culture, language, ethnicity, ability, gender identity, and family structure.

two
Early Childhood Education

Contemporary Perspectives on the Profession

America's future will be determined by the home and the school. The child becomes largely what it is taught, hence we must watch what we teach it, and how we live before it.

Jane Addams (1860–1935)

Chapter Objectives

After reading this chapter, you should be able to:

- Explain the importance of early childhood education in contemporary America.
- Identify careers available to early childhood professionals and describe the settings in which they take place.
- Identify the major early childhood professional organizations.
- Describe the differences between appropriate and inappropriate reasons for choosing an early childhood career.
- List and explain the professional teaching standards of the early childhood professional.
- Describe the major educational traditions of early education.

As you think about and apply chapter content on your own, you should be able to:

- Begin to identify the best options for your own future career.
- Start formulating a metaphor for yourself as an early childhood professional.

The quotation at the top of the page is as true now as it was during the two previous centuries. One day soon it will be your job to provide care, instruction, and guidance to infants, toddlers, preschoolers, or primary school boys and girls. Early childhood educators hold a significant responsibility, not only for the young children we teach, but for the people those youngsters become and the contributions they make to their future communities and society at large.

You have chosen to study early education at a time when the field is undergoing a period of significant growth and change. For a variety of reasons, infants, toddlers, and preschoolers in the United States are increasingly being cared for and educated outside of their homes. Parents often return to the work force when their children are still quite young, either out of choice or economic necessity. Also, during the decade between 1995 and 2005 the general public became widely aware of the results of research in early development, and the importance of early education as a foundation for success in school. Brain development research, for example, began to explain the effects of very early experiences on humans' lifelong capacity to learn. Additionally, the long-term benefits of early education became apparent as a large group of low-income children of the 1960s—some urban, some rural—grew to adulthood, demonstrating greater successes in all aspects of life than did their peers who had not had the benefit of preschool (Schweinhart, Montie, Xiang, Barnett, Belfield, & Nores, 2005). It began to be apparent to parents and policy makers alike, that although love and kindness are vitally important for infants and young children, something more is necessary if youngsters are to grow successfully into adulthood.

Currently there is a large body of research that shows clearly the social, academic, and economic benefits of early education (Barnett & Hustedt, 2003). High-quality early care and education have been shown to have an enduring impact on children's social and cognitive development, and on the early academic skills necessary for success in school, which in turn support a more skilled work force and a higher standard of living for post-secondary students (Barnett & Masse, 2007; Magnuson, Ruhm, & Waldfogel, 2007). As a result, federal funding for Head Start programs continues to increase, and many state governments have begun to fund education for 3- and 4-year-olds, particularly for those at risk in their development and those from low-income families. Many early childhood professionals are advocating for universal prekindergarten programs as an efficient and effective approach to preparing young children for school and closing the achievement gap.

At odds with the acknowledged importance of early education is the fact that the profession and the people who represent it are often underestimated and undervalued in our society and in educational circles. Many of us have heard how nice and patient we must be, to spend time with young children all day. We are too often considered by many to be glorified baby-sitters, who "just play" with children, as opposed to the "real teachers" of academic content. Few people outside of the profession acknowledge the intelligence, competence, and creativity necessary to design and implement curricula across such widely divergent ages and skill levels. Such attitudes exist despite the fact that a number of the more progressive educational practices currently being promoted in public schools, such as multi-age groupings, team teaching, integrated curricula, activity-based instruction, and multi-cultural curricula, originated in early childhood settings. Particularly for the primary grades, there is still disagreement about how best to teach early academic skills, and questions about the relative application of "early childhood" manipulative materials and "hands on" activities, versus more structured and teacher-directed learning experiences.

The undervaluing of early educators is perhaps most obviously expressed in their insufficient pay—parking lot attendants and grocery clerks have until recently made better wages. Wages in child-care programs seem to reflect the sentiment that the only qualifications required are enjoying children and being older than those in your charge (Cost, Quality & Child Outcomes Study Team, 1995). One argument in favor of universal preschool is the notion that early childhood teachers would enter the workforce with the same rigorous preparation as public school teachers, and thus be compensated on a similar pay scale. As standards for professionalism in early childhood education are raised, salaries are also improving. Still, at this time, although there are many good reasons to become an early childhood educator, pay is not one of them.

The beginning of the 21st century is a good time to be considering early childhood education as a career. The profession is moving forward quickly, applying research findings in teaching and child development to the art of providing meaningful and effective learning experiences for young children. New knowledge and innovative practices are being integrated into a long early childhood tradition of working with families, collaborating with peers, and respecting the individuality of each child. It is your generation of early childhood professionals that will be most responsible for deciding the directions that the profession will take as the new century unfolds. A strong formal educational preparation in early childhood should garner you the career choices, respect, and wages of a professional. As you read this book, take your education courses, and work in the field, reflect on the issues that face the profession of early childhood education, and then determine your place in it.

Should I Choose Teaching Young Children as my Profession?

> Young children are interesting and appealing, but they are also sensitive and vulnerable. How we care for them, what we do and say each day affects their happiness and well-being as they grow.
>
> (Hendrick, 1987, p. 1)

Young children soak up knowledge about their world with the eagerness of thirsty sponges. Because they don't yet have the cognitive sophistication to sort through those things that are valuable to learn and those that are less worthy, they take in just about everything. Thus, this quote by Joanne Hendrick, a leading writer in the field, suggests that people who work with young children have an ethical obligation to choose a career in early childhood education with serious intent and for the right reasons. Here are a few of the reasons you may be planning a career in early childhood education, as suggested by Hendrick, with some observations and considerations to accompany each one.

- *Because you like to teach.* It is possible, even probable, that you have had experiences with children already and that these have been sufficiently positive to lead you into the field. If you have not, then do acquire some experience before you go much further. After all, you probably wouldn't buy a car or even a new outfit without trying them out first. It is even more important to try out a career to be sure it fits you. If, on the other hand, you have had some experience but it has been of only one type, find time to try out some related options. Babysitting and tutoring with individuals and small groups of children are quite different from working with groups. Teaching Sunday school is quite different from spending an entire day with toddlers, which is quite different from teaching a classroom of second graders, and so on. If you think you would like to teach young children, but find that classroom groups are not to your liking, be sure to investigate the many other options for careers beyond teaching.

- *Because you can make an important difference in children's lives.* At the start of this chapter, we described briefly the long-term benefits of early preschool experiences for children; those who attend preschool are found to reach adulthood with much more success in their professional and personal lives than those who do not. The research that has reported these benefits infers that what teachers of young children do has enormous impact! Because the growth in young children is often concrete and visible, one satisfaction for their teachers is seeing positive changes on a day-to-day basis. Perhaps a new kindergartner overcomes his shyness and asks to join others in the dramatic play area, and they accept him graciously. Or a whole class of 3-year-olds suddenly understands the art of getting both arms into their coat sleeves. Or a third grader who has been unable to relate rote-learned arithmetic tables to real life begins to show her understanding of the processes by creating story problems of her own. Such small victories collect and build toward successful lives for children and satisfying careers for their teachers.

- *Because you can enrich the lives of the families you serve.* Children are tied to their families more intimately in the early years than at any other time in their lives. The ensuing three-way relationship among parents, teachers, and young children also tends to be closer than in later years. Parents are often welcomed into the classroom not just for formal and informal meetings, but as observers or helpers. Some careers in early childhood send the professional to the homes of the youngsters. Whatever the setting, the opportunities are many for interaction with families about children's learning and development, and the effectiveness of various approaches to fostering growth in the early years. If the diversity and energy of working with young children within the context of family life appeals to you, a career in early childhood education may be a good choice.

- *Because you like diversity and challenge.* People who teach young children are seldom able to rest on their past accomplishments but, rather, must prepare each day carefully, thinking through a variety of options before creating an hours-long schedule. Furthermore, that schedule generally includes long periods of time when several activities are occurring at once, and the teacher must be aware of what is happening with each activity at any given time. A kindergarten teacher once found herself dealing with the following: several boys in the block corner negotiating for increased space in the next-door housekeeping corner that was inhabited by three territorial and angry girls; one boy "flying" around the room knocking games and books off shelves; two children at a woodworking table having trouble sawing a piece of lumber; several others quietly looking at books in the library corner; three or four at the sand and water table that was just beginning to leak out one side; and all while she tried to get a stuck zipper opened for a boy who was in desperate need of the toilet. She could only laugh, realizing—as any teacher of young children must—that flexibility and a sense of humor are important traits for success in the early education profession. Additionally, the children themselves are likely to spread out over 2 or 3 years of age, have a wide variety of family backgrounds, and speak a variety of home languages.

- *Because you are needed.* The population of young children is growing and will continue to do so. As we continue to have high numbers of marriages with two parents working, as well as single parents in need of child care while they work, the demand will be steady or will increase. As society and the workplace become more complex, learning experiences during the earliest years become ever more important, and the need for caring, dedicated, well-educated professionals grows. Perhaps you should be one of them!

Although these reasons for choosing a career in early childhood are sound, there are others that, as Hendrick says, are "based on illusion rather than reality" (1987, p. 5). She lists three that can be observed or heard frequently. If any of these is your primary reason for choosing this career direction, it might be a good time to reflect on your choice, perhaps spending more time in a teaching situation before making a final decision.

- *Because young children are so cute and lovable.* This reason is often stated as, "I just want to be a teacher because I love children and I always have." Of course it is good to love children, but as a primary reason to choose the profession, it comes up lacking. Almost no child is lovable at all times. Furthermore, in every group of children there will be some who are easier to love than others. Frequently, it is the children who appear least lovable who are most in need of adult attention and for whom the attention, care, support, and intervention of early educators will make the biggest

FIGURE 2.1 As the demand for child care increases, the need for caring professionals grows.

difference. The professional teacher regards his or her children as real human beings and understands that they can be moody or calm, enthusiastic or disinterested, happily obedient or strongly independent. And sometimes cute.

■ *Because young children are easier to control than older children.* Some prospective teachers have tried working with older children and have found management and discipline to be a barrier to success. They assume that working with younger, smaller children will be easier. This is definitely not the case! Young children are egocentric, as yet unable to see things very well from another's point of view. They haven't yet developed much skill at patience and want their way n-o-w. Although they will bend to the will of an authority figure while he or she is in view, they often revert to their own desires once the authority isn't looking. Furthermore, they are in constant motion, but tire quickly, and are impulsive rather than planful in their actions. It takes a skilled professional to know how to attain an atmosphere of well-managed calm in a classroom of younger children. The most successful early educators are those who are intrigued and amused by the more challenging aspects of young children's behavior, rather than frustrated and impatient.

■ *Because working with young children is fun, like babysitting and play.* Yes, play happens in an effectively taught class, but it is assuredly <u>not</u> babysitting (although caring for and about youngsters is always a crucial element of this work). Teachers of young children do not just provide play and hope or trust that learning will follow. For play to be an effective mode of learning, it must be carefully orchestrated, planned, and integrated with a wide variety of learning experiences. Successful teaching through play is a skill acquired through study and practice. Students looking for an easy and fun position will be disappointed to find that early childhood education, while often fun and funny, can also be very demanding, sometimes sad, and rarely restful.

FIGURE 2.2 While much of early education involves play, this is an insufficient reason to choose teaching young children as a career.

A career in early childhood education can be highly rewarding in many ways, particularly if it is chosen for some of the better reasons discussed previously. For the benefit of children as well as the career satisfaction of the teacher, it is also a career that should be chosen only by those who plan to take it seriously, as professionals.

Where Young Children Learn

This book is intended to provide the reader with information about being a teacher of young children; thus, the focus of our discussion is on learning experiences that have been created by educators. Yet it should always be remembered that humans begin to learn before birth and continue to do so for a considerable time before they enter educational settings. Furthermore, even after formal education begins, youngsters continue to learn both before and after school or caregiving hours. Parents and other family members are children's first teachers, both chronologically and in importance. Professionals must always remember this and give these teachers the greatest respect, turning to them for advice and suggestions and with a willingness to collaborate in their children's education.

As an early childhood educator, you will have a choice of age groups with which you can work. Although the early childhood years typically cover from birth to age 8, different programs divide these ages in different ways. Some schools and centers segregate each age group, making it possible to focus on the changing needs of the child at

FIGURE 2.3 It is important to remember that parents and other family members are a child's first teachers, both chronologically and in importance.

each identifiable stage. Others place two or more age groups together so that children can learn from each other and also share their growing knowledge and expertise. There are advantages and disadvantages to each approach, and as you work with children of different ages, you will no doubt discover that you have some preferences. There may even be some ages you are not comfortable working with at all. Try to identify your preferences and capabilities during your teacher education, as this is the time when it is easiest to experiment, take risks, and learn from others' feedback.

Following are descriptions of places young children learn outside of their homes, and the ages generally associated with each setting.

Nursery School and Preschool

The concept of nurturing very young children lay behind the creation and naming of the *nursery school*. At the turn of the 20th century, Margaret and Rachel McMillan noted with dismay the sad state of health of many of England's youngsters. The sisters were inspired to create a school designed to give children plenty of fresh air, good food, and hygiene in addition to academics and socialization through play. Their employees were qualified both as nurses and as teachers (Osborn, 1980). When transported to the United States, nursery schools often became cooperatives, with parents sharing the responsibilities of running them, thus keeping costs down. Children who attend nursery schools are generally between the ages of 2 and 4, or even 5.

The term *preschool* is often used interchangeably with nursery school. It is, however, a more modern term, implying a strong focus on academics and socialization as preparation for school, and less emphasis on nutrition and hygiene. Many community colleges and four-year universities offer preschool programs for student parents, and as field experience sites for early childhood education students. Attendance ages are the same.

Early Intervention Services

Specialized services for infants and toddlers (ages birth to 3 years) who experience disabilities or have delayed development have been available in the United States and Canada for more than 20 years. Early intervention services provide individually designed assessment, therapeutic, and developmental programs and are funded by a patchwork combination of federal, state and provincial, school district, and private sources. Recommended practice guidelines (Sandall, Hemmeter, Smith, & McLean, 2005) indicate that services for newborns to 3-year-olds be centered in the lives of individual families, with caregiving activities and parent–child relationships the primary context and content for intervention.

Early intervention professionals work across a variety of settings and with a number of professionals from other disciplines. They make visits to homes, hospitals, and center-based classrooms to assess, design, implement, and monitor developmental interventions in movement, socialization, cognition, self-care, and communication domains. Early interventionists coordinate educational and developmental services with physical, occupational, and speech therapists; pediatricians; family-service specialists; and early childhood professionals. Because so much of early intervention work occurs within family and community settings, infant and toddler specialists must also be competent at working across cultures and with adults as well as with infants and toddlers.

Kindergarten

Typically, kindergarten is a single-year learning experience, immediately preceding first grade. As originally created by Friedrich Froebel in mid-19th-century Germany, it was for children between the ages of 4 and 6. In many countries it remains so today. However, as public elementary schools in the United States added a one-year kindergarten to their regular programs, and as more and more children began to attend preschool and child care, the role of kindergarten began to change. It may still be the bridge that Froebel envisioned between home and the primary grades for many children, but it has also become a transition experience following preschool or child care. Kindergarten curricula vary depending on the philosophy of the school or district. Traditionally, the focus was on play with one academic purpose—readiness for first grade. In recent years, kindergartens have become much more academic, a move that has produced some degree of controversy. You will become acquainted with the issues in coming chapters.

Transitional Kindergarten, Pre-First Grade, and Interim First Grade

Some children do not seem ready to enter the primary grades after one year of kindergarten. To ensure success in later years, transitional programs were created. Some educators, referring back to the work of Arnold Gesell, believe that if children appear to be at risk for academic failure, it is better to hold them back at this time than later, when the feeling of failure can be more damaging, academic momentum is lost, friends may be forever separated.

Others argue that the primary reasons for holding children back in kindergarten tend to indicate a first-grade education that is developmentally inappropriate for the age, with too great a focus on early academics. Yet in today's climate of rigorous academic standards in all grades, it is considered essential that children enter first grade with a good start on identifying letter–sound relationships, counting, following directions, working on paper-and-pencil tasks, raising hands, and following other classroom protocols such as speaking only in turn. Many states have some form of transitional kindergarten, to insure that children enter first grade ready to engage in learning how to read, write, add, and subtract. If you enjoy the accomplishment and excitement of helping young children master basic skills, transitional kindergarten may be a good career option for you.

Developmental Preschool and Kindergarten

In the United States, federal legislation (IDEA, 2004) requires that local school districts provide special education services for all eligible children beginning at age 3. Half-day developmental preschool classrooms are the most common setting for delivery of specialized instruction and related therapeutic services for 3- to 6-year-olds. Because public schools do not routinely serve the general population of preschoolers, developmental preschools have traditionally served only children with disabilities and developmental delays. The benefits of inclusion, however, have prompted many districts to explore creative alternatives to self-contained special education classrooms for preschoolers. Many districts have begun to enroll typically developing preschool peers in developmental preschool classrooms, or to provide special education services to eligible children in community child-care and preschool programs.

The timing of kindergarten entry can be a complicated issue for young children with special needs. Youngsters who are eligible for special education services may have already attended public school programs for two or three years by the time they are 5, yet many 5-year-olds with disabilities or delays lack the social and pre-academic skills expected in kindergarten. In addition to the transitional programs previously described, a number of larger American school districts have designed alternate models rather than adhering strictly to age 5 or a specific group of skills as kindergarten entry requirements. One such program is supplementary kindergarten, which young students attend every day and for increasingly longer days to receive additional instruction in preparation for first grade. Another model is the continuation of developmental services in a special education kindergarten classroom, sometimes offered as a supplementary program to regular kindergarten attendance.

The role of developmental preschool and kindergarten teachers emphasizes enhancement of specific skills that will increase children's chances of success in the primary grades. Families are still a big part of youngsters' lives during the preschool years, so teachers and parents work together as partners. Developmental services often include speech and motor therapies integrated into classroom activities and coordinated with the teacher's curriculum.

Head Start

Head Start is a federally funded preschool program for children at risk for school failure because of economic disadvantage; children are eligible for Head Start based on family income. The program primarily serves children over the age of 3, but there are some home-based services for younger ages, Early Head Start for children ages birth to 3, and a few primary-grade pilot programs. Although it is now comprehensive in scope, with benefits for the entire family, Head Start was begun in 1965 as a summer-only program focusing on pre-kindergartners' health and social development. President Lyndon Johnson's War on Poverty promoted much creative thinking from the various governmental "warriors," and a number of social programs were begun almost simultaneously. Head Start was one of them and was viewed as a way to close the gap between the lives of economically disadvantaged children and those of their wealthier peers during the summer before the start of school. Today, children may attend Head Start for two years, and programs have academic orientations along with health and socialization. Chapter Three describes several current Head Start programs in depth.

Primary Grades

Traditionally, early childhood education has been thought of as encompassing children from birth to age 8. In some ways, ages 6 through 8 are transitional years between early and middle childhood. The primary grades, 1 through 3, are concerned with educating children during this transition. The changes that begin to occur in youngsters' lives cover all aspects of their development. Socially, they become less focused on self and more interested in group interactions, less concerned with what adults think of them than with the opinions of their peers. Physically, they become stronger and more coordinated; more able to accomplish the fundamental movements that will enable them to participate in sports; and more adept at hand–eye coordination, leading to the ability to do pencil-and-paper or computerized school work. Cognitively, they begin to understand the world as adults see it, making academic learning possible.

Of course, not every child attains the same understandings and skills at exactly the same time in just the same way. Because children develop so unevenly during these years, it is important that primary teachers have a strong understanding of child development. Thus you will observe that teachers in the first three grades often have training in early childhood as well as in elementary education. Primary teachers are charged with introducing young children to all the academic subjects they will encounter for the next several years of their lives: literacy, oral and written language, mathematics, science, social studies, and the arts. However, because these are transitional years, separating the subject areas and teaching them formally is not usually the best approach. Primary-grade teachers generally find themselves seeking ways to integrate the curriculum into more meaningful themes, topics, or projects.

Child Care

The purpose of child care is to provide a secure and happy place for young children while their parents work. Typically it serves children from birth to school age, but it can also provide after-school care for older children. Types of child-care centers vary widely. Family day care is common and popular and is usually provided by a mother who wishes to stay home with her own children while earning income by caring for other children. Corporate or employer child care is provided by a company for its employees, although outsiders are often permitted if space is available. Proprietary child care is offered by for-profit organizations, some of them regional or national chains or franchises. Educational components in child-care settings vary widely and at times may not exist at all.

In many countries, child care is supported for all working parents by public money, but this has not been the case in the United States. Finding good care continues to be a nationwide problem for many families. It is an especially difficult problem for poor single parents in states with welfare-to-work laws. Just as their work skills increase sufficiently to apply for entry-level jobs and their public assistance payments run out, they are faced with an inability to find affordable child care. Some states have developed child-care networks and referral agencies that provide parents with information on licensed centers and financial assistance.

Career Choices in Early Childhood Education

In addition to selecting particular age groups and program settings for your work in early childhood, you will be able to focus on specific roles within the early childhood profession and throughout your career. In part the professional roles you fill will be determined by the level of training you undergo, but there is quite a bit of flexibility at all levels of preparation. You may decide to own your own school, and that could mean caring for a small group of children in your home or creating a larger enterprise with its own buildings and a large staff. Eventually you might not work with children at all, preferring instead to become director of a center or even to attend law school and specialize in education-related legal issues. As a teacher, you can work in privately run centers that are either nonprofit or for profit; teach in public preschools, kindergartens, or primary grades; or be employed in corporate care centers. Some public libraries hire people with early childhood training for their children's rooms, and there are hospitals that run small centers for their patients or even the patients' visiting siblings. Wherever young children gather, there is a career waiting for you. Here are some of the more traditional jobs in early education, along with expected preparation, responsibilities, and rewards.

Teacher Aide or Teacher Assistant

This job requires little or no training, as reflected in the pay, which is minimum wage or close to it. An aide helps the teacher in whatever ways are needed, usually assisting children in activities that require adult help: preparing supplies, grading projects and papers, keeping the environment cleaned and straightened. Primary qualifications for an aide are to enjoy, respect, and relate well to young children. Often, people who begin working with children by being an aide discover that they enjoy the work and would like to take more responsibility. Naturally, this requires more education. There may be people in your class now who have followed this route.

Associate Teacher or Assistant Teacher

An associate teacher has more credentials than a teacher aide, the most common being an associate of arts (AA) degree or a child development associate (CDA) certificate. The CDA program is offered by many community colleges and vocational–technical institutes that have early childhood programs, although it is also possible to be informally educated through in-service workshops. These programs require the student to demonstrate specific competencies in order to receive the certificate. The associate teacher, like the teacher aide, works under the direction of the regular teacher, usually in a center-based (as opposed to school-based) environment. The associate teacher supervises children as the teacher directs and may do some team teaching, particularly by reading stories or singing songs. Although this job generally pays more than the teacher aide position, the salary is still low.

Teacher, Including Regular and Special Education Preschool Teacher, and K–3 Entry-Level Teacher

In an early childhood center, a teacher will usually have an AA degree, possibly with the CDA certificate. Centers may also have teachers who hold bachelor's degrees, but the pay is generally lower than in the public schools, so this is less common. In public schools, kindergarten through the grades, entry-level teachers must have baccalaureate degrees, although some states are moving toward a required master's degree. As more states pass legislation to create publicly funded preschool education, decisions must be made concerning teacher training. In some cases, only an AA is required, thus lowering the personnel cost for the state; in others, a bachelor's degree is required.

In a school setting, the teacher is usually the highest-level person to come in contact with the children. In early childhood centers, the teacher may also answer to a head teacher. In either case, the teacher makes lesson plans based on the school's philosophy and goals, arranges and maintains the environment, keeps records of children's progress, and does the actual day-to-day instructing.

Head Teacher or Lead Teacher

Typically found in an early childhood center or in special education public school preschool classrooms, the head teacher coordinates the curriculum and classroom functioning with the other teachers and staff. The head teacher takes a leadership role in meetings and planning sessions and may do some training of aides. Depending on the center and the head teacher's experience and capabilities, his or her background might include an AA, a bachelor's degree, or even a master's degree. Head teachers can often, but not always, expect to earn as much as public school teachers. Head Start lead teachers are now required to have a four-year degree, and salaries have improved with the requirement for a bachelor's degree.

In public schools there may also be a head teacher, who is appointed by the principal or elected by other teachers, usually in the same grade. In this case, the head teacher is not expected to monitor the teaching or organization in other classrooms but coordinates the curriculum, calls meetings for the group, and speaks for the group in communications with administrators. There may well be no extra remuneration for this task, but the teaching load might be reduced in some way. Most people reading this book will be training to be a teacher or head teacher.

Program Director or Supervisor, Assistant Director, Educational Director, Curriculum Coordinator, or Resource Teacher

People in these positions have had experience, often in-depth, teaching young children. They have been successful at it and are willing to accept responsibility on a broader level. Their positions can be defined as a midway point between the administration and the teaching staff and generally provide pay that is above a teacher's but lower than an administrator's. These supervisors and coordinators are responsible for monitoring the programs of each teacher, coordinating curriculum, providing in-service programs, maintaining teaching materials, supervising testing, and spearheading program development. People in these positions may have an AA but can usually be expected to have at least a bachelor's degree and often some graduate work.

Director or Principal

Whatever the setting, these positions require the most responsibility and the most unpredictable working hours. They also provide the highest pay. A director or principal must be able to work well with faculty, staff, parents, and the community as needed. In addition to overseeing the staff, this person must also manage the school's budget, coordinating it with the school's academic and caregiving goals. A director or principal generally holds a bachelor's degree and, increasingly, a master's or specialist's degree. In some places, principals and directors even hold doctoral degrees. In this case, they are usually expected to contribute professional research or extra programs for the community. Directors and principals have almost always had several years of teaching experience.

As described, professional positions in early childhood education generally follow a *career ladder* of increasing training, responsibility, and compensation, as shown in Table 2.1. The National Association for the Education of Young Children (NAEYC), which will be discussed later in the chapter, has expanded the concept of the career ladder to describe an early childhood *career lattice* (Johnson & McCracken, 1994). The concept of a career *lattice* was chosen to reflect the variety and complexity of the early childhood profession. Think of the horizontal levels of the lattice as the steps of the career ladder described in previous pages, with teaching assistant positions at the bottom and center directors/principals at the top. Vertical strands of the lattice represent the many roles and settings described at the beginning of this chapter, woven across each step of the profession. Finally, diagonals on the lattice demonstrate the movement that professionals can make across the various roles. Taken together, all these interconnected strands add up to the unique and varied fabric of the early childhood profession.

As you take your courses and have opportunities to work in classrooms, centers, and homes, think about the roles, responsibilities, and settings within which you will feel most comfortable. Then, choose an appropriate career direction and try setting goals for the next five years or so. Finally, be sure that you are acquiring the necessary training and credentials when you need them. This advice might sound obvious, but many prospective teachers ignore such suggestions and eventually find themselves taking redundant courses, going back to school for requirements they overlooked, or changing careers because the credentials they need require too much time, effort, and money. It is

TABLE 2.1 Early Childhood Positions, Credentials, and Responsibilities

Position	Minimum Education	Responsibilities
Director or principal	Usually BA or BS degree or MEd	Oversees and manages enrollment, parent relations, curriculum, budget, general running of school
Program or educational director, curriculum coordinator, resource teacher	Usually BA or BS or MEd, teaching experience	Monitors programs, materials, and testing; coordinates curriculum; provides in-service programs and program development
Head teacher	AA degree and/or CDA certificate, or BA or BS degree	Coordinates curriculum and schedules; calls and runs meetings; represents teachers; may be responsible for personnel issues and aide training
Teacher	AA degree and/or CDA certificate in preschools; BA or BS in K–3 grades; state certificate in public schools	Designs curriculum; plans schedule; has primary teaching responsibility for a single class
Associate or assistant teacher	Usually AA degree and/or CDA certificate	Supervises and/or teaches under direction of teacher
Teacher aide or teacher assistant	Depends on site or local regulations	Helps teacher as directed

well worth the effort to think through now what professional roles you will want to play over the next several years.

What is an Early Childhood Professional?

The dictionary defines a *profession* as an occupation or vocation that requires advanced education and training as well as intellectual skills, and teaching is often included as an example. To be a *professional*, dictionaries tell us, requires an active commitment to the chosen profession's high standards.

One educator, researcher, and writer (Fromberg, 2003) lists six characteristics of a profession that expand on this definition:

- An expectation of ethical performance.
- The required high level of expertise and skill.
- A body of knowledge and skills not possessed by lay people.
- Considerable autonomy in its practice, including control of entry into the profession.
- Commensurate compensation.
- A professional organization.

To become and be a professional, then, requires a good amount of self-motivation, effort, and integrity. It also includes the need to continue one's education over a long period—probably for the duration of one's professional life—and to participate in, as well as agree to the tenets of, the applicable professional organizations.

More specifically, to be an early childhood professional, your task will be to fulfill your state's requirements for certification; demonstrate your capabilities as you interact with children; keep up to date on research, theory, and developments in the understanding of best practices; and participate at some level in your choice of professional organizations, at the very minimum by subscribing to the organization's code of ethics. At the end of this chapter, you will find a list of professional organizations that will be helpful for you to know about. Here we will describe the two largest professional organizations in the United States for early childhood and early childhood special educators.

National Association for the Education of Young Children (NAEYC)

The National Association for the Education of Young Children (NAEYC), headquartered in Washington, DC, was founded in 1926 and has consistently grown in size and influence as a professional organization. There are currently almost 90,000 members who have joined NAEYC in a commitment to excellence in promoting the well-being of young children from birth to age 8, with an emphasis on developmental and early educational services. NAEYC's infrastructure includes over 300 regional, state, and local Affiliate Groups, with membership options that include student memberships at reduced subscription fees.

NAEYC provides a wide variety of resources for early childhood professionals, including the journal *Young Children*, a catalog of publications on an array of relevant topics, a long list of position papers on current issues, and an annual conference. In addition, NAEYC supports a comprehensive system of accreditation for programs that serve young children, and for two- and four-year personnel preparation programs.

NAEYC is an essential resource for the improvement of early childhood education nationwide, and collaborates with many other related professional organizations in this effort. Joining NAEYC as a student member is one of the best bridges from your preparation to your role as a professional.

Division of Early Childhood (DEC)

The Division of Early Childhood (DEC) is one related professional organization with which NAEYC has worked extensively; for example, NAEYC and DEC have produced joint position papers and sponsored joint conference presentations. The mission of DEC is to promote policies and evidence-based practices that support families and enhance the development of young children who have, or are at risk for having, developmental delays and disabilities. DEC is the largest of the 17 divisions of the Council for Exceptional Children (CEC), and like NAEYC supports a network of local, regional, and state subdivisions, as well as international chapters. Membership in DEC has grown dramatically since the mid-1980s, when preschool special education became a national mandate in the United States. The executive office for DEC is currently housed in Missoula, Montana and the CEC national office is in Arlington, Virginia.

In addition to position papers and an annual conference, DEC publishes the *Journal of Early Intervention* and *Young Exceptional Children* monograph series, maintains a large catalog of publications, sponsors webinars, and has an active legislative advocacy network. DEC membership is an option for division membership under CEC, and there is an incentive for CEC student membership that extends reduced subscription rates into the first year after graduation.

The trend toward inclusion of young children with special needs in early childhood programs is reflected in collaborative activities between DEC and NAEYC. The DEC and NAEYC alliance is a powerful force and resource on behalf of all young children and their families. Publications on inclusion can be found on each organization's Web site and in joint publications such as *The Joint Position Paper on Inclusion*.

Think about the boxed statement you find here. It accompanies the NAEYC code of ethics and speaks to the commitment we need to make as early childhood professionals. Take a moment to reflect on your own readiness to adopt it. To get you started along this road, we have included a copy of NAEYC's code of ethics in Appendix A; Appendix B is the code of ethics from DEC.

STATEMENT OF COMMITMENT

As an individual who works with young children, I commit myself to furthering the values of early childhood education as they are reflected in the NAEYC Code of Ethical Conduct.

To the best of my ability I will:

- Ensure that programs for young children are based on current knowledge of child development and early childhood education.
- Respect and support families in their task of nurturing children.

- Respect colleagues in early childhood education and support them in maintaining the NAEYC Code of Ethical Conduct.
- Serve as an advocate for children, their families, and their teachers in community and society.
- Maintain high standards of professional conduct.
- Recognize how personal values, opinions, and biases can affect professional judgment.
- Be open to new ideas and be willing to learn from the suggestions of others.
- Continue to learn, grow, and contribute as a professional.
- Honor the ideals and principles of the NAEYC Code of Ethical Conduct.

Career Standards

In 1987, the National Board for Professional Teaching Standards (NBPTS) was founded by educators with support from school boards, college officials, business executives, and state governors. The core challenge embraced by the board was "delineating outstanding practice and recognizing those who achieve it" (NAEYC, 1996, p. 55). The philosophical foundation underlying any definition of outstanding practice, the board proposed, should include five assumptions about teaching at all levels from early childhood through secondary grades:

1. Teachers are committed to students and their learning, treating them equitably while recognizing their individual differences.
2. Teachers know the subjects they teach and how to teach them.
3. Teachers are responsible for managing and monitoring student learning, and know how to engage students in disciplined learning.
4. Teachers think systematically about their practice and learn from experience, exemplifying in themselves the virtues they hope to instill in their students.
5. Teachers are members of learning communities, working with colleagues and parents to make decisions for their students' benefit.

From these five assumptions or propositions, age-related professional teaching standards were developed. For the early childhood years, there are eight standards. It is understood that these are standards to which only accomplished, experienced teachers should be held. Think of them as goals for your not-too-distant future. They are presented here in brief summary form; actual descriptions as available from the NBTPS or NAEYC appear in much richer detail.

- *Understanding young children.* There are three ways in which teachers need to understand their children: 1) They must have a knowledge of universal principles of physical, social and emotional, and cognitive development; 2) they need informed awareness of the roles that culture, history, and the values of community and family have in children's development and learning; and, 3) they must know the attributes of the children in their own classrooms. With a good understanding in all three areas, teachers are then able to plan programs to engage children in meaningful learning and to assess their progress.

- *Promoting child development and learning.* Based on their understanding of young children, teachers must be able to structure a physical, social, and emotional environment that successfully fosters development and learning. Teachers need to emphasize the importance of play in all aspects of children's development, incorporate play throughout the day, and be able to explain its use as a learning tool to parents, colleagues, and administrators. To promote health and physical growth, teachers need to provide movement and rest, fine- and gross-motor activities, and education in health and hygiene. To enhance social development, teachers have to educate children about behavioral expectations, learning in groups, and the importance and meaning of rules. To support emotional development and self-respect, teachers must know how to encourage independence, risk taking, and persistence. To foster language acquisition, teachers should provide plenty of opportunities to use both oral and written language. And to encourage growth in knowledge, teachers will provide appropriate resources and opportunities for children to engage their curiosity while learning to take risks, be persistent, and work with peers.

- *Knowledge of integrated curriculum.* Integrating the curriculum involves crossing academic disciplines to create learning that is personally relevant and meaningful to children. The core academic subjects for young children include literacy, language arts, mathematics, science, social studies, and the visual and performing arts. A multidisciplinary approach to teaching might include organizing a learning project according to key concepts, themes, or topics of interest to the children; in each case, appropriate learning would be pulled from each of the academic areas. Accomplished teachers have learned to do this to such an extent that the casual observer might find it difficult to sort out what subjects are being taught when. Still, teachers also know that each academic area has its own integrity, major ideas, and concepts and are sure to incorporate these within the learning experiences of their classes.

- *Multiple teaching strategies for meaningful learning.* Referring back to the first standard, we see that teachers need to be aware of universal development principles, cultural and societal influences, and the needs and interests of their individual children. The complexity of this awareness ultimately leads to complexity in teaching approaches. Master-level teaching includes a good mix in the classroom of varying activities, discussions, and social interactions. Teachers must observe, listen, ask skilled questions, facilitate discussions, select and adapt materials, and know when to intervene and when to let children alone. They are able to arrange and rearrange the physical environment, including technology, to implement activities appropriately. Accomplished teachers recognize when children are developing outside the typical range or are learning English as a new language. They make curricular and environmental alterations as necessary, knowing when to seek assistance from others, including children's families.

- *Assessment.* Teachers need to judge the effects of their work and make decisions about the things that happen next in the classroom. They also need to be held accountable to children and their parents as well as to the general public. Expert teachers of young children know that assessment of their work must go on daily as they observe youngsters working and playing, interacting socially, engaging themselves physically, and gaining cognitive knowledge. Their assessment strategies are varied and include observations, questions, listening, anecdotal records, systematic sampling of work products, and standardized instruments when they are appropriate.

■ *Reflective practice.* Effective teachers engage in ongoing self-examination, by considering the role of their experiences, cultures, biases, and values on their decision-making and interactions with children. They remain open to innovation and positive change, while being aware of the difference between important breakthroughs and momentary fads. Accomplished teachers see the need for self-renewal to strengthen the quality of their work and know that this means lifelong learning. As effective teachers reflect, they make use of and select from research studies, theories old and new, and current discussions about best practices. Experienced teachers remain accomplished and expert by continually looking for ways to grow personally and professionally.

FIGURE 2.4 Effective teachers reflect continually on their work and seek to strengthen its quality through lifelong learning.

■ *Family partnerships.* Accomplished teachers know that positive outcomes result from viewing families as allies in their work. They know that young children are especially dependent on their families and those children who feel as though home and school are well connected will be happier, more self-confident, and more motivated. These teachers know that families come in varying types and sizes and are respectful of them all. They are able to evaluate parents' special abilities and interests and then engage them effectively in the classroom, with projects that can be done at home, or in support of their own children's growth. Important teacher skills include the ability to listen to and learn from family members as well as to share information about children's progress and events in the classroom. And they are able to share information about children's development, as well as an understanding of child behavior, in ways that are useful to parents.

■ *Professional partnerships.* This final standard is based on the need for teachers to take what they have demonstrated within the other standards and share their knowledge with others, to receive information from other knowledgeable professionals, and to work effectively with colleagues from all levels. Effective teachers can be supportive as they offer criticism and stay positive and open-minded as they receive it. They can skillfully challenge those who engage in behaviors that are detrimental to children, and they are diligent in finding other teachers' classroom activities to celebrate publicly. They give and attend workshops, network with others in the profession, participate in professional organizations, perhaps become involved in child-related community issues or service, and even write or make presentations about what they have learned and experienced as teachers.

The NBPTS early childhood committee responsible for delineating the eight standards just summarized recognized that their expectations might "seem extraordinarily demanding," yet "every day they are upheld by teachers ... who are hard at work in our schools inspiring the nation's children." The committee hoped that the standards would "promise to be a stimulus for self-reflection on the part of teachers at all levels of performance" (NAEYC, 1996, p. 101). Thus, they have been included here for you to think about as you consider the demands of a profession that has always been of critical importance in the lives of young children and their families, and is now becoming recognized as such in the media and by the general public.

Traditions and Trends in Contemporary Early Childhood Education

In the first chapter, we acquainted you with the rich traditions in developmental psychology, general education, compensatory education, and special education that inform contemporary early childhood education. Developmental psychology has for decades evolved a sophisticated body of research that early educators draw upon for information about how children develop in cognitive/academic, social-emotional, motor/physical, and communication areas. General education in the United States provides a system of publically funded classroom services, and our colleagues in the primary grades are some of the strongest advocates of universal preschool programs. Compensatory education, as reflected in Head Start entitlement programs for young children, has supplied decades of successful efforts to provide equitable opportunities for success when children enter public school, and a strong emphasis on partnerships with families. And special education provides both a legal framework and a body of evidence-based practices for identifying and remediating developmental and early academic problems. Early intervention for infants and toddlers offers both a legal requirement and recommended practices for working within the family context. Taken together, these different traditions form a strong foundation for our profession in early childhood education, and as our traditions continue to evolve, so will our work with children and families.

NAEYC Developmentally Appropriate Practices and DEC Recommended Practices

One of the most influential contributions from NAEYC has been a document first published in 1987, and known in shorthand as DAP: *Developmentally Appropriate Practice in Early Childhood Programs Serving Children from Birth through Age 8* (Bredekamp, 1987). DAP organized appropriate and inappropriate interactions for early educators and children across the age range from infancy to primary school. Over the next decade, reactions from the field informed NAEYC of alterations that should be made to the document and of additional voices that needed to be heard as decisions about these modifications were made. Revised editions of the book have been published in 1997 and again in 2009 (Bredekamp & Copple, 1997/2009), with accompanying practice guides, ancillary materials, and training for educational leaders. DAP has for over 20 years now ignited serious and meaningful professional conversations, become integrated into personnel preparation programs, and catalyzed changes in programs for young children.

Developmentally Appropriate Practice was originally written in response to a wide-spread trend toward the use of teaching practices more appropriate for older students: rote learning, out-of-context skills, too much whole-group instruction, and readiness tests that unfairly retained children or denied them enrollment entirely. NAEYC's response was to create a series of position papers that laid out the results of research showing that young children usually learn best through active learning approaches, and these statements eventually led to the first major DAP document, as well as subsequent editions of the work. The perspective encouraged by DAP can be characterized as a *constructivist* approach, with an emphasis on internal processes that allow young children to be actively engaged in constructing their own knowledge and experiences.

The collaboration between NAEYC and DEC soon brought to light the fact that some children, often those eligible for special education, were more successful in preschool and primary grades if more structured approaches were used than those recommended in DAP. Special educators have a vast array of teacher-directed strategies that break skills into smaller skills, provide clear cues and reinforcement for learning difficult skills, and structure the environment for learning and behavior management. The teaching strategies that proved most effective in special education apply many tenets of the behavioral theory you learned about in Chapter One to individualized interventions for young children in specific areas of need.

In 1993, DEC published a compendium of practices that currently form the basis for professionals wanting to apply research-based special education practices with young children (DEC Task Force on Recommended Practices, 1993). The DEC book on recommended practices was updated most recently in 2005 as *DEC Recommended Practices: A Comprehensive Guide for Practical Application in Early Intervention/Early Childhood Special Education*, covering 240 practices in seven strands that emphasize the connection between research and practice (Sandall, Hemmeter, Smith, & McLean, 2005). DEC *Recommended Practices* materials also include video, toolkit, workbook, program level assessment, and other application resources for professionals.

Following a brief period of scholarly arguments between general and special early educators at conferences, in journal articles, and in the popular media, DEC and NAEYC began productive collaboration on the topic of including children with special needs in early childhood programs for typically developing peers. *Inclusion* holds great promise and has been shown to be a very successful program model for young children with and without disabilities and delays. After all, children with disabilities are more like their typically developing peers than they are different, so it stands to reason that DAP would be appropriate for them much of the time. Likewise, it is not only children eligible for special education who need extra support and structure as they learn to manage their own behavior and acquire difficult developmental and early academic skills. Educating young children with and without identified disabilities and delays together has made it clear that there is no one approach or tradition that is most successful for all children. As a result, interactive theories and philosophies have again become popular in our profession.

While theories and philosophies may seem too abstract to have many implications for practice, any kind of teaching in any setting will require you to knowledgeably choose materials for learning, activities to fill the day, management and discipline options, and teacher–child interaction styles. Learning how to make these decisions comprises much of a college student's teacher education program. Underlying this learning must be the development of a philosophy of early education, based on the philosophies and theories from the long history of early childhood education you studied in Chapter One, and practices based on the specific information in the remaining three chapters of this text.

EXTENDING YOUR LEARNING

The first two Suggestions are a continuation of the first two Suggestions in Chapter One (pages 33 and 34). Refer back to it if you have not yet started your philosophy and metaphor position papers and would like to.

 1 Now that you have read about modern-day careers in early education, do your initial views from Chapter One still sound practical and philosophically sound? Adjust your positions as necessary or make statements that verify your original ideas.

 2 It is time to attach a metaphor to yourself, to the children you'll teach, and to the classroom itself. You can do this in a short statement that identifies all three, and then explain your choices. Do you see yourself, for example, as an orchestra conductor or perhaps a mother hen? (Use different metaphors for yourself.) Imagine yourself teaching, working with colleagues, and meeting with parents as you build your metaphor, and strive for a coherent symbol that captures all aspects of your work.

3 From the career options discussed in this chapter, choose at least two that interest you. Interview someone who holds each position. Some questions you might ask:

   ■ What prompted you to choose this career?

- What are your goals for the future? Are you planning for any changes in your career?
- What are the most satisfying elements of your career? The most frustrating?
- What are some ways you can prepare well for this kind of career?
- What characteristics do you think someone needs to do this?

4 Observe a preschool class and a primary grade class. List similarities and differences in the teacher's style, children's interactions with each other, children's interactions with the teacher, kinds of materials, and the amount of freedom the children have.

5 Observe a center or classroom for 30 minutes, writing down everything that happens. Then, make a map of the room(s), noting the principal materials and furnishings. Refer to the orientations toward early education described in this chapter, and determine which elements of each you observed. Try to identify the primary orientation of the site.

6 Observe in an inclusive classroom and identify one child with a disability or delay, and one without. (You may have to ask the teacher for help identifying the child with a disability/delay if you are not familiar with the class.) Take notes on similarities and differences between the two.

7 Look at the NBPTS standards for early childhood and think about your teacher training program. Where in your training will you address each of the standards? Which classes in your program of study align with each of the standards? Which of the standards strike you as most interesting? Identify any special interests you have and start to develop your own plan for professional growth.

Professional Organizations

Administration for Children and Families
Office of Head Start
1250 Maryland Avenue SW, 8th Floor
Washington, DC 20024
P: (202) 205-8573

American Montessori Society
281 Park Avenue South
New York, NY 10010-6102
P: (212) 358-1250
F: (212) 358-1256
E: ams@amshq.org

Association for Childhood Education International
17904 Georgia Avenue, Suite 215
Olney, MD 20832
P: (301) 570-2111, (800) 423-3563
F: (301) 570-2212
E: headquarters@acei.org

Association Montessori Internationale/USA
410 Alexander Street
Rochester, NY 14607-1028
P: (716) 461-5920, (800) 872-2643
F: (585) 461-0075
E: ami-usa@montessori-ami.org

Center for the Child Care Workforce
555 New Jersey Avenue NW
Washington, DC 20001
P: (202) 662-8005
F: (202) 662-8006
E: ccw@aft.org

Council for Exceptional Children
1110 North Glebe Road, Suite 300
Arlington, VA 22201
P: (888) 232-7733, (800) 224-6830
F: (703) 264-9494
E: service@cec.sped.org

Council for Professional Recognition
2460 16th Street NW
Washington, DC 20009-3547
P: (202) 265-9090, (800) 424-4310

National Association for the Education of Young Children
1313 L Street NW, Suite 500
Washington, DC 20005-4110
P: (202) 232-8777, (800) 424-2460
F: (202) 328-1846

National Black Child Development Institute
1313 L Street NW, Suite 110
Washington, DC 20005-4110
P: (202) 833-2220
F: (202) 833-8222

Internet Resources

Web sites provide much useful information for educators and we list some here that pertain to the topics covered in this chapter. The addresses of Web sites can also change, however, and new ones are continually added. Thus, this list should be considered as a first step in your acquisition of a larger and ever-changing collection.

American Montessori Society
www.amshq.org

Association Montessori Internationale
www.ami.edu

Center for the Child Care Workforce
www.ccw.org/

Child Welfare League of America
www.cwla.org

Children's Defense Fund
www.childrensdefense.org

Division for Early Childhood, Council for Exceptional Children
www.dec-sped.org

Head Start
www.nhsa.org
or www.acf.hhs.gov/programs.ohs
or www.eclkc.ohs.acf.hhs.gov/hslc

National Association for the Education of Young Children
www.naeyc.org

Stand for Children
www.stand.org

Vocabulary

Child Care Centers. Facilities that provide out of home care for young children. Centers may offer educational programs or simply custodial supervision.

Child Development Associate (CDA). Graduate of a program offering the CDA certificate. CDA programs are usually offered in community colleges or vocational institutes and focus specifically on training for effective child care.

Constructivism. A psychological theory largely attributed to the Swiss Jean Piaget. It postulates that humans construct their own knowledge, intelligence, and morality through a series of stages.

Inclusion. An early childhood program that enrolls young children across all ability levels, including children with and without identified developmental delays and disabilities.

Kindergarten. A German word meaning "children's garden" first coined by educator Friedrich Froebel in the mid-19th century. An educational setting for children about 5 years old.

Kindergartner. Child of kindergarten age. A kindergarten teacher (obsolete).

Maturationism. A psychological theory largely attributed to the U.S. psychologist Arnold Gesell. It holds that humans are biologically destined to mature in a regular, sequential pattern.

Norms. Age-related expectations for what children should know and be able to do. Norms are often used in scoring and interpretation of standardized tests of early development, comparing each child's scores to those of a group of typically developing peers.

Nursery School. A group program that emphasizes caregiving and social interaction for young children, typically between the ages of 2 and 5; a less academic program than preschool.

Preschool. A classroom program for young children between the ages of 2 and 5, that emphasizes preparation for school; a more academic version of nursery school.

Readiness. A determination of a child's preparedness for the demands of formal schooling. Currently also used to indicate the preparedness of schools for meeting the needs of all children.

Transitional Kindergarten. A classroom program, generally after kindergarten and before first grade, for children who are old enough to be in first grade but not considered ready for formal, school-based learning.

References

Barnett, W. S. & Hustedt, J. T. (2003). Preschool: The most important grade. *Educational Leadership, 60*(7), 54–57.

Barnett, W. S., & Masse, L. N. (2007). Comparative benefit–cost analysis of the Abecedarian program and its policy implications. *Economics of Education Review, 26*(1), 113–125.

Bredekamp, S. (Ed.) (1987). *Developmentally appropriate practice in early childhood programs serving children from birth through age 8* (Expanded ed.). Washington, DC: National Association for the Education of Young Children.

Bredekamp, S., & Copple, C. (1997). *Developmentally appropriate practice in early childhood programs: Serving children from birth through age 8* (2nd ed.). Washington, DC: National Association for the Education of Young Children.

Bredekamp, S., & Copple, C. (2009). *Developmentally appropriate practice in early childhood programs: Serving children from birth through age 8* (3rd ed.). Washington, DC: National Association for the Education of Young Children.

Cost, Quality & Child Outcomes Study Team (1995). *Cost, quality, and child outcomes in child care centers, Public Report* (2nd ed.). Denver: Department of Economics, University of Colorado at Denver.

DEC Task Force on Recommended Practices (1993). *DEC recommended practices: Indicators of quality in programs for infants and young children with special needs and their families.* Reston, VA: Division for Early Childhood, Council for Exceptional Children.

Fromberg, D. P. (2003). The professional and social status of the early childhood educator. In J. P. Isenberg & M. R. Jalongo (Eds.), *Major trends and issues in early childhood education: Challenges, controversies, and insights* (2nd ed., pp. 177–192). New York: Teachers College Press.

Hendrick, J. (1987). *Why teach? A first look at working with young children.* Washington, DC: National Association for the Education of Young Children.

IDEA (2004). Individuals with Disabilities Education Improvement Act of 2004. PL No. 108-446.

Johnson, J., & McCracken, J. (Eds.) (1994). *The early childhood career lattice: Perspectives on professional development.* Washington, DC: National Association for the Education of Young Children.

Magnuson, K. A., Ruhm, C., & Waldfogel, J. (2007). Does prekindergarten improve school preparation and performance? *Economics of Education Review, 26*(1), 33–51.

NAEYC (National Association for the Education of Young Children) (1996). *Guidelines for preparation of early childhood professionals.* Washington, DC: Author.

Osborn, D. (1980). *Early childhood education in historical perspective.* Athens, GA: Education Associates.

Sandall, S., Hemmeter, M. L., Smith, B. J., & McLean, M. E. (2005). *DEC recommended practices: A comprehensive guide for practical application in early intervention/early childhood special education.* Missoula, MT: Division for Early Childhood.

Schweinhart, L. J., Montie, J., Xiang, Z., Barnett, W. S., Belfield, C. R., & Nores, M. (2005). *Lifetime effects: The High/Scope Perry preschool study through age 40.* Monographs of the High/Scope Educational Research Foundation, Number 14. Ypsilanti, MI: High/Scope Educational Research Foundation.

three
How Theoretical Perspectives Shape Early Education

Selected Models

The best school, after all, for the world of childhood, is not the school where children know the most answers, but the school where children ask the most questions.

Joe Coe

Chapter Objectives

After reading this chapter, you should be able to:

- Describe, compare, and contrast six current models of early childhood education.
- Relate the six models to the theories and philosophies described in Chapter One.

As you think about and apply chapter content on your own, you should be able to:

- Begin to make your emerging philosophy of early education practical by developing a list of the kinds of places you can envision yourself happily working.
- Observe schools and centers with some understanding of their underlying theories and philosophies, whether overtly stated or not.

A glance around any selection of schools and centers for young children should inform the viewer that every site is not equal or the same. Without some explanation, however, it may be difficult to put one's finger on just what the differences are. There are schools that are directly influenced by theories or philosophies past or present, and the titles and mission statements of these schools make their identification obvious. As well, it is possible to visit schools and centers in which teachers are permitted to base educational practices on their personal philosophies. Then, there are numerous child-care centers with no other guiding educational philosophy than the locally mandated standards for safety.

In this chapter, we visit six quite different schools and centers for young children. Their philosophies may differ widely, the youngsters vary in age from infants to children in primary grades, but in all cases the directors, caregivers, and teachers are committed to providing the best possible learning experiences. It should be pointed out that each of these visits was a snapshot in time and, by the time you read this, personnel and even sites may well have changed. Where connections can be made to this book's first two chapters, this has been done, so that application of theory to the real world becomes apparent and job descriptions are seen in action.

Our first visit takes us to a complex of centers and activities all under the guiding concepts of the Head Start movement that began in the 1960s.

Head Start: A Uniquely U.S. Model

The U.S. social and political turmoil of the 1960s was, in part, instigated by top-down political development. President John F. Kennedy's administration was committed to finding new ways of improving the economic status of the nation's poor, estimated at that time to be one fourth of the population. After Kennedy's death, President Lyndon Johnson enthusiastically took up the challenge, declaring a "war on poverty" whose goals were to both cure and prevent poverty in the United States.

As a first step, the Office of Economic Opportunity (OEO) was created in 1964, and a few months later Project Head Start was begun under its sponsorship. From the beginning, the focus of this program was to provide poor children of preschool age with some of the benefits middle-class society could more easily afford: day care, academic experiences, medical and dental care, and involvement of parents in their children's early education. Originally planned as a pilot program for 100,000 children in the summer of 1965, the national clamor to be part of this unique creation led to an initial enrollment of more than 550,000 children in over 11,000 centers. For the next few years, Head Start grew in size and popularity, while also extending the summer program to a full year at most sites. Then the first national review of its effectiveness was published.

In 1969, the Westinghouse Learning Corporation was commissioned to evaluate the impact on school achievement of children who were graduates of the Head Start program. The results were dismaying. Although the children's cognitive and affective gains were positive during their time in Head Start, any growth flattened out and diminished during the primary years. By this time, Richard Nixon was president, and his initial enthusiasm for the program quickly abated, as did congressional funding (Washington & Oyemade, 1987).

Over the next several years, Head Start fought for its existence. As a beginning, the OEO published a review of all Project Head Start research, demonstrating that the program was more successful than the Westinghouse study indicated (Kirschner Associates, 1970). Yet, many thought Head Start had died, particularly after its demise was prematurely reported in some major newspapers (Washington & Oyemade Bailey, 1995). Congressional support varied and waivered over the years until the first longitudinal studies showed what happened to Head Start children as they moved toward and into adulthood. The most widely reported study was one that followed 123 children from the Perry Preschool in Yspilanti, Michigan, into their 27th year (Schweinhart & Weikart, 1993). The researchers found that in adulthood, the preschool graduates were more likely than their peers who had never attended preschool to own homes, complete higher levels of education, require fewer social services, and be in less trouble with the law.

In recent years, such reports of success have gone a long way to promote public and congressional awareness of and support for Head Start and its several programs. Always a work in progress, Head Start has continually experimented with a variety of programs to meet differing needs while being moved from one government agency to another (it is currently housed in the U.S. Department of Health and Human Services.) By 2008, more than 908,000 children between the ages of 3 and 5 were enrolled in more than 18,000 centers. Children with disabilities accounted for 12% of the total.

Although the original model for preschoolers is the most widely known and commonly found, other programs have evolved over the years as well. Some, but by no means all, of Head Start's innovations, national demonstration models, and strategies include:

- *Early Head Start.* Established in 1994 as research was showing the critical importance of healthy development in the first three years of life. The purpose of Early Head Start is to foster the cognitive, social and emotional, and physical growth of newborns to 3-year-olds while helping parents to be better teachers and caregivers of their infants and toddlers. Included too is help for parents in meeting their own life goals, including financial independence. In this program, education can take place either in the home or at a Head Start center; help for parents can be provided on an individual basis, through peer support groups, or both.

- *Home Start.* Provides home-based educational, health, and social services, primarily in rural areas. The Head Start teacher works with both the at-home parent and child(ren). In some cases, children may participate in Home Start while they are 3 years old, and then attend a Head Start preschool the following year.

- *Even Start.* Unites early childhood education (through age 7) and adult basic education. While their children attend a Head Start center or elementary school, parents are provided with help in literacy acquisition, vocational training, and/or study for the GED (general equivalency diploma). Parenting education is an integral part of the program with goals that include building stronger family networks and improving parent and child self-esteem.

- *Child Development Associate (CDA).* This national credentialing program, once part of the Head Start framework, is now operated by the Council for Early Childhood Professional Recognition in Washington, DC. More than 90% of Head Start's teachers have teaching certification, and most of these hold the CDA. The credential can be earned through a combination of on-site mentoring and coursework, often through a local community college. The core curriculum is determined by the four foci of the Head Start program: education, health, parent involvement, and social services.

To see some Head Start initiatives in action, we will visit a rural area in northwestern Washington State, close to the Canadian border.

Head Start Preschool and Much More, All Under One Local Umbrella

It is unusual to see such a large variety of Head Start-related resources in one rural community, but strong leadership and community cooperation have led to an increasing number of family services in the Nooksack Valley School District, Center for Children and Families Program. In addition to the services described here, also included is an alternative high school complete with child care.

The Head Start Program

We will begin our several visits at the Head Start center. In general, when people think of the national program, a setting such as this for 4- and 5-year-olds is what they envision. Like many centers, the Nooksack Head Start is located in a homelike building next to a public school, in this case the local high school. In a large room that serves about 20 children, Michael Marsh and Julie Emerson share teaching responsibilities with the help of a classroom aide. Several of the children are just learning English and whereas Michael can speak Spanish to those who come from Mexico, children who have immigrated from Ukraine, Russia, Vietnam, and the Punjab must use other clues to understand what is going on.

It is 9:30 A.M. when we begin our visit, the time that the children are divided into two groups of 10 for special projects and snack with their assigned teachers. Michael divides his group of children further, for a choice of planting popcorn seeds or an art project, but Julie's group works together on a counting lesson involving fish-shaped crackers that are eaten by her 10 "hungry sharks." It is about 10:00 A.M. when both groups finish their activities and begin to prepare for snack.

Head Start academic curricula and teaching styles can vary considerably in different sites across the United States, but snack and meal times share a focus on nutrition, community building, traditional family serving styles, and growth in good manners. To see how this works, let's observe Julie and her group during the 30 minutes it takes to complete the entire experience.

A kitchen helper has wheeled in a large serving cart with small bagels already placed on plastic plates and applesauce served up in small bowls. With everyone seated at a single rectangular table, their hands freshly washed, Julie demonstrates how each plate and bowl should be passed in one direction. She then carefully helps herself to some cream cheese, shows how it should be placed on the plate, then passed around the table. Spreading the cheese on the bagel, Julie points out that it is important to spread after passing so that people don't have to wait so long for their food. Finally, a pitcher of milk is also passed, with Julie demonstrating proper pouring techniques. When a bit is spilled by one child, she assures him that "It's okay—this happens sometimes" and helps him wipe up the spill.

When all the food has been distributed, Julie reminds the children that she always likes to wait until everybody has their food before she begins eating. This comment, and those that have preceded it, are not news to the children but rather are daily reminders of proper behavior. When Julie makes this final suggestion, not a single child has begun eating.

For the next few minutes, as everyone eats, Julie engages the children in polite conversation, asking what they have enjoyed doing during the extended weekend that has just passed. When the children are finished, they clear their own places, putting spoons and knives to soak in soapy water and plastic dishes in the trash. Circle time and free-choice centers round out the half-day program.

The curricular framework for this Head Start center was developed cooperatively with a local expert in early childhood education. It is based, for the most part, on the positions taken by the National Association for the Education of Young Children (NAEYC) regarding developmentally appropriate practices. In addition, each child has an individual learning plan (ILP) developed cooperatively with his or her parents. Because there are many varieties of curriculum and teaching methodologies found in Head Start centers, visits to one or more nearby sites are recommended for our readers.

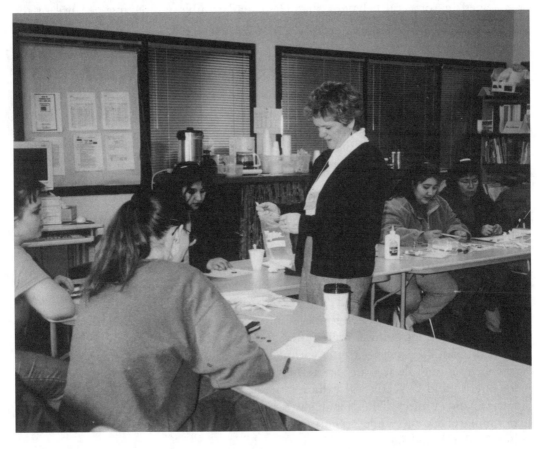

FIGURE 3.1 Head Start programs are not only for children. Their parents also have opportunities for learning.

The Home Start Program

Heidi Bugby's time is split between the Nooksack Head Start center and her visits to the homes of 3-year-old children who are scheduled to begin the Head Start program when they turn 4. She meets each of her 10 children once a week in their homes, then works with them again on Thursdays when they all join the 4-year-olds at the center.

Each home visit is two hours long and is divided into three typical Head Start components: social services, parenting and child development, and one-on-one educational work with the child. Heidi enters each home with planned topics for discussion with the parent and activities for the child, but she remains flexible. On the day of our visit, she spends more than her usual time with the parent, although there is still plenty of time left for a major activity with the child, as we shall see.

Alexei, his older sister, and parents live in a mobile-home park located in a wooded area at the foot of a mountain range. This is an area populated to great extent by immigrants from the former Soviet Union; Alexei's family immigrated from Ukraine eight years ago. Although his father has been able to find well-paying work, his mother, Ivana, has not. In addition, Alexei, who speaks almost no English, will begin school at the Head Start center in a few months. At his last weekly visit with the other 3-year-olds, he engaged in some misbehavior that Heidi had trouble redirecting because of the linguistic barrier between them. These issues will guide today's visit as each of the Head Start components is met.

A small but comfortable dining room serves as Heidi's classroom, and she begins by discussing with Ivana a combination of information about upcoming Head Start activities and progress on finding a job appropriate to Ivana's training, work background, and bilingual capabilities. Heidi has brought a letter she has written as reference and discusses Ivana's résumé, which they are working on together. Conversation then moves to Alexei's behavior the previous week, and Heidi suggests one or two ways that Ivana might talk to Alexei about it "without making him feel bad." The discussion of Head Start activities, job hunts, and Alexei's behavior takes just over an hour and combines, in a friendly and informal way, the first three components of the Head Start program (social services, parenting and child development, educational work with the child).

During this discussion, Alexei has been happily involved in creating ever more complex structures from a set of snap-blocks brought by Heidi. For the most part, he has played by himself, though occasionally he walks shyly around Heidi and whispers to his mother, usually to share a description of what he has just made.

During the second hour, Heidi, Ivana, and Alexei all participate in the making of a piñata, a craft activity designed to allow informal conversation in English and to help children from varying cultures represented at the center learn more about each other. As they work, Heidi practices learning various color words in their language while Alexei learns them in English. It is an important aspect of Head Start that immigrant children learn English and U.S. cultural values while at the same time retaining their original languages and cultures. Thus, Heidi shows her respect for what she sees in this Ukrainian immigrant home while preparing Alexei for the experiences he will have in the culture of the United States.

As we leave, Heidi admires the pots of flowers Ivana has planted near the front door, reminds Alexei that she will see him Thursday and that he should wear something green (*ziloni*) because it is the color of the week.

The Even Start Program

Across the street from the center, in an out-of-the-way wing of the high school, a comfortable classroom and adjacent office space have been assigned to the local Even Start program. Here, parents whose reading skills are less than those of an eighth grader and who lack high school diplomas, gather several times a week for an array of educational services. Parent education is provided by a nearby technical college. Adult basic education comes from the county's community college. Much or most of the curriculum is individualized, since each parent comes in with his or her own educational accomplishments and goals. (Currently, all the parents are mothers.)

In addition to the on-campus education, there are home visits provided if the family has a child in Head Start. Public health nurses, social workers, and bilingual educators all provide services as needed.

The success of this program can be seen in parental comments such as these:

"I never thought I'd get a second chance to go back … and here I am, six months into my high school diploma! I'm watching my kids grow and they're watching me, too!"

"I wasn't doing anything … just sitting at home and watching TV. Now, I spend time reading to my kids and I'm almost done with my GED!"

The Infant–Toddler Program

While their mothers attend Even Start classes, those children too young to attend the Head Start preschool class are provided with care in a light and open portable classroom on the school grounds. Infants and toddlers from the Early Head Start program join the group once each week for peer socialization. Just as the other programs we described focus on enhancing each individual child's learning, so too does this program. It emphasizes providing the children with stability, predictability, and consistency through scheduled naps, meals, and other healthful routines. The staff also works to create a safe environment in which nothing is off-limits to beginning explorers.

Once each week, Even Start parents join their children at the child-care center for a special Parent and Child Together (PACT) session. Here, the skills learned in the parenting classes can be discussed and put into practice with support from peers and instructors.

Early Childhood Special Education Programs

Children with special needs, and their families, are also included in the Nooksack Center for Children and Families Programs. Preschool children ages 3 to 5 years who are eligible for special education receive specially designed instruction in the Head Start preschool classroom, with individualized instruction to address motor and communication needs. Infants and toddlers with disabilities attend Early Head Start socialization groups with their parents. Advantages of this model include peer interactions for children, convenient services for parents, and the availability of specialists to provide extra support for all children in the program.

All the programs described here grew in conjunction with the federally funded Project Head Start, but they also receive funding and other support from local agencies and schools. There is a strong emphasis on collaboration and cooperation along with a continual assessment of every program so that improvements can be made and new ideas instituted. As mentioned earlier, Head Start has always been a work in progress.

Montessori's Influence on U.S. Early Education

Working parents' need for child care has been with us since the advent of the industrial revolution. It has been about a century since the owners of slum apartments in Rome contracted with Maria Montessori to provide a day-care center for the children who played unsupervised while their parents were at work. The owners' interests were less with the children than with the survival of their buildings. Happily for the children, Montessori's interests were with them. Here is the story of the schools that grew from that experience.

Chapter One presented an overview of the life and ideas of Maria Montessori, Italy's first female medical doctor and influential leader in the development of 20th-century early childhood education. Because of her continuing influence more than a half century after her death, we include here a more in-depth description of the schools that bear her name.

The social environment of a Montessori class, as you will recall from Chapter One, is designed to foster in children independence, cooperation, sharing, responsibility, even grace and courtesy—all qualities necessary for the creation of a pre-democratic *society in embryo*, as Montessori called it. Montessori believed that it was unnecessary, even futile, to attempt to goad young children into developing these qualities through intrusive adult teaching methods, and so the teachers in her schools rely on a carefully crafted environment instead. The focus is on letting children develop as individuals, and as they do, they come naturally into the beginnings of a successful society. Materials and furniture are designed and arranged in such a way that children can choose whether to work independently or with others; the teacher intervenes in a child's decisions only if a continuing problem arises. Generally, there are few materials found in multiples. Instead, a single sample of each type is available, thus making it necessary for children to take turns and share. The teacher's responsibility is to work with the children to design an equitable system, thus providing them with an opportunity to develop as individuals and create their embryonic society.

The social structure in a Montessori classroom is also enhanced by the mixing of ages and abilities. This provides children with an experience more representative of real life than a single-age class would. More specifically, the younger children learn to rely on the older ones for assistance while the older children experience responsibility and caring.

The academic environment of a Montessori school is a bit different—at times it can be profoundly different—from that in most other preschools. The social structure just described plays an important part in academic learning. For example, more knowledgeable children take an active part in teaching what they know to their classmates. At the same time, young children are more likely to work on their own than they are in most preschools or centers. Montessori observed that there was a *sensitive* or *critical period* at the younger ages for self-development best fostered, she believed, by not forcing group work and play.

Academic materials in a Montessori preschool tend to be quite structured with very specific purposes. Whereas there is certainly room for creativity, the Montessori philosophy is that creativity grows best from the experience of reality. Thus, when a new skill or learning is encountered, children are provided with self-correcting materials and direct instruction. Later, exploration and creativity are permitted. Even at this more advanced stage, however, there may be limits. For example, a series of 10 wooden (usually pink) cubes that increase in size from 1 to 100 square centimeters may be built into a vertical tower, a horizontal tower, or even combined with other similar materials to make intricate patterns. The cubes, however, may not be turned into a choo-choo train or a dollhouse, but instead must always keep their original academic intent.

The role of the teacher in a Montessori school is considered that of guide, director, or facilitator. It is with the purpose of serving the children's needs and interests that the teacher steps back when possible in order to observe independent child behaviors and to allow the embryonic society to develop. In all ways, teachers model appropriate behaviors: carrying chairs and materials carefully, taking care not to bump into children's work and helping to fix things if they do, speaking and moving with a sense of quietness.

In the following description of a Montessori school, you see examples of these elements in action. In addition, two different classrooms within the school are described so that connections between what children learn at a young age and carry forward over the years can be seen.

The Montessori Approach at the Aidan Montessori School in Washington, DC

Originally founded as the St. Aidan School by Roman Catholic parents, the school has now been secularized and moved to a central location so that it might serve all of the city. The ethnic diversity of the children as well as of the teaching staff reflects the success of this venture. There are four age levels represented in the multi-age classes: 18 months to 3 years, 3 to 6 years, 6 to 9 years, and 9 to 12 years. Our visit takes us to two of these classrooms on the second day of a new school year.

FIGURE 3.2 Montessori classrooms are designed so that children can choose to work either in groups or independently.

Denise Merkel, teacher of the toddler class, considers the development of independence an issue from the first day of school and provides the children with careful instructions for such skills as washing their own hands, using the toilet, and taking coats on and off. Beginning socialization skills include choosing their own work, waiting turns, pushing chairs in carefully, and becoming more graceful in their movements throughout the room. Denise introduces all of these skills by demonstration and modeling, then providing encouragement to the children as they endeavor to repeat what she does.

Most of the eight children in her class are returnees and have some familiarity with the expected behaviors and routines. Still, one of the 2½-year-olds suddenly becomes homesick on this, her second day of the new year. Denise goes to her and a few of the others crowd around as well. "I want my daddy to pick me up," Annie cries. Soon, Denise has all the children telling the group who will be picking them up and Annie becomes calm.

During the discussion, Edward is at the other end of the room spooning hazelnuts from one bowl into another, a *practical life* exercise designed to help the youngest children learn to participate skillfully in everyday life. Occasionally he contributes a comment to the discussion with Annie and finally goes to join the group. Gently, Denise tells him, "You need to finish your work. Go finish your spooning." He returns to his little table with its single chair and spoons the nuts for another minute or two, finally returning the materials to their proper place on the open-shelving system. Denise notices, however, that Edward has left his chair out, and she sends him back to replace it correctly. She does this without any trace of criticism in her voice and Edward accepts the correction with equanimity, pushing the chair in as well as a 2-year-old can, then joins a group beginning to collect around the guinea pig cage.

For the next half-hour, the children wander the room, sometimes deciding on materials to work on alone or with others, sometimes following the teacher as she shows a child a table-washing activity and demonstrates to others how to water a plant. At one point, Annie asks, "Is Daddy here yet?" but seems undisturbed to be told he isn't. Forty minutes into their two-hour day, the entire group settles happily into self-chosen activities, occasionally exchanging them for others after correctly returning the originals to their proper places.

Meanwhile, the primary class (3- to 6-year-olds) is also adjusting to its first week of school. All the children are returnees, with new children scheduled to begin a few days later, after the rhythm of the class has been established. The teacher, Kajal Guha, displays much the same behavior as Denise does in the toddler class, roving quietly through the room looking for opportunities to teach and lend support. In both classes, this roving is not casual and unplanned. The teachers have ideas in advance about the children they plan to work with and the materials they will introduce.

In this, the middle of the second morning of the first week of school, Kajal is most concerned with the social processes that must be established early on if learning is to flow smoothly the rest of the year. Like Denise, she keeps an eye out for the social processes that would benefit from some practice.

As she observes and interacts with children working, sometimes alone and sometimes in pairs, on such activities as puzzle maps, easel painting, and table scrubbing, Kajal notes that one clean-up routine is not being accomplished easily by several children. Since many of the children work on the floor in a Montessori classroom, they are provided with small rugs that are kept rolled up in a storage bin when not in use. The children in Kajal's class have had much practice in unrolling and rerolling the rugs, but after the summer vacation, several have lost their earlier expert touch, and the rugs are beginning to flop chaotically from their bin.

Kajal decides that a reminder demonstration of rug-rolling techniques would be useful for the entire group of 12 children. She gathers them around her on the large oriental rug that is used at group time, with the children using the exterior border as a guide for sitting. Three children, however, have not finished the work they started on the far side of the room and show no interest in joining the larger group. Kajal determines that it is more important just now for these three to experience the satisfaction that comes with completion of an activity than to join the group in an activity that can be repeated later, so she makes no suggestions to them about hurrying to join the class or interrupting their work for the demonstration.

The nine remaining children watch as Kajal shows them how to roll the rug. She makes no comments about the fact that they have known this before and seem to have lost their expertise; all is done without criticism or even coaxing children to improve. Then, the children take turns rolling several mats with the teacher encouraging their effort and complimenting their skill. At the other end of the room, the classroom aide helps the remaining three children finish their work and, eventually, they join the others in rug rolling.

Suddenly, Georg shouts a question to the aide, shattering the serenity of the moment. Everyone except the teacher looks a bit startled. Kajal simply asks quietly, "Can anyone tell us why we don't shout?"

Children raise their hands and answer, "It bothers the other classes," or "We can't work," or "It's rude," and "It can get annoying."

"What do we do instead?" Kajal asks.

"We walk to the other teacher," someone answers, and Georg walks to the other end of the room and talks quietly to the aide.

Translating Philosophy to Different Settings

If we look closely at the two classrooms in this very typical Montessori school, we see different teaching approaches that reflect the different ages of the children. We also see close connections and careful transitions between the ages. Both Denise and Kajal take time at the beginning of the year to establish routines that show respect for the materials as well as one another and contribute to the smooth functioning of the classroom. In addition, there are underlying values of personal independence coupled with the creation of a pre-democratic group ethic—Montessori's society in embryo. For example, when Denise and Kajal carefully teach a specific method for rolling a rug or placing a chair at its table, their intent is to help the children achieve independence and competence while learning that what they do is a courtesy to the children who wish to use the materials next. Such simple activities, multiplied over time and among children, lead to a cohesive group that is, nevertheless, made up of very independent individuals.

The Aidan Montessori School was chosen for its excellence in demonstrating Montessori's ideas, but one could visit almost any other Montessori school and recognize the philosophy in action, even though historically there have been schisms among various groups, all of which purport to teach the "real" Montessori curriculum. There is, for example, a core collection of manufactured materials, all of them containing some form of self-correction. All the manufactured materials as well as those made by the teachers are placed on child-height shelving with divisions made according to categories (for example, math, language, practical life, and materials for learning through the various senses.) The observer of this environment in action would see children making their own choices of work; deciding whether they wish to work alone or with others; and, for that matter, a focus on *work* as opposed to *play*, although this terminology is more for the purpose of showing respect for the children's activities than it is for taking away their enjoyment. The children would seem, to most observers, to be quite content with their school lives.

Educating the Whole Child: The Aesthetic Perspective of Waldorf Schools

Our next model of early education is, no doubt, the most unusual one we will study. It is also the one that is least likely to be adopted by public or more traditional schools, although in some respects, it has influenced education in ways both subtle and global. For this reason, we now look at the history of Waldorf schools and view an example in British Columbia, Canada.

The unusual nature of Waldorf education has been described by one writer (Kotzsch, n.d., p. 2) as:

> like passing through Alice's looking glass into an educational wonderland. It is a surprising, sometimes disorienting world of fairy tales, myths and legends, of music, art, physics demonstrations, class plays and seasonal festivals, of workbooks written and illustrated by students, a world without exams, grades, computers or televisions. It is, in short, a world where most of the standard ideas and practices of American education have been stood on their heads.

The history of this approach to education began in a most unlikely place, a German cigarette factory. In April 1919, just a few months after the end of World War I, a philosopher named Rudolf Steiner (1861–1925) gave a talk about politics, economics, and education to a gathering of workers at the Waldorf-Astoria cigarette factory in Stuttgart, Germany. It was Steiner's view that people such as the Waldorf workers and their children should not be subjected to an education that simply trained them for an industrial society. Rather, they should have an education that developed their natural talents and permitted their individual personalities to bloom.

The owner of the factory was so impressed with Steiner's talk that he immediately asked him to begin a school for the workers. Steiner agreed to do so as long as children of all social and economic backgrounds could attend, the curriculum would cover an entire 12 years, and its religious orientation would be nondenominational. His conditions were agreed to, and by fall of the same year, the Waldorf School had opened (Uhrmacher, 1995).

During the next few years, similar schools were founded in Germany, the Netherlands, and Great Britain. In 1928, the first Waldorf school opened in the United States, in New York City. By 2010, more than 950 schools could be found worldwide.

The influences on Steiner's philosophy and views of education were several and included both Western and Eastern thought. Putting them together, he created a new philosophy that he named *anthroposophy* (from *anthropos* or man and *sophia* or wisdom). A key tenet of anthroposophy is that even the most ordinary human being is capable of becoming more spiritual. The activities Steiner suggested for achieving a spiritual state include several that had immediate application for education from the earliest ages: "cultivating one's sense of the beautiful, sympathizing with fellow beings, thinking ... and developing powers of observation" (Uhrmacher, 1995, p. 387).

Anthroposophy defines human development as a journey of the soul from birth to death to rebirth through reincarnation, but it is the stages of child development Steiner posited that are reflected in a Waldorf school. In some ways, the Steiner stages are similar to those Piaget theorized in that their divisions appear at about the same chronological time and their cognitive elements have implications for classroom teaching (Ginsburg, 1982). Piaget's views, however, are those of the scientist whereas Steiner's come from a philosophical orientation. To Steiner, the development of cognition was only part of an educator's focus; the journey of soul and spirit was equally important, if not more so.

Steiner viewed the first stage of child development, birth to age 7, as a time of imitation, of learning through empathy and by doing. Thus, it becomes important for influential adults to model only the behavior they wish to see imitated. Everything from tone of voice to "physical touch, bodily gesture, light, darkness, color, harmony and disharmony" comprise influences that "are absorbed by the still-malleable physical organism and affect the body for a lifetime" (Barnes, 1991, p. 52). Education for this age, according to Steiner, should not push children into academic pursuits. Reading instruction, which could actually cause more harm than good if provided too early, should wait while more important activities are engaged in. These include various art activities, in which imitation of the teacher does not carry the negative stigma it does in other models of early education; story time, in which the teacher creates and tells stories appropriate to a particular class, so that children can imagine the pictures for themselves; and *eurythmy*, an art form created by Steiner that involves movement, rhythm, language, and music.

Middle childhood begins, in Steiner's philosophy, about the time children's baby teeth are lost and the *etheric life force*, or vital energy that differentiates living beings from minerals, emerges, somewhere around age 6. Whereas the first stage is characterized by imitation, this second stage focuses on feeling and rhythm. As children learn their arithmetic tables, they chant them rhythmically or sing songs to help them memorize. Eurythmy is continued from the earlier years, as is story telling. The latter is focused on fairy tales in the first grade, fables in the second, and Old Testament stories in the third—all with the idea that these forms of literature appeal to the feeling mode of children in the second stage of development.

One major component of Waldorf education for all ages is the two-hour block of study at the beginning of each day. This was originated to counteract the fragmentation of the curriculum in early 20th-century Germany, but Waldorf educators could just as easily point to the same problem in American education today.

Another component is the division of faculty into *class* and *specialty* teachers. The class teacher stays with a single group of children from first through eighth grade, providing continuity while also being mindful of the children's changing needs and interests. Specialty teachers are experts in particular areas such as eurythmics or art. In the early grades, the teacher is viewed less as a facilitator than as the classroom leader—not in an authoritarian way, but as one who is definitely in charge of the learning that goes on. There is sensitivity to children's interests, but it is the teachers, not children or administrators, who determine the curriculum.

Third, classroom environment and tools of learning are created with an eye focused closely on the aesthetic. This is probably to be expected in an approach to education that focuses on arts and crafts more than any other model does. Natural materials are used where possible. Thus, walls are painted with careful attention to both color and texture, fabrics are often hand dyed, and beeswax is prized as the best material for crayons and one of the most aesthetic substances for modeling projects. Few commercial textbooks are used, technology is reserved for later years, and teachers, often with the children's help, create most learning materials.

Finally, although anthroposophic philosophy guides curriculum and teaching methodology, Waldorf schools do not intend to create new generations of anthroposophists. Children are not in any way indoctrinated; indeed, they may attend their school for years and never hear the words *anthroposophy* or *Steiner* (Kotzsch, n.d.).

Putting all these elements together into a unified whole creates schools that emphasize both the arts and nature, with close attention paid to children's development. In recent years, this has meant adopting and adapting in some 100 United States Waldorf schools, the "forest kindergarten" model, begun in the 1950s in Scandinavia (Leyden, 2009). A forest kindergarten's curriculum is taught mostly outdoors, except in extreme or dangerous weather, and includes time for pretend play as well as for learning about nature.

More traditionally, however, Waldorf education is to be found indoors and we go now to North Vancouver, British Columbia to see such a school in action.

Aesthetics in Practice at the Vancouver Waldorf School

It is 9:00 A.M. and Pat Tatum's 25 third graders sit in rows of two-person desks, facing the blackboard in front and practicing songs on their recorders. At first, the scene appears much like that of any traditional third-grade class led by their teacher in a direct instruction lesson. Then, subtle differences become noticeable. The children sit in beautifully crafted wooden chairs. The contours of the room form an indefinable geometric shape with corners in unexpected places. The walls are painted in restful pastel shades. And on the chalkboard is a large, teacher-drawn picture of a *sukkah*, an integral part of the Hebrew Sukkot holiday the children have been studying. Next to the picture is a story the teacher has written in a beautiful cursive hand, words alternating in three colors of chalk. The story tells of the children's experiences in making their own version of a sukkah:

> In honor of the harvest we made a little house. It had three walls. We made a roof by nailing boards across the top. We put branches on top also. When people climbed on it our shelter fell down.

At this moment, however, story and picture await the appropriate time for the class's attention. The focus is on memorizing the recorder music and, eventually, on singing.

When it is time to move on to the morning's arithmetic lesson, the class does so, quite literally. Pat clasps two large wooden sticks in her hands, beating them and chanting in rhythm, "Move those chairs. Work those muscles." The children know just what to do, and soon everything has been placed close to the walls leaving a large space for very active learning. After a couple full-group songs that place everyone in a large circle, sub-circles are formed with each one in turn playing a chanting game that includes the multiplication tables they are currently studying. Next, children return to the larger circle where they divide into pairs to chant and clap the same tables. This time, however, they also work backward, starting with the answers ("50 is 10 times 5"). Occasionally, Pat taps her foot in rhythm to keep the children on track, then returns to her rhythm sticks when it is time to replace the furniture.

The point of the multiplication games has been review, in preparation for a more in-depth division lesson. Using a small slate as her prop and the Sukkot holiday as the theme, Pat leads the children in a discussion of ways that varying numbers of apples might be divided among different numbers of guests. At first, just a few children understand what she is doing, but within a few minutes, hands are going up everywhere. When Pat is satisfied that everyone sees the division process as the reverse of the multiplication they practiced earlier, she has them write the tables they are learning in their class-made practice books.

At last it is time to study the story Pat has written on the board. In large, class-made *main lesson books*, the children turn to the carefully drawn pictures they have made of sukkahs. Now, on the following page, they draw their own light green lines for writing, in preparation for copying the story from the board. Pat is aware that, for some, the copying exercise itself will be a challenge in language learning whereas others could quite easily compose a similar story on their own. It is her intent to maintain group cohesion by keeping them all together for this activity, and she will rely on the more advanced children to help those who may be struggling, thus providing a challenge for everyone while promoting unity.

Just drawing the lines has taken enough time that the two-hour block is coming to an end. Copying the story will have to wait. It is snack time, and the children know just what to do next: Main lesson books are placed in wooden bins at the edge of the room, chairs are pushed into tables, children stand behind them with hands crossed over their chests, and they then recite together, "There lives in me an image of all that I should be. Until I can become it, my heart is never free." A child lights a single candle and a brief blessing is recited. Then, everyone enjoys the snack they have brought from home along with the day's first opportunity to chat with their friends.

On the way to the recess that follows, one of the girls comes to Pat with a concern. A new student, a boy with no Waldorf background, has been assigned the seat next to her. Michelle explains the frustration of working with someone who seems to make fun of the rhymes and songs. She imitates him briefly then states, "It's really annoying. He just doesn't get it!" Pat reminds Michelle that the boy is new but also agrees that she will talk to him.

For the other 24 children in Pat Tatum's third grade, "getting it" comes easily after being together for more than two years. They are not consciously aware of it, but much of Steiner's philosophy for this age group has been demonstrated during the morning's main lesson: children have participated in music, one of the arts, and they have used rhythm and movement to solidify their knowledge of multiplication tables. In addition, the teacher has shown herself the authority when it was time to present new knowledge and demonstrated her sensitivity to a difficult interaction between peers. The Steiner-recommended Old Testament literature has provided an important segment of curriculum content. The class furniture and learning materials have been natural ones, and technology has been totally absent. Finally, awareness of the spirit within has been verbalized by the pre-snack recitation. In a two-hour time block, the growth of the whole child, as defined by Rudolf Steiner, has been attended to in one way or another.

For our next visit we enter a very different sort of classroom. Although its teacher shares with the Montessori and Waldorf teachers a desire that children grow to their fullest potential, this teacher approaches the goal from an entirely different direction.

Letting the Curriculum Emerge Through Children's Projects

A new–old way of teaching young children has been the focus of considerable interest in recent years. With this method, the curriculum is not set but emerges from children's intellectual needs and interests; specific topics and learning experiences are chosen through negotiation among children and teacher. When put together as a whole, the experiences create thematic projects that incorporate many or most areas of the academic curriculum without overtly focusing on one or the other.

The roots of what is now called *the project approach* are in the works and ideas of John Dewey and other similarly inclined American educators, as well as in the *integrated day* or *informal education* adopted by many British schools in the 1970s. In the late 1980s, two North American educators, Lilian Katz and Sylvia Chard (1989) determined that the time was ripe to bring the focused thematic approach back to the forefront of early education. Through workshops, courses, presentations, and a book, *Engaging Children's Minds*, they coaxed teachers to abandon their more traditional ways of teaching in favor of using projects that would stimulate and enhance children's development, both cognitive and social.

Arguing that the best projects are those that help children understand the world that surrounds them, they defined a project as:

> an in-depth study of a particular topic that one or more children undertake. It consists of exploring a topic or theme such as "going to the hospital," "building a house," or "the bus that brings us to school." Work on a project should extend over a period of days or weeks, depending on the children's ages and the nature of the topic.
>
> (Katz & Chard, 1989, p. 2)

Although they do not see projects as the whole curriculum, Katz and Chard argue that they are an important complement to standard academics and play. They believe, as did Dewey, that projects help develop a sense of community among the children and that they reflect real life better than does an arbitrary division of the curriculum into discreet subjects. Katz and Chard (1989) even see one aim of the project approach as giving teachers a way to view their work as challenging. They wrote that a "curriculum that limits the teacher primarily to daily instructional lessons or to setting out the same toys and equipment day after day can quickly become dreary and devoid of intellectual challenge" (p. 8).

The Katz and Chard (1989) approach to project learning is more structured than its predecessors, at least in its explanation to teachers. They define three phases in the development of any project:

- *Phase 1* provides time for planning and getting the project off the ground. The teacher can introduce a topic or it can be negotiated with the children. Then, current knowledge is pooled through discussion, dramatic play, drawing, and shared materials from home. This is followed by planning for future study and, perhaps, some preliminary investigations.

- *Phase 2* is the period in which children gain new information by following through on the plans made in phase 1. The teacher guides the children to use research skills appropriate to their age, such as observation and drawing in the earlier years and with writing, reading, and calculating added on for older children.

- *Phase 3* draws everything together as children reflect on what they have learned. Older children might apply their skills in music, drama, dance, various forms of art work, and the creation of class books. They might even invite family members to a presentation. Younger children might reflect primarily through dramatic play, which may help them "integrate their modified and fuller understanding of the real world" (p. 84).

To see how the Katz and Chard vision of project learning can work in an early childhood setting, let's visit a kindergarten–first-grade classroom in which it has been in action for several years.

How One Teacher Applies the Project Approach

When Pam Morehouse, a public school teacher in Washington State, first heard of the Katz and Chard approach to projects, she was excited to learn more. In her K–1 classroom she was already engaged in similar methodology and was intrigued by the structure that they brought to it. Eventually, Pam not only attended Katz's and Chard's summer institute for teachers but began to offer workshops of her own, even presenting with Sylvia Chard.

The first project Pam and her class engaged in after she attended the summer institute was one she was only partially prepared to teach. The children asked her for help in making an airplane that could "fly" in the classroom. Pam is a licensed pilot and could supply the necessary technical information, but she had no background in construction. Fortunately, a local building contractor agreed to help out, accepting as payment the fishing worms the children offered from their compost bin. As the project grew ever more complex, Pam turned to the Boeing Corporation for funding and advice. They, in turn, invited the children to present their finished airplane and their knowledge of flight at a major air show. As a final step, Pam wrote an informative and entertaining description of the project for a national education journal that is read not only by teachers but by principals and superintendents as well (Morehouse, 1995).

A year or two later, another group of first graders, with quite different interests, noted with excitement a new building with golden arches rising above the freeway. It was time, they decided, to learn what they could about this kind of restaurant, and so, Pam said, "the inquiry and investigation began."

One indication of the seriousness and respect with which Pam regards her children's interests is her use of the words *inquiry* and *investigation*. In the project approach, even very young children are believed capable of research that is guided, but not directed or taken over, by adults. What does a research project look like when the participants are just 5 or 6 years old? Some of the activities included in the fast-food project were:

- *Classification, by type, of the questions the children generated for their research.* Four categories were defined, and committees were formed to learn about workers, buildings, food, and machines. The children then discussed ways of learning what they wanted to know and decided on first-person interviews, observations, and looking in books.

- *Memory drawings with accompanying stories preceding visits to local restaurants.* The stories demonstrated what the children already knew and remembered about fast-food establishments and inspired questions for upcoming research.

- *Visits to a nearby Dairy Queen and a local drive-in for field research (not just a "field trip," Pam emphasizes).* Here, first-person interviews as well as observations were possible, and each committee had its list of questions to be answered. Topics ranged from length of time it takes to serve a customer to the measurements of each room.

- *A collection of spelling words that began during phase 1 as the children talked about the words they would need to know.* As time went on, Pam wrote individual words generated by the children on small pieces of poster board and glued to another very large piece that hung on the wall for everyone's reference.

- *Sharing time, in which each committee explained what it had learned in its research.*

- *The grand finale, the creation of an in-class fast-food restaurant.* This was only possible after each committee had shared its expertise with the class and after much hard work to ready the restaurant for customers. Creating a menu and price list required ingenuity and math skills. More math was needed as the children made bills and coins to fill their cash register, then learned to make change with some degree of accuracy. Of course, signs of various sorts had to be created and placed in appropriate places in the carefully designed restaurant facility.

As children took turns being employees and customers, they learned lessons in courteous service. Because their project drew the attention of interested adults, drop-by customers included the district curriculum director, the principal, and university students and professors. Just as previous youngsters had been able to speak to an interested public about their airplane, so were these children able to share their knowledge, with poise and self-confidence. In both cases, they had behind them many weeks of knowledge building, interactions with people in the community, and experiences in both independent and cooperative research. They had been taken seriously by the adults who facilitated their learning, and they had the air of children who expected that such treatment would continue.

FIGURE 3.3 When children choose and develop their own projects, they not only participate in role-play experiences but in the more traditional curriculum as well.

In the next section, you will learn about a somewhat similar approach to be found originally in Italy and now in a good many early childhood centers in the United States. Differences between the Italian centers and Pam Morehouse's class include the ages of the children (3 to 6 as opposed to 5 to 6), general focus (child-care centers rather than a public school), and adult–child ratios (aides and special resource teachers to assist the regular teacher vs. Pam's assignment as the lone teacher in the classroom). Attitudes toward children and their capabilities and teaching methodology, however, contain striking similarities. After reading about the Italian approach, you will visit a U.S. school where many of their ideas have been adapted.

Adapting Reggio Emilia Ideas to a U.S. Setting

At the end of Chapter One, you were asked to consider what direction your own thinking might take as you progress in your understanding of early development and education. One possibility, of course, is to take the best that each has to offer, thus creating a tool kit of ideas that work. This is the approach that was adopted by an educator from northern Italy shortly after the end of World War II.

Loris Malaguzzi (Edwards, Gandini, & Forman, 1993) was a middle school teacher from Reggio Emilia in northern Italy when, less than a week after the end of the war, he came across a group of parents attempting to build a school for young children. From the rubble of bombed-out buildings, women were finding bricks and washing them by hand; they planned to sell military vehicles left behind by the Germans to finance the rest. Inspired by their vision and determination, Malaguzzi spent the next several years working with the growing numbers of such parent-run schools, all while keeping his position as a teacher and, later, as the founder of a mental health center for children.

By 1963, it had become possible to receive local tax support for the schools, and to this day, parents in Reggio Emilia may choose between sending their preschool children to municipally funded schools, federally funded schools, or private—largely Roman Catholic—schools. It is the municipal schools that are the descendants of those parent-run centers begun with hand-washed bricks and money from German tanks. Until his death in 1994, Malaguzzi was the driving intellectual force behind the development of curriculum and method.

Both he and the teachers made it their commitment to study the ideas of everyone alive or long deceased who might have something of value to tell them. Most of the philosophers and theorists presented in this book's Chapter One, and others besides, provided a foundation for thought and discussion. Because Malaguzzi had been favorably impressed by the Rousseau Institute in Geneva, Switzerland, one of the Reggio Emilia schools' early and important influences was Jean Piaget. Piaget's argument for early exploration in mathematics became an integral part of the curriculum. In addition, his concept of children as builders of their own knowledge or, as Malaguzzi described them, children as "protagonists" in their own learning experiences, was adopted. As time went on, this view of children led to a teaching method much like Katz's and Chard's project approach, although for several years neither knew of the other.

As the Reggio Emilia schools became known to the outside world, explanatory articles and books were published, visitors arrived from around the world to observe and learn, videos showing the children in action were created, and internet discussion groups were begun. Despite the intense interest that the Reggio schools have provided in recent years, it remains difficult to describe them in such a way that they can be emulated, because there is no established or approved curriculum and no set of materials to guide one's teaching. This is as it should be, for the core idea of the schools is that they should be flexible, responding to the needs and interests of the children while taking into account the local culture and society. Thus, it would be inappropriate to study these northern Italian schools and then bring their philosophies and practices, without any alteration or adaptation, to the United States.

Nevertheless, there are certain elements contained in the schools that set them apart from most others. Although each of these elements could certainly be found elsewhere, it is the combination of them that makes the Reggio Emilia schools unique. First, they owe much to the ideas about constructivism held by Piaget and Vygotsky, but the ongoing research by teachers and staff ensures that the schools' philosophies undergo continual growth. One example in recent years has been an interest in Howard Gardner's concept of multiple intelligences (and Gardner's interest in Reggio's application of his theory). Second, a central curricular emphasis is the use of the various arts as a means of communication by children who are, for the most part, preliterate. This emphasis is of such importance that each school is provided with an *atelierista* (art teacher) who works out of his or her own *atelier* (workshop or studio) as well as in the classrooms and in planning sessions with the other teachers. Third, although many of the materials and activities are those that would make any traditional preschool or kindergarten teacher feel at home, there are also in-depth projects throughout the year that are the product of negotiation between children and teachers. These projects may emerge directly from the children and simply be guided by the adults. One example is an amusement park created for the birds that frequented the school playground; this experience was one of such depth and interest that a video was made of it (Forman & Gandini, 1994). There are also projects that are suggested by the teachers, based on their continual observations of the children.

One admirer of the Reggio Emilia schools is Lilian Katz (1993) whom you met in the previous section. She suggests that our teaching of young children could be improved if we gave some thought to the following six lessons she believes these schools can teach us:

1) The view of preprimary children in regard to visual representation is that they can "communicate their ideas, feelings, understandings, imaginings, and observations ... much earlier than most U.S. early childhood educators typically assume." This attitude makes it possible to put art at the core of the curriculum.

2) Visual representations are not treated simply as decorative products as they are in the United States. Instead, they are used as resources or reference materials for further study.

3) Even though art work is used in such a serious and realistic manner, it does not keep children from being competent in unrepresentative and abstract visual expression as well. In other words, there is art for the sake of artistic expressions as well as art as a substitute for written communication.

4) Teacher–child interactions tend to be focused primarily on the content of the children's work and less concerned with daily routines and obedience to rules. In the United States, the focus is more often the reverse.

5) Teachers take the children's interests and intellectual efforts seriously and convey their sincere respect.

6) The buildings are homelike, with spaces and furnishings designed to "create a comfortable, warm, and cheerful ambience and pleasant environment."

(Katz, 1993, pp. 25–32)

To understand how the Reggio Emilia ideas might work in a United States setting, we describe next a school with similar interests and philosophy.

A Visit to the Clifton School in Atlanta, Georgia

The school you are about to visit was chosen not only for its enthusiasm for the Italian Reggio Emilia approach, but for its continuing evolution as a high-quality American child-care site. Situated near Emory University and a variety of medical establishments, the building's architecture was designed, according to Clifton's written history, "with spaces that foster relationships, exhibit transparency, and allow for investigations." Thus, there is a wing, or "village," for each of four age groups, infancy through preschool. Each village has its own "piazza," an open space that might be described as an indoor town square. Surrounding each piazza can be found four to six classrooms. In this welcoming and comfortable setting, more than 200 youngsters are provided both child care and education.

On hallway walls, and on the walls of the piazzas and classrooms, are no commercially made posters or pictures. Instead, there are photos of children engaged in ongoing investigations and projects, along with dictated commentaries from the children or narratives by the teachers. Such documentation is a core component of Reggio Emilia schools and the Clifton teachers take this responsibility seriously, carrying their cameras and notepads with them throughout the day. Evidence of parent involvement can be found on the walls too: In one hallway is a list of reflections by teachers and parents entitled "Dialogue on the Rights of the Child." The 65 entries include examples such as children's rights to solve their own problems, be nourished with healthy foods, experience uninterrupted play, be comforted and loved, be encouraged rather than forced to learn, and even to be able to argue with each other.

The classrooms themselves vary, as one would expect, based on the children's ages. The infant rooms are similar to infant rooms in most high-quality centers. Even here though, Reggio-inspired "light tables" seen throughout the school, have been introduced in a made-to-order size that permits crawlers to explore. Light tables have translucent surfaces with electric light shining from beneath. Teachers or children can place interesting materials on top, then experiment and observe as desired. The teachers use found objects and natural materials to design "provocations" to invite the infants to pat, pound, grasp, pull, push, or fill and empty. The focus of these materials is on multisensory exploration.

Once Clifton's children begin to toddle, their classrooms contain increasingly complex materials, including those from nature, for exploration. Their expanding interests are noted by the teachers who then guide them in investigations that might be short-lived or ongoing as the children choose.

In the preschool village, the 3- and 4-year-old children begin to engage in projects that can be in-depth and detailed. At the same time, the more casual investigations of the toddler years continue. Here is an example of each of these two modes of learning:

An investigation. In the Toddler II classroom, LaTisha Flowers, Lisa Kato, and the children have just begun an exploration with the overhead projector. The machine has been placed on the floor with its light shining on a wall about 8 feet away. Next to the projector are several wooden bowls containing flat, plastic translucent discs of several colors ("gems," purchased at a local craft store). Throughout the morning youngsters experiment, first just emptying the contents on the glass and replacing them in their bowls, mostly repeating the activity and noticing the sounds, and then trying out different designs and noises. This goes on for some time until, at last, one child notices that the far wall seems to be lit up and contain shadows of discs and that, as his friends move the discs around, the shadows move too. Ms. LaTisha, busy with other children elsewhere, has been keeping an eye on this activity as well. Noting the boy's discovery, she goes to him and asks what he thinks is happening. He isn't sure, but she asks directive questions for as long as he is interested. Only one or two other children eventually express interest in the wall, but this exploration will be an ongoing one, with time for expansion of children's interests and knowledge.

FIGURE 3.4 Children in Clifton School's Toddler II classroom investigate a fascinating new material.

A project. The previous summer, a number of children in a preschool class had been on airplane trips. Returning to school in the fall, the children were still discussing their experiences, sharing them with the rest of the class, some of whom also became intrigued. Eventually, an airplane project ensued. Earlier in this chapter we described the airplane project in Pam Morehouse's K–1 class. At Clifton, the children were younger (3- and 4-year-olds), so their interests and abilities were quite different. By the time their engagement and attention had waned, the Clifton children had made maps, sketches, and airplane models using connecting blocks, building blocks, a globe, paints, and wood to explore, demonstrate, and represent their knowledge. These various means of expression are what Loris Malaguzzi termed "the hundred languages of children," noting that preliteracy most definitely would not hinder younger children from communicating.

As in the original Italian schools, the children's efforts are supported by an *atelier* (art studio) and *atelierista* (art teacher) who helps them visualize and communicate their ideas through graphic representations. As in Reggio, the children are encouraged to take risks, experiment, and learn from their mistakes. When participating in atelier activities or such investigations as the discs on overhead projector, their misperceptions are not directly corrected. Instead, the children try out their ideas and hypotheses, and then reformulate them as they gain experience and knowledge.

Teachers at Clifton, as at Reggio, learn of children's needs and interests through careful observation and documentation. Administration and staff are committed to providing the children with an emergent curriculum, that is, a curriculum that emerges from the interests of the children as opposed to one that is stamped out beforehand by adults in authority positions. And as in Reggio, they are equally committed to an emergent curriculum for themselves, leading to teachers' meetings that focus less on administrative details and more on expanding their knowledge. At one preschool staff meeting, for example, teachers shared demonstrations of projects recently undertaken by children in their classrooms. No two were the same and the exhibits included an exploration of autumn leaves, a study of plant parts, and an in-depth study of corn. All projects grew from observations of children's interests and were developed from principles based on the teachers' shared reading. A tradition of continued scholarly study by teachers is one that began with the earliest Reggio Emilia schools.

Of course, as in Reggio Emilia, there is more to the curriculum than projects large and small. The classrooms at Clifton School are filled with materials that might be found in any quality center such as clay, storybooks, and building materials. It is the provision of opportunities to explore and research based on children's own interests, coupled with intense observation and support from the teachers, that sets this Reggio-inspired center apart.

Project-based approaches, including the Reggio Emilia model in all its variations, are particularly appealing because young children are usually self-directed in their learning, appreciate hands-on activities, and can make connections among a series of events and activities. Some children, however, have difficulty acquiring new skills and knowledge while negotiating the social demands of ongoing activities; others have sensory or physical disabilities that prevent them from moving around and interacting independently with materials and people; still others need specialized instruction to help them focus their attention on learning. Early childhood special education services are important resources for young children who need individualized support to realize the benefits of early education.

Helping Children Meet Difficult Challenges: Early Childhood Special Education (ECSE)

Until the mid-1970s, children who experienced developmental delays or disabilities were often excluded from public schools, and families were responsible for finding and organizing their children's educational programs, especially for preschoolers. Families who could afford the expense sent their children to special private schools, and those who could not cared for their sons and daughters at home. When families were faced with overwhelming demands in raising children with special needs or could not provide the level of care necessary, the only other option was residential institutions where children often became wards of the state. In the 1960s and 1970s, courageous parents formed advocacy groups and pressed lawsuits on behalf of their children, claiming that denial of public education for children with disabilities was discriminatory. The courts agreed and ruled that children with special needs had the same rights to public education as their typically developing peers.

In 1975, on the heels of many other pieces of civil rights legislation, the United States Congress passed a law requiring local school districts nationwide to provide special education to all eligible school-aged children. This legislation, now known as the Individuals with Disabilities Education Act (IDEA, 2004), represented a remarkable level of commitment for the federal government, since regulation and control of K–12 education had previously been the responsibility of each state.

IDEA legislation has been amended many times, most recently in 2004, and currently mandates special education services for all eligible children beginning at age 3. In other words, preschoolers with identified disabilities and delays are the only 3- to 5-year-olds the public schools have a legal responsibility to educate. (States have also been encouraged, but not required, to serve eligible infants and toddlers. A few states have laws that mandate services to eligible birth to 3-year-olds under IDEA.)

Eligibility for preschool services can be determined in two different ways. The first is by disability categories that apply to children from age 3 to age 21: mental retardation; hearing, vision, language, or orthopedic impairments; serious emotional disturbance; autism; traumatic brain injury; and specific learning disabilities. Parents and professionals alike, however, always voiced significant concerns about premature labeling and misdiagnoses when applying such disability categories to very young children. In 1991, Congress added a more appropriate, less specific, eligibility category for preschoolers: *developmental delays* in physical, cognitive, communication, social, emotional, or adaptive development. This category is strongly preferred to the disability categories for children under age 5 (Division for Early Childhood, 1996).

Evaluation of special education eligibility for infants, toddlers, and preschoolers usually involves interviews with parents and reviews of available medical records, as well as a comprehensive interdisciplinary assessment of the child's development. Eligibility evaluation teams generally include a school psychologist, either a speech or motor therapist or both, special educators, family members, and perhaps a social worker or medical personnel. As a preschool or primary teacher, you will no doubt be involved in early identification of special needs, and the information and concerns you have about children will prove valuable to the eligibility evaluation team.

Because comprehensive evaluations are quite expensive and time consuming, short screening tests are often given first. If the tests indicate a likelihood of delay or disability, then a full-scale assessment, including both formal testing and observation, is scheduled. Each state defines its own conditions and test scores that qualify children for special education services.

As a preschool or primary teacher, you may well work with children in your classrooms who receive special education services, or you might decide to pursue special education as a career. For our final site visit, let's go to a preschool special education classroom. The classroom is part of the public school system with a program for children ages 3 through 5. Although it is primarily for those who qualify for special education, the class also includes a few typically developing children. (Because of strict confidentiality guidelines in special education, the actual class is not identified by district or teacher.)

The Special Education Preschool

Two preschool children, one boy and one girl, walk confidently into the classroom and look around for the teacher. The little girl's mother calls her back for a quick good-bye kiss, waves at the teacher, and leaves. The children hang their coats and backpacks on hooks under their names.

"Good morning, Lea; good morning, Kyle. How was your weekend? Did you bring your journals?" The children go to their backpacks and produce small hand-bound books with covers decorated in colorful preschool style. Kyle says, "Me wented farm see horsie." He seems to have more to say. "Grandma's," he adds after a moment.

"Oh, how fun. You went to your grandma's farm and saw horses." The teacher repeats his sentence using more proper syntax, reads his parents' account of the weekend in the journal, and asks two more questions. Each of Kyle's statements is reflected back to him in extended and expanded form.

Lea stands patiently but expectantly waiting for her turn to show the teacher her journal. She doesn't say any words, but nods, points, and makes some sounds in response to the teacher's questions. Other children enter the room during the next 15 minutes, and by 9:00 A.M. there are seven youngsters present. Most have shared their home–school journals with the teacher, and she has learned that one child was sick over the weekend, one had a toileting accident, and one began drawing pictures for family members. The last two arrivals are talking with the teacher, two boys are building a tower in the block corner, and three girls are using small paper punches at the art table, with help from the teaching assistant when needed, punching out shapes and pasting them on index cards.

At 9:00 A.M. the teacher sings a song about cleaning up. All the children put their materials away and congregate on the rug area in a semicircle around the teacher's chair. Circle time commences with a hello song, each verse greeting a different child. The teacher uses sign language as she sings and most of the children hum, sing, or sign along. The teaching assistant sits behind one boy and helps him follow the motions of the song (pointing, waving, clapping.) The children who are present hang up their name cards on the "In" board and "read" the name card for the child who is absent.

After these traditional early childhood circle-time social activities, the group stays and works briefly on recognizing letter sounds. The teacher starts by using the name cards and asking the group to make the initial sounds of each name as she points to the letter. Some of the children are learning to associate the letters with their sounds; others are choosing pictures that begin with certain sounds.

At 9:20, the speech–language pathologist (SLP) and occupational therapist (OT) come into the room and join the end of circle time while the teaching assistant moves about setting up activities at centers around the room. The SLP goes to the dramatic play center with two children and the OT takes two others to the art table. The teaching assistant goes to the toy shelf with two children who select barn and garage sets, and the teacher works at a small desk with one girl who is learning to recognize numerals. These group activities last 15 minutes, and then the children rotate around to a different adult. After two rotations, the SLP leaves and the children go outside with the teaching assistant.

Outdoor play is a rather rambunctious affair for the first few minutes with much noisy running around before children sort themselves onto tricycles and climbing equipment and to the sand table. Afterward, everyone has a chance to practice or learn washing hands, and help get the snack together. The SLP returns and sits at the snack table, talking with the children and adults, clearly eliciting, expanding, and modeling communication skills. The teacher weaves number, color, time, and size concepts into the conversation as well and reminds children to take turns and share.

Children leave the snack table whenever they are finished, telling an adult the center they will play in next. The two adults cruise from center to center listening, observing, making comments, and asking questions until parents begin to arrive and children depart. The room is quiet as the assistant cleans up and the teacher records each child's progress in individual notebooks. "Every moment counts for these kids," says the teacher. "We are always teaching, even when it just looks like play. Every interaction is intentional and designed to move children toward meeting their individual goals."

Influences on ECSE Preschools

You have probably noticed a number of similarities and differences among the special education preschool and the other models described in this chapter. Like Head Start, the ECSE preschool is supported by federal law and funding that flows through the states to local programs. Both Head Start and ECSE programs are designed to provide support for a particular group of children who are at risk for school failure, although the eligibility criteria differ. The types of specific materials, structured curricula, and direct instructional strategies found in Montessori preschools can also be found in ECSE classrooms, sometimes giving an impression of more work than play. The teachers in ECSE classrooms are more directly responsible for the content and outcomes of individual children's learning, however.

Teaching teams with specialized expertise are the norm in both ECSE and the Waldorf models, although the particular specialties are quite different and both models have children with the same teachers for several years. Project-based approaches are increasingly being modified for use in ECSE classrooms, with an emphasis on *individual education plan (IEP)* objectives that promote repeated practice and generalization of functional skills across a number of related activities. The individualization inherent in the Reggio Emilia model, along with the partnerships among school, families, and communities, is also reflected strongly in ECSE programs. Perhaps the most important thing to remember about ECSE programs, however, is that the professionals working in them are generally familiar with the full range of approaches in early childhood education, and they work in close partnership with other early childhood programs in the best interests of each child.

EXTENDING YOUR LEARNING

As in the previous chapters, Suggestions 1 and 2 focus on your developing philosophy of teaching and learning.

1 Read Suggestion 6 below and think it through or discuss it with others. Then, return to your emerging philosophy of early education. What would you change and what would you keep the same? Use your response to Suggestion 6 to justify your choices. Add these notes to your ongoing ideas.

2 Imagine yourself as a teacher with three or four years of experience. What age or grade would you like to be teaching? Now, on a large sheet of art paper, and using crayons or markers, draw a picture of yourself teaching in your ideal classroom. Whether you feel comfortable in your art work or not, do not just use pencil and avoid the use of stick figures. (This might take some courage but, as you will see in upcoming chapters, this requirement has a goal.)

3 Choose one of the models of early education you have studied in this chapter. Make a list of the most important elements pertaining to its philosophy or point

of view. Visit a center or school that represents this model, making notes of examples of the philosophy in action.

4 With your instructor, make a list of questions you would like to ask a teacher or administrator about each of the models. Singly, in pairs, or in small groups of students, interview teachers or administrators in schools that represent the models. Compare the responses and discuss possible reasons for similarities and differences.

5 Extend your knowledge of the history, philosophy, and ideas of any one model by reading the original writings of its founder(s), exploring any studies related to the model's effectiveness, or researching government documents for developmental history.

6 Imagine yourself as a well-trained teacher in any one of the models discussed in this chapter. List the three or four most important reasons you would choose your model. As you contemplate your best choice, think about the model's amount of structure: Is it highly structured providing you and the children with a planned curriculum and/or materials, or is it less structured leading to more flexibility? Which approach is more comfortable for you? In a small group, share your thinking and listen to others'.

7 Interview parents of children from two or three different models of early education. Explore their reasons for choosing the programs they have and the types of parent involvement they experience. Share the results of your interviews with your peers who have interviewed parents from other programs.

Internet Resources

Web sites provide much useful information for educators and we list some here that pertain to the topics covered in this chapter. The addresses of Web sites can also change, however, and new ones are continually added. Thus, this list should be considered as a first step in your acquisition of a larger and ever-changing collection.

Association of Waldorf Schools of North America
www.whywaldorfworks.org

Head Start
www.acf.hhs.gov/programs/ohs

Montessori (American)
www.amshq.org

Montessori (International)
www.Montessori.edu

The Project Approach
www.projectapproach.org

Reggio Emilia
www.reggioalliance.org

Vocabulary

Anthroposophy. A term coined by the German Rudolf Steiner. A religious or mystical philosophy that rejects Judeo-Christian theology in favor of the mystical insight of individuals.

Critical or Sensitive Period. A window of time during which a child is believed to learn a skill or gain an understanding with the least amount of effort and the greatest amount of receptivity.

Developmentally Appropriate Practices. Teaching practices that take into account a child's developmental stage, individual needs and interests, and culture.

Embryonic Society. A social structure created by the children in a group, though not fully realized according to adult definition.

Emergent Curriculum. Curriculum that emerges from children's interests and teachers' understanding of children's needs.

Eurythmy. A method of teaching dancing or rhythmic movement that includes the recitation of verse or prose, usually with musical accompaniment.

Field Trip/Field Research. A field trip is a learning excursion outside the class room, generally for no more than one day. Field research incorporates the same idea but emphasizes the learning entailed, particularly as it relates to classroom work.

Individual Educational Plan (IEP). A plan of individualized goals and objectives that guides instruction for children who are eligible for special education services.

Practical Life Exercise. A classroom activity in which a task from home life is isolated for the purpose of providing children an opportunity to practice and master the necessary skills pertaining to the task.

Provocations. The questions, opportunities, and materials or other elements in the environment used by Reggio Emilia teachers to provoke curiosity and a desire to research in their children.

References

Barnes, H. (1991, October). Learning that grows with the learner: An introduction to Waldorf education. *Educational Leadership*, 52–54.

Division for Early Childhood. (1996). *Developmental delay as an eligibility category: A concept paper of the Division for Early Childhood for the Council of Exceptional Children*. Reston, VA: Council for Exceptional Children.

Edwards, C., Gandini, L., & Forman, G. (Eds.) (1993). *The hundred languages of children*. Norwood, NJ: Ablex.

Forman, G., & Gandini, L. (1994). *The amusement park for birds* [a video]. Amherst, MA: Performanetics Press.

Ginsburg, I. (1982). Jean Piaget and Rudolf Steiner: Stages of child development and implications for pedagogy. *Teachers College Record, 84*(2), 327–337.

IDEA (2004). Individuals with Disabilities Education Improvement Act of 2004. PL No. 108-446.

Katz, L. (1993). What can we learn from Reggio Emilia? In C. Edwards, L. Gandini, & G. Forman (Eds.), *The hundred languages of children*, 25–32. Norwood, NJ: Ablex.

Katz, L., & Chard, S. (1989). *Engaging children's minds: The project approach*. Norwood, NJ: Ablex.

Kirschner Associates (1970). *A national survey of the impacts of Head Start centers on community institutions*. Albuquerque, NM: Author.

Kotzsch, R. E. (n.d.). *Waldorf education: Schooling the head, hands and heart*. Massachusetts: Author.

Leyden, L. (2009). For forest kindergartners, class is back to nature, rain or shine. NYTimes.com/2009/11/30/nyregion/30forest.html.

Morehouse, P. (1995, May). The building of an airplane (with a little help from friends). *Educational Leadership, 52*(8), 56–57.

Schweinhart, L., & Weikart, D. (1993). *Significant benefits: The High/Scope Perry preschool study through age twenty-seven*. Ypsilanti, MI: Author.

Uhrmacher, P. (1995). Uncommon schooling: A historical look at Rudolf Steiner, anthroposophy, and Waldorf education. *Curriculum Inquiry, 25*(4), 381–406.

Washington, V., & Oyemade, U. (1987). *Project Head Start: Past, present, and future trends in the context of family needs*. New York: Garland.

Washington, V., & Oyemade Bailey, U. (1995). *Project Head Start: Models and strategies for the twenty-first century*. New York: Garland.

four
Diversity in Early Childhood Settings

When someone with the authority of a teacher, say, describes the world, and you're not in it, there is a moment of psychic disequilibrium, as if you looked into a mirror and saw nothing.

Adrienne Rich

Chapter Objectives

After reading this chapter, you should be able to:

■ Define diversity in broad terms and apply the concepts to early childhood education settings.
■ Apply issues of diversity to previously read chapters.
■ Identify characteristics of several U.S. cultures, particularly as they apply to interactions with families and young children.
■ Begin establishing a classroom atmosphere that respects, values, nurtures, and provides equitable opportunities to all children.
■ Begin establishing classroom practices that teach young children how to stand up for fairness and oppose bias, prejudice, and discrimination.

As you think about and apply the chapter content on your own, you should be able to:

■ Recognize various characteristics of diversity among the children and families you encounter.
■ Understand your own culture more fully.
■ Embark on a lifelong process of learning about others.
■ Collect a bank of ideas for handling diversity issues with skill.
■ Incorporate issues of diversity into your developing philosophy of early education.
■ Apply the four core goals of anti-bias education (ABE) to your own identity, life, and work in early childhood. Identify challenges, immediate goals, and long-term goals for development in each of the ABE goal areas.

One of the most intriguing aspects of early education is observing and supporting young children as they develop their individual identities. Discovering who they are can be a joyful journey of self-discovery as children learn about personal characteristics such as race, language, culture, ability, and gender. There can also be many bumps, potholes, and threats along the way as children encounter racism, sexism, discrimination, teasing, and exclusion. Helping young children build healthy and positive internal identities requires an understanding of the many facets of diversity, an awareness of opportunities to teach about similarities and differences, and a desire to expand your knowledge of self and others in collaboration with parents, other family members, and colleagues. And often it demands that early educators be courageous, stretch the boundaries of their comfort zones, and address issues that are sensitive and sometimes controversial.

It is critical that every child and every family feel recognized, valued, and included in early childhood programs. A child's identity is first awakened within the context of family, and early education is most effective when families are involved. One of your most important tasks as an early educator will be to establish and maintain positive relationships with all families, regardless of their various backgrounds, family structures and membership, or *social economic status (SES)*. In this chapter we will provide an overview of the types of diversity you are likely to encounter in early childhood education settings, and suggest some useful strategies and resources to combat prejudice and inequity in your daily work with children.

FIGURE 4.1 When teachers interact with families of cultures other than their own, they will generally have more success if they take time to learn about the families' cultures and communication styles.

Early childhood classrooms are becoming increasingly diverse. Preschool attendance has been increasing steadily for the last four decades, and a large majority of American children now spend time in classroom settings before they enter kindergarten. The increase in attendance in group settings prior to kindergarten reflects a greater need for out-of-home care among dual-career and single-parent families, as well as a rising demand for quality preschool education among the middle class (Barnett & Yarosz, 2007). Federal and state appropriations have increased over the same period for publicly funded preschool programs for children from families with low incomes, although children from affluent families are still more likely to attend preschool than their less advantaged peers. Along with the increase in preschool enrollment has come a marked increase in the diversity of children in early care and education programs.

Head Start, for example, has been a national leader in serving children from diverse cultures and language groups, and as early as 1993 served children from over 140 primary language groups. Estimates are that the number of cultures represented in Head Start programs is even larger. In 2008 almost 30% of enrolled children came from families who had home languages other than English, and nationwide just 16% of Head Start programs enrolled only *monolingual* English speaking children (U.S. Department of Health and Human Services, 2008). Head Start's mission is to serve children from families with low incomes, a population that often includes an unusually high number of families who have immigrated to this country and children who are not yet proficient in English. Nonetheless, Head Start programs also illustrate well the increasing diversity that early childhood educators will encounter in preschool programs.

Early childhood educators will also find increased emphasis on diversity in public schools during the primary years. There has been much national conversation and debate about the *achievement gap*, a term which describes unequal patterns of educational performance among groups of students in American schools. In specific, students of color (especially Hispanic, African-American, and American Indian) and those from lower income families tend to have poorer scores on measures of academic proficiency and higher drop-out rates than Caucasian peers from middle income and affluent families (U.S. Department of Education, 2003; Children's Defense Fund, 2008). Children from lower SES backgrounds start kindergarten with significantly lower achievement in the skills necessary for school success (Burkam & Lee, 2002), so early childhood educators have a very important role to play in closing the achievement gap during the primary years.

Cultural Influences

The term *diversity* as used in this chapter is defined in the broadest and most inclusive manner possible. We will discuss diversity among young children and their families that you are likely to encounter as an early educator, whether you work in home-based programs, center-based models, public schools, or private primary classrooms. Our discussion will address diversity among young children in areas of culture, race, language, social-economic status, family structure (including same-sex parents), ability, and gender identity. We will describe trends in demographics and education that have increased diversity in classrooms, introduce you to concepts related to gender and ability, and provide information to stimulate your thinking about the importance of your own heritage and the backgrounds of the children and families with whom you will soon be working.

Social scientists are forever creating new definitions for that elusive word *culture*, but the one that follows is sufficiently broad for use in this chapter's discussion of early education. *Culture: The knowledge, art, morals, laws, customs, values, attitudes, belief systems, behavioral expectations, and norms that give a society and the individuals in it their identity.* Another definition of culture is *life ways*, or the routines, activities, and roles of daily life for children and their families (Derman-Sparks & Olsen Edwards, 2010). For young children, important aspects of culture include daily routines and practices in their families: eating, sleeping, interacting, roles of children and adults, language, education, religion, and social activities. Although we have not yet addressed the issue of culture directly in this book's first chapters, it has been an important presence nonetheless.

For example, history and culture have a significant impact on our view of many of the central concepts of early learning: development, parenting, families, and the role of formal education in the lives of young children. An illustration of this impact is demonstrated by the variety of historical figures you met in Chapter One. All of these people observed children within approximately the same age range, witnessed approximately the same development and behaviors, yet emerged from their observations with very divergent ideas for education. In great part, these differences can be explained by variations in the cultures of the times, places, and people who have provided the foundation for our field.

In Chapter Two, a variety of career options were presented for your consideration, with the caveat that some of your choices would be of little financial benefit. In the culture of the United States, there has been a long history of strong reluctance to provide government support for the care and education of our youngest citizens. Without such support, living wages are out of reach for caregivers and teachers, and tuition rates are out of reach for many parents. Our cultural belief system includes both a desire for freedom from government intrusion, and the belief that young children are a valuable asset for the future. The inconsistency between two strong, opposing cultural values remains unresolved, and the result is a very tenuous foundation of early education in America, and young children and their teachers remain the unfortunate victims.

In Chapter Three, we visited several classrooms and centers, some of them influenced by the historic figures from Chapter One, all of them products, at least in part, of their own times and cultures. The project approach, for example, provides young children with the power to choose their own curricula, to decide their own methods of learning, and to make decisions as individuals and as groups both large and small. Giving such decision-making power might be dangerous in an autocratic culture; it is more appropriate, even expected, in a democratic society such as the United States.

These descriptions of cultural influences are but examples from each previous chapter. You are invited to discover other ways in which culture has shaped careers in early education, the views of educationists, and the various models of classrooms and centers.

The Role of Immigration

Complementary to influences of the immediate culture on early education are the diverse backgrounds of the children who attend the schools and centers. In the United States, such diversity has been growing in recent years as immigrants and refugees enter from an expanding number of countries and our own culture increasingly values and honors the backgrounds and variations in personal characteristics among all children. Arguing that we must look at the education of young children in new ways, one group of authors summarized the situation, particularly in relationship to immigration:

> The dramatic increase in immigration in the past 20 years, the young average age of immigrants, and the higher birth rate of several of these groups relative to that of white Americans is changing the face of America's people. This rapid demographic change has been called "the browning of America."
> (Swiniarski, Breitborde, & Murphy, 1999, p. 82)

In the decade between 1990 and 2000, the population of foreign-born people living in the United States increased by over half for naturalized citizens and non-citizens alike, from 19.8 million to 31.1 million. Over half of U.S. residents born elsewhere were from Latin America (Central America, South America, and the Caribbean), and 30% of the total immigrant population was from Mexico (U.S. Census Bureau, 2003). These statistics explain the fact that Spanish is the second most frequent home language in the United States. When countries were counted singly, Mexico was the greatest contributor of new arrivals, with China a distant second. Perhaps even more telling, the United Kingdom, the original source of American citizens and cultural heritage, was ranked 17th with just 1.5% of the new population. Germany, the leading contributor of new immigrants as recently as the 1950s, did not even make the top 30 countries listed by the U.S. Immigration and Naturalization Service.

From these statistics, it is possible to predict what school and child-care-center populations will look like in the near future. For example, it has been predicted that the 70% White population in 1990s American schools will be reversed by 2026 so that 70% will be non-White. Another prediction is that between 1990 and 2050, the percentage of Whites will fall from 74% to 52% (Swiniarski et al., 1999).

Many people believe it would be a good idea to close the door against the flood of outsiders who want to belong to the American family. The newspapers are full of stories that verify this opinion, and you may be or know someone who agrees that "America should remain American." This is not a new attitude, yet America has always been a nation of immigrants. After all, every group of citizens in the United States, with the exception of American Indians, comes from immigrant backgrounds. Despite the fact that most American families hailed originally from other countries, our country has a long history of anti-immigrant sentiment. Some members of immigrant groups and their heirs, ironically, have even become strong advocates for keeping out new immigrants.

Yet, immigrants continue to arrive, and their numbers steadily increase. Despite resentment and prejudice, the vilified groups of the last two centuries have managed to overcome most or all of the barriers erected against them, becoming full participants in the ever-changing U.S. culture. One of the most important tasks for early educators is to design environments and cultivate interactions with children that affirm and honor each and every family background, and to teach young children to follow that example.

The Demise of the Middle Class

> The United States has the unwanted distinction of being worst among indus-
> trialized nations in relative child poverty, in the gap between rich and poor, in
> teen birth rates, and in child gun violence, and first in the number of incarcer-
> ated persons.
>
> (Children's Defense Fund, 2008, p. 1)

Compared to other industrialized countries, the United States ranks first in the number of
millionaires and billionaires, but close to last in the gap between rich and poor children.

We are first in health technology but 25th in infant mortality; our country's standing
in infant mortality rates fell from 18th to 25th between 1998 and 2008, meaning that by
2008 more babies in America died before their first birthdays than in 24 other developed countries. The United States is ranked first in military technology but last in
protecting children against gun violence. On the average, states spend almost three times
as much for each person in prison as for each public school student (Children's Defense
Fund, 2008). These statistics illustrate clearly that our society's collective desire for
autonomy from government intervention is stronger than the combined will to protect
and support the well-being of young children.

One in six children in the United States, a total of 13.3 million, lived in poverty in
2008, an increase of over 500,000 from 2006. Young children are more likely to live in
extreme poverty than are school-aged children. Child poverty rates are three times
higher for Black and Hispanic children than they are for White children, and children of
color are least likely to have health insurance (Children's Defense Fund, 2008). This
means that a rather large proportion of children may arrive at the doorsteps of their
centers and schools with insufficient nutrition for effective learning, untreated chronic
medical conditions, and undue stress and anxiety from unsafe living conditions and/or
the threat of homelessness. Their language skills may also be inadequate to meet the
middle-class expectations of the school curriculum, and their enthusiasm for learning
may be dampened by the hardships and distress of not having basic needs met. Early
educators encounter a lot of inequity in the lives of children, particularly in urban areas
and in states with policies that are particularly unsupportive of children and families.

As the gap between rich and poor widens, early childhood programs tend to be segre-
gated by SES: affluent families send their children to private preschools and primary
schools, and families with the lowest incomes are eligible for Head Start. The demographics of public schools are becoming increasingly diverse, with marked differences in
quality between low- and high-income neighborhoods. As families from increasingly
varied backgrounds move into and across the country, early childhood schools and
centers are enrolling children with more diversity in languages and cultures. An additional influence on diversity in early childhood programs is the recent trend toward
inclusive early childhood environments where children with a variety of ability levels
play and learn together.

The Influence of Inclusion Policies

In the mid-1970s, federal legislation for the first time mandated that children with
special needs were entitled to a free public education that was tailored to meet their indi-

vidual needs. Previously, many children with disabilities stayed at home or went to private schools, and public schools often did not have well-trained special education teachers. This initial special education legislation, the *Education of All Handicapped Children Act* (EAHCA), was passed following a number of civil rights cases addressing the rights of racial minority students.

The EAHCA was quite a landmark, amended in 1986 to include eligible preschool children (ages 3 to 5) and older secondary students (ages 18 to 21) under the federal mandate for special education services. Since the mid-1980s public schools have been providing special education services to eligible students from age 3 until age 21. Special education services, by law, begin two years earlier and end three years later than general education does. The 1986 amendments to the EAHCA also included an optional provision for states to provide special education services to eligible infants and toddlers: 1986 was a banner year for special services to young children with special needs!

In 1991, the name of the special education law was updated to its current *Individuals with Disabilities Education Act* (IDEA), reflecting a national preference for the term "disability" over the use of the outdated "handicapped" label. The EAHCA and IDEA and subsequent amendments have addressed the responsibilities of school districts to eligible students and their families, including a provision for students ages 3 to 21 to be educated in the *least restrictive environment (LRE)*. The big idea of LRE is that students with disabilities receive educational services with their peers and/or in environments that are as close to the general education classroom as possible.

Most recently, the 1997 and 2004 IDEA amendments emphasized the importance of access to the general education curriculum for all students, including those eligible for special education. In 2002, the Elementary and Secondary Education Act (ESEA) was amended under the title No Child Left Behind Act (NCLB). NCLB emphasized accountability to high standards and educational achievement outcomes for all students. The combination of IDEA legislation and No Child Left Behind legislation during the George W. Bush administration was a powerful force for *inclusion* of students with disabilities and delays in general education settings with their peers. If you teach in the primary grades, it is almost a certainty that you will have children in your classrooms who also receive special education services.

There is no federal legislation requiring school districts to provide public preschool services, unless they are from poor families or have identified disabilities. The only entitlement programs for preschoolers are Head Start and IDEA services for 3–5-year-olds, so most American children start public school in kindergarten at age 5. For this reason, the concept of LRE isn't relevant for preschoolers in special education classrooms, because rarely are there general education classrooms available in the public schools.

The most progressive approaches emphasize *inclusion* of young children with disabilities in community-based preschool programs or in Head Start classrooms. Head Start programs are required to reserve 10% of their enrollment for preschoolers with identified disabilities. Infants and toddlers who receive special education services are required to be served in *natural environments*, meaning at home or in their child-care settings. There are still many self-contained special education preschool classrooms, but you are likely to have the opportunity to care for and educate young children with special needs in community-based child care or preschool settings.

The focus of special education services has shifted progressively over the years from exclusion of students with special needs, to an emphasis on separate programs and individualized instruction within school buildings, and more recently to specialized instruction delivered within general education classrooms, community preschools, homes, and child-care programs. The diversity in U.S. schools has most definitely been enhanced by inclusion of students with a wide range of abilities.

Diversity Issues Related to Gender

The final aspects of diversity to be discussed here relate to gender. During recent decades, research findings have led to mixed conclusions about the influences on and causes of behavioral differences between the sexes. Do girls play in the housekeeping corner whereas boys gravitate to the large blocks because society reinforces such choices or because their biology is sending them preprogrammed messages? Or is it a combination of the two? Definitive answers have yet to be discovered, but it is known that young children are still developing their sense of gender identity as well as their beginning understandings of societal expectations and roles for each sex.

Many younger children are not yet sure what makes them boys or girls, believing that the answer may lie in concrete and visible factors, such as how they dress, their hair styles, or the games they choose to play. In addition, they have an incomplete understanding of biological permanence, sometimes believing that they might change genders as they get older, perhaps even becoming someone else entirely. Parents may not think to explain biological differences to them, or may find the prospect uncomfortable. Thus, young children sometimes take their confusion to school (Derman-Sparks & Olsen Edwards, 2010). Teachers who simply and matter-of-factly provide information about gender can set the stage for children to discover their own identities and negotiate societal expectations.

> Janice was a mother who purposely chose a female pediatrician for her children so that they would see the normality of girls growing up to take on a traditionally male career. When her daughter Kelly was 4, Janice was startled to overhear her say to the boy visiting from next door, "Okay. You'll be the doctor and I'll be the nurse. Boys are always doctors and girls are always nurses." On reflection, Janice realized that a medical TV show Kelly liked to watch with her parents reflected the more traditional gender roles in the medical profession, and she came to understand that society's messages could be stronger than the reality of the children's own lives.

We can say that one important goal for any early childhood classroom is "to free children from constraining, stereotypic definitions of gender role so that no aspects of development will be closed off simply because of a child's sex" (Derman-Sparks, 1993, p. 49). At the same time, the example of Janice and her daughter tells us that achieving this goal involves a major commitment of time, effort, and awareness. Once you begin paying attention to gender roles in your classroom, you are likely to hear children say things that are startling reflections of the messages society sends about how boys and girls are supposed to behave, dress, play, talk, and think. In addition, families often have very definite ideas about gender roles that may or may not match the goals you have for children in your classroom.

Diversity in gender identity and gender roles is evident in the variety of young

FIGURE 4.2 Children do not always conform with efforts by teachers and families to free them from traditional gender roles.

children's family structures. There are single-parent families with just a father or mother, and two-parent families with mother and father, or two same-sex parents. Some families have two working parents; others have a stay-at-home mother or father. Grandparents and other extended family members may all live under one roof and share child care. A very thoughtful article by Burt, Gelnaw, and Lesser (2010) makes the point that children are harmed when their families are not acknowledged and included in early childhood programs. Teachers often unintentionally harm children of gay, lesbian, bisexual, and transgendered families, for example, through unconscious bias and by never using words, reading books, or having pictures in the classroom that show same-sex parents. Families who are invisible are excluded, with a detrimental effect on their children's developing identities and sense of self-worth.

Gender identity is a product of both biological and social/societal factors. Most often children's biology aligns with their gender identity, but not always. One other aspect of gender role and identity that is beginning to be recognized in early childhood settings is captured in the terms *transgender* and *gender variant* or *gender fluid*. Transgender children have an internal gender identity that does not match their anatomical gender: a biological male who identifies as a girl, or vice versa. Gender variance or gender fluidity are terms that describe children whose gender identity is variable, and/or shows aspects of both male and female (Brill & Pepper, 2008).

Being transgender or gender variant is not a choice for young children, shown clearly by young children who identify strongly across biological genders before they have a fully developed concept of what it means socially or biologically to be male/female. Early childhood teachers have a dual role in supporting children's optimal individual development, and supporting parents who may themselves be struggling to understand a complex and confusing aspect of their children's development.

We wrote in Chapter Two about the misperception that teaching young children is easy, perhaps just a form of babysitting. By now it should be becoming increasingly clear that the actuality is much more complex, that the tasks of meeting all children's needs fairly and positively are not easy ones. Yet, it is only in recent years that professionals at all levels have come to realize that the issue of diversity deserves specific and increased attention.

Valuing All Children and Their Families

In 1987, the National Association for the Education of Young Children (NAEYC) published its first edition of *Developmentally Appropriate Practice in Early Childhood Programs* (Bredekamp, 1987) and differentiated between appropriate practice for groups of children at particular stages of development and appropriate practice given an individual child's own context. Cultural differences, in the first edition, were deemed a part of variations among individuals. A decade later, NAEYC published a revised edition, with the realization that the original view did not sufficiently take into consideration the strong influence that culture has on children's development and on what and how they learn.

NAEYC concluded many years ago, and continues to maintain, that ignoring the important influences of culture on the development of young children can lead to many different problems in practice. When the cultural rules of the home and the early childhood program are congruent, the process of learning is eased. However, when the expectations of the cultures of the home and the school or child-care program are different or conflicting, children can be confused or forced to choose which culture to identify with and which to reject (Bredekamp & Copple, 1997/2009).

An important role for all teachers and caregivers, then, is to help youngsters bridge the disparities between home and school or center. Not to do so can be damaging to children, in both great and small ways. Many beginning teachers choose to ignore cultural differences, declaring that they love all children the same. "Few of us have developed tools to address difficult issues such as discrimination and oppression, and likely naively believe that if we respect the individual child, all will be well" (Boutte, 2008, p. 165). The result of this attitude, however, is that the teacher's cultural view tends to be unconsciously imposed on the children, sometimes with an implicit sense of superiority. When teachers convey that their own cultural views are better, the next step may well be children's differences are interpreted as deficits, as illustrated in the following vignette:

> A teacher educator once looked forward to assigning a practicum student to a particular class of 4-year-olds. The majority of the children were learning English as a second language, seemingly a perfect opportunity for this student, who professed an interest in an international teaching career. Just two days into the experience, however, the practicum student began referring to the "language barrier" that was preventing her from teaching anything of value to the children. Her professor discussed with her the fact that the children, although beginners at English, were already proficient in at least one other home language, and some of them—at just 4 years old—already spoke two. This was a feat that the education student had yet to accomplish, as she only spoke English. Nevertheless, the student continued to focus on the "barrier" that kept her from teaching, and soon she began to speak of

the children derogatorily, as "English deficient," seeing the barrier as the children's rather than her own.

Continued work with the student on the part of her university supervisor and the classroom teacher eventually led her to new teaching methods and respect for the children's capabilities, but her original attitude is a common one. Perhaps because teachers have an ingrained disposition to fill in gaps of knowledge, they often look for weaknesses rather than strengths in children. A child who brings another culture and another language to class can be evaluated as having a clearly visible set of deficiencies to be fixed. Yet, it is through honoring the child's abilities and strengths while respecting the family's culture that a teacher can best reach the child. As one writer has said, young children:

> deserve to be in programs where it is safe for them to be who they are. ... Children have the right to feel good about themselves, to learn to be courageous, and not to feel like victims. Children are entitled to their cultural heritage and to be proud of it.
>
> (York, 1991, p. 23)

The NAEYC Code of Ethical Conduct states that "Above all, we shall not harm children. ... This principle has precedence over all others in this Code" (NAEYC, 2005). Burt, Gelnaw, and Lesser (2010) argue that early educators can inadvertently harm children and families by making assumptions based on their own experience and the majority rule, for example that all children have both a mother and father, that all children will grow up to be heterosexual, or that it is better for children to speak English than any other language. Providing children with the respect they deserve requires that teachers and caregivers know something about the cultural similarities and differences their youngsters bring with them each day.

To understand children's backgrounds most fully, teachers and caregivers also need to know something about their own cultures. This can be even more difficult than learning about another's culture, because our own daily lives have a ring of reality and neutrality, making other points of view seem alien, even unreal. Sociologists describe our unquestioned views as taken-for-granted realities. One example that is frequently given refers to the preference of U.S. mainstream culture to look directly in another's eyes when speaking. This is particularly important when coming across as honest is an issue, or a topic of urgency is being discussed. There are, however, some people who find such physical directness inappropriate, some Hispanic and American Indian cultures, for instance. An illustration of the complexity of this issue is the notion, voiced by an American Indian researcher, that looking down to indicate respect began when Indian children were taken to mission boarding schools (Demmert, 2005). Thus, a child from one of these groups might look at his feet out of respect for his teacher just when she is saying, "Look at me when I talk to you!" Each person in this unfortunate interchange is, at this moment, in possession of a taken-for-granted reality that is a disservice to the occasion. However, it is the teacher's responsibility, not the child's, to comprehend this and to move to a better understanding of the cultural complexities that make up a classroom.

One aspect of cultural complexity that should be considered is the fact that there is great variability among individual practices and values <u>within</u> any cultural group.

Stereotyping can result from generalizations that all American Indian children will look at their feet while the teacher talks, that all Asian Americans will work hard in school, or that all Anglo-European children are programmed for competitive individualism. Cultural values commonly held by mainstream Americans do include individualism, privacy, equality, informality, wise use of time, achievement, materialism, and directness. Yet, individual Americans, natives and immigrants alike, accept these values at differing levels of intensity. Or, they may fully accept most of the values but completely opt out on one or two (Lynch & Hanson, 2004). One way to begin handling such complexities in our own teaching lives is to take steps toward a better consciousness of the realities we take for granted, to see our own cultures more clearly.

Learning to See Ourselves More Clearly

How we see ourselves and our backgrounds has direct bearing on our views of teaching and learning. The first step in dealing with the cultural complexities of teaching is to become consciously aware of our values and beliefs and the influence of those values and beliefs on our behaviors.

> Robin was a first-year teacher being observed by her principal for the first time. For the occasion, she placed the children's chairs in a horseshoe shape and planned a question-and-answer session around a story they were all reading together. The principal sat quietly in the back, taking occasional notes, until she noticed a disturbing pattern. Robin rarely called on any girls, ignoring their raised hands in favor of answers from the boys. Bit by bit the girls began to wilt visibly, their early enthusiasm soon replaced by looks of boredom or resentment. Eventually, Robin began calling on children in what appeared to be a left-to-right order around the horseshoe. The principal breathed a sigh of relief; the girls would finally get a chance. To her amazement, Robin did go around the room in order, but continued to ignore the girls by jumping right over them to call on the next boy. When the principal later brought this to Robin's attention, she denied the possibility that it had happened until the principal showed her the chart she had made of the experience. Together they discussed solutions, finally settling on the idea that Robin should make a mental checklist as she called on children, consciously alternating boys and girls as much as possible.

It takes continuing efforts toward self-awareness, and sometimes the observations of a colleague or friend, to prepare ourselves well for handling cultural complexity. A good place to start is to reflect on our own cultural backgrounds, particularly in regard to education. Perhaps you come from a family with many educators in it, so that teaching was a natural choice for you. Or, your family may not particularly value education, but you are pressing ahead anyway, because you believe in the career you have chosen. Perhaps your family takes a different view of education entirely, valuing it for training in specific, hands-on trades and not for the more academic approach you are experiencing.

> Caroline, an experienced kindergarten teacher, thought she treated all her children with equality and made sure she gave positive feedback and encour-

agement in appropriate doses to everyone. One day, a friend on vacation from teaching in another state came to visit Caroline's class. She enjoyed her time with Caroline, but she observed a behavior that bothered her and decided it presented issues that should be discussed. Caroline was stunned to hear that she regularly hugged and touched the White and Hispanic children but not the Blacks. In fact, she couldn't quite believe it and spent the next week in some self-observation and soul searching. Finally, she admitted to herself it was true, realized that it was most probably related to her southern upbringing, and immediately went to work changing her behaviors.

Whatever your family's values and beliefs regarding education, and whether you have accepted or rejected those views, you have been shaped by their influence and will take your attitudes with you into the classroom.

At the end of this chapter, in the section Extending Your Learning, there are suggested activities that are intended to help increase your cultural self-awareness. We urge you to try at least one activity. In the meantime, as you have opportunities to work with children, try to observe your own behaviors with English language learners, boys and girls, and with children of different abilities, economic backgrounds, and ethnicities. See if you are drawn to or uncomfortable with one group or another. Do you tend to talk with girls more than boys and engage in physical play more with boys than with girls? Do you avoid physical contact with children whose hygiene is less than ideal, or whose clothing is dirty? Once you identify some of your biases, make specific plans for expanding into new patterns of behavior and thinking, so that all children will feel safe, included, recognized, and satisfied in their interactions with you.

Learning About Others

In addition to increasing our own self-awareness, an important step in serving children well is to learn something about their cultural backgrounds, particularly if their families have recently immigrated or have influential members—grandparents, perhaps—who influence the families' views on education and childrearing. This section provides overviews of several cultures commonly found in U.S. centers and schools at the beginning of the 21st century. It is important to restate, however, that there are degrees and variations in acceptance of and participation in any culture, even by those who have known only one culture from birth. Additionally, cultures evolve over time, ensuring that some elements may take new forms or even disappear. This is especially true following immigration.

Anglo-European Culture

In the United States, the traditional mainstream culture is Anglo-European. Its roots are seen in documents such as the Constitution and the Declaration of Independence that underlie legal decision-making and the rights and privileges that most citizens have come to expect. The culture's roots are also in the nation's mythology of pilgrims seeking religious freedom, patriots fighting their war for independence, and brave families heading west with few possessions but plenty of dreams. Built into this heritage can be found a Puritan work ethic that only permits play once all tasks are done; independent decision-making based on enlightened self-interest; and risk-taking that allows for failure but generally expects success. Few people today undergo the same strenuous challenges of these earlier settlers, but the founders' attitudes can still be found, even in early education settings. The work ethic remains in the requirement that children finish all their work before heading out to recess; independent decision-making occurs when learning choices are made by children at centers rather than by teachers; and risk-taking is valued when creativity is nurtured at the expense of a single standard of success.

Other values (see Althen, 1988; Lynch & Hanson, 2004), most of which can be traced back to the country's early days and the Anglo-European, include:

- *Equality.* American history is replete with the struggle to live up to this value. From freeing Blacks from slavery to providing women with voting rights, from mandating public education for children with disabilities to grappling with ways to make access to higher education more equitable, the vision of equality continues, slowly, to come closer to reality.
- *Focus on the future, belief in progress and change.* When settling their new land, early Anglo-European Americans had few historical frames of reference for what they did; every decision, every move to a new home site was an act of pioneering. Their descendants carry with them a belief that people are in charge of their own destinies; that progress is almost always possible, given one's own effort and self-confidence; and that change is generally for the good. This value is maintained sometimes in the face of resistance to change, for example in many reoccurring political debates about health care, immigration, education reform, and the role of corporate influence on the political system.
- *Respect for action and achievement, inclination toward materialism.* For people focused on progress, change, and self-determination, hard work is, not surprisingly, a concomitant value. Increasingly, the material rewards for hard work have become a strong emphasis, and the growing materialism that outsiders comment on has become a matter of concern for Anglo-European Americans themselves.
- *Attention to time.* Progress, change, and achievement may come about through hard work, but respect for the clock is seen as an underlying requirement. Value is placed on being on time and on timely efficiency, not only in the work place but in social interactions. Just as it is important to be on the job at the stated starting hour, so it is expected that arrival at a social function won't be much later than the time provided by the hosts' invitation. In the first case, a few minutes early may even be preferred.
- *A preference for informality.* To many outsiders, Anglo-European Americans both at home and abroad may be seen to be rude or lacking in class or culture because of their informality of speech, dress, and interaction style. In recent decades, the respect accorded a new acquaintance by using his or her last name has almost entirely disappeared, even for younger children. Jeans and T-shirts are worn everywhere, even on formal occasions. It is possible that such an increase in informality may, in part, be due to the greater emphasis on equality.
- *Communicating with directness and openness.* Subtlety and indirect statements are almost foreign to Anglo-European Americans. "What you see is what you get" and "telling it like it is" are valued sentiments in most interactions, and communication of feelings often accompanies a sharing of thoughts and ideas. However, in situations such as talking with a business superior or a new acquaintance, typically

Anglo-European Americans will be more reticent; moving to the next stage of more open sharing is a sign of increasing friendship.

- *The family.* The nuclear family—parents and children—defines the core concept of family for Anglo-European Americans. Members of the extended family, who may live at great distances, are referred to as relatives. Although parents do take charge, in America children are also accorded a say in decision-making, attaining an early equality not found in many other cultures. The self-determination valued by the larger culture is also manifested within the family, as young adults generally prefer to live outside the home and elderly members also prefer their independence, trying to avoid becoming a burden on the younger generations.

- *Childrearing.* Anglo-European American parents essentially begin training their children to grow up and leave home from the time they are born. Newborns are most likely to sleep in their own beds, often in their own rooms. Solid foods are introduced earlier than in some other cultures, and efforts at self-feeding and independent toileting are encouraged and praised. Youngsters may arrive at school wearing mismatched clothing with various fasteners poorly attended to, not because of parental neglect but because the children have been encouraged to choose their own outfits and to dress themselves. In supermarkets and restaurants, young children may be observed making their own choices of foods.

- *Views of illness and disabilities.* Explanations for disabilities generally follow a scientific model that focuses on specific causes: genetic disorders, accidents, disease, prenatal trauma, and so forth. It is believed by most Anglo-European Americans that better diagnoses, health treatments, education, and living conditions can be of help. The view that the attitudes and behaviors of parents, especially mothers, are responsible for some disabilities, for the most part, has been replaced by the focus on genetic causes for even emotional disorders.

Interactions Between the School or Center and Families

Some cultural customs of Anglo-European Americans are important for teachers to keep in mind (Lynch & Hanson, 2004). These include:

- Equal treatment for everyone, no matter their gender or station in life.
- Freedom of speech on most subjects, although topics related to sex, politics, religion, and physical traits (such as body odor) are typically not discussed in a formal situation.
- Open, warm greetings that often include a handshake (even if the ensuing meeting is expected to be difficult). Making eye contact and looking at each other talking indicates honesty and courtesy.
- Except for shaking hands, an expectation that people do not touch during interactions. Personal space of about an arm's length is most comfortable.
- Meetings and conferences that begin on time, or a brief explanation and possibly an apology if a delay is necessary.
- Parents generally expect to be informed of their children's progress and are less likely than parents in some cultures to defer to the teacher's expertise and superiority. Parents of children with disabilities are often strong advocates of their children's rights and are aware of the teacher's responsibilities.

- Teachers should expect variations in the Anglo-European culture as determined by section of the country, rural or urban lifestyles, and national or religious heritage. (This is good advice for all the cultures discussed in this chapter.)

African-American Culture

Before pilgrims landed in what was to become New England, about 20 Africans arrived in Virginia. Like many of the Whites arriving at the same time, they had been kidnapped and sold, then bound to their masters for a set number of years until they had earned their freedom. Blacks and Whites alike were treated abusively, and at times ran away together or bore children together. Either action was punishable, but a subtle difference in the treatment of the two races set the stage for the imminent move to slavery. In 1640, the Virginia legislature passed a law decreeing that masters should provide firearms to White but not Black servants. The same year, three servants, one Black and two White, ran away and were captured. All three men received 30 lashes, but here the equality of punishment stopped. The White servants were indentured for four more years; the Black servant was indentured for "the time of his Natural life" (Takaki, 1993, p. 56). In other words, he became a slave, one of an increasing number during the 1640s. The spread of slavery throughout the Americas led to the forced emigration of 20 million Africans between the 16th and 19th centuries. Of these, 4 million came to North America.

After the American Revolution, in which Black soldiers from each of the 13 colonies participated, slavery was abolished in the northern states. The Civil War in the 19th century may have freed the rest of the slaves legally, but racism continued and grew alongside the increasing participation by Blacks in all aspects of mainstream life. For example, the Ku Klux Klan was organized in 1866, just before the South Carolina House of Representatives found itself with a Black majority. By 1896, the U.S. Supreme Court determined (in *Plessy v. Ferguson*) that states were free to provide separate but equal institutions, and many states, particularly in the South, seized the opportunity, most notably in regard to schools.

Looking for better opportunities, Blacks began to leave the South, only to arrive at the same time European immigrants were also crowding into northern cities. For the most part, help with education, housing, and employment was provided for the Europeans but not for the African-Americans, who soon settled into city slums. "The impact of prejudice, poverty, and urban ghettos continues to affect many African Americans disproportionately to the present day" (Willis, 1998, p. 169). Yet, by the first half of the 20th century, the exodus of Blacks from the South only grew. Sharecropping in the South was at the whim of floods and insect infestations, and Black farmers found themselves encumbered by increasing debt.

Meanwhile, the influx of Europeans to the North halted during World War I, causing factory managers to send labor recruiters to the South. Widespread institutionalized racism continued in both North and South until World War II, when the military was desegregated, and even until 1954, when the *Plessy v. Ferguson* ruling was replaced by the Supreme Court's *Brown v. Board of Education* decision, which desegregated schools nationwide. In various ways, some of them controversial (e.g., the repeal of affirmative action in some states in the late 1990s), the deinstitutionalization of racism continued throughout the remainder of the 20th century. Yet informal or social racism continues. "Negative attitudes, instilled by years of institutionalized breeding of fear and contempt, are still evident" (Willis, 1998, p. 170). According to Derman-Sparks and Olsen Edwards, "In every aspect of society, White children are more likely to have access to resources that support healthy development and future success, such as safe neighborhoods and good schools" (2010, p. 77).

Teachers and caregivers can expect, in their encounters with African-American families, to see both the results of this history of maltreatment and the influences of the Anglo-European mainstream culture described above. Within each family, the extent of these influences will vary, as is the case for any culture and its subsets. The influences and values listed and discussed next reflect an African heritage but also, at times, input from the U.S. mainstream culture as well.

- *Language.* The Africans who came to the United States as slaves brought with them a diversity of languages, although there were commonalities within them. It was generally required of Blacks that they learn English, but their interpretation of it was influenced by their native languages. Generations later, some linguistic patterns from these times remain in the speech of many African Americans.
- Linguists who have studied the speech patterns of African Americans in recent decades have altered their previous belief that this language is substandard English to an understanding that Black English has its own standardized rules. It has been observed that Black English tends to be used more broadly among people of lower socioeconomic status (SES) and selectively, depending on the social situation, by those of higher SES (Dillard, 1972).
- *The family.* From the time of slavery, when family members could be sold individually, to the present day, when single mothers are often the official head of household, the African-American nuclear family has been endangered. In its place has been an extended family model with its roots in African traditions. This heritage has led to a valuing of group effort over private gain. With support from the extended family, however, independence is also valued:

> This may seem at first to be in conflict with the group-effort ethic, but it actually extends that ethic. It has to do with the empowerment that comes when as many as are able can earn a living, meet their family's basic needs, and have a little bit left over to help others in the extended family who may need temporary assistance.
>
> (Willis, 1998, p. 183)

Respect for elders, although eroding in most facets of U.S. society, is historically an African-American value. From Africa came the belief that the oldest members of society are the closest to God; centuries later this idea still leads to the assumption that these are the people who lead prayers in any group setting. Obedience to parents and older siblings has been emphasized more than, for example, the discussions and reasoning often favored by those of Anglo-European heritage.

- *Childrearing.* Guidance from adults has traditionally emphasized discipline and obedience. The African proverb that it takes a village to raise a child is born out in the expectation that extended family and responsible community members will participate in the child's discipline and training. Children are expected to obey the family's rules and treat others with respect as soon as they are old enough to understand. "Although these beliefs are not acted upon by all African Americans because of their life circumstances, they form a core set of beliefs that continue to be valued by many" (Willis, 1998, p. 189).

- *Views of illness and disabilities.* These views can vary from an acceptance of the scientific model described in the Anglo-European section, to a belief in simple bad luck or misfortune, to the belief that a child's disability is the result of sinning on the parents' part.

Interactions Between School or Center and Families

Again we emphasize that it is important not to over-generalize the cultural influences on any one group. Some ideas to think about with that necessary caution, however, include:

- Communication is likely to be "high context," that is, less verbal and more through shared history, intonation, facial expressions, and other body language.
- Emphasis may be placed more on the situation than on time. Thus, it is more important to finish the business of a meeting than to watch the clock.
- Addressing parents and other adults by their last names and titles until invited to use the first name is considered polite. Not to do so indicates disrespect.
- Telling ethnic jokes of any kind should be avoided. African Americans often feel as though the joke would be about them if they were out of the room. (This is good advice for all teachers at all times with all cultures.)
- If an African-American child lives with an extended family, it may be someone other than, or in addition to, a parent who is responsible for home–school communication and who should be invited to conferences and special events.

American Indian Culture

It is estimated that before Europeans began to explore and settle North America, the American Indian population numbered about 5 million. By the 1800s, warfare and infectious diseases brought by White settlers had caused a drop to just about 600,000 people. The great loss of population led to a weakening of tribal alliances, leaving an opening for aggressive European advancement.

From the American Indian point of view, interactions were more or less negative, depending on the motives the outsiders brought with them. For the French, economics was the driving force. Trappers and traders lived with the American Indians, learned from and worked with them, and sometimes married them. The English looked more toward building permanent settlements in their own style. American Indians were at times viewed as impediments to success and were thought of as savages and pagans, scarcely worth noticing unless it became necessary to remove them from the land that the English claimed for their king. The Spanish, like the French, brought economic motives but were swayed more by valuable metals than by furs. In addition, they expended their energies spreading their Roman Catholic faith through the establishment of a system of missions. American Indians became a source of free labor as well as potential Christian converts. Faced with the powerful English and Spanish forces of expansion, the American Indians lost hope for keeping either their land or their cultures, and for the most part, they lost both.

As the United States began to form a nation, then expanded geographically, policies toward American Indian populations fluctuated wildly. Throughout much of the 19th century, negotiations took place by treaty. By the end of the century, tribes were relocated to reservations on lands deemed undesirable for the ever-growing numbers of settlers. "Such forced relocation not only broke the spirit of many once-proud Indian nations, but also destined them to a life of poverty and hopelessness—conditions that continue to haunt American Indians today" (Joe & Malach, 1998, p. 130).

Toward the end of the 19th century, the government decided that individual land ownership would make the American Indians more civilized, more productive, and more American. The reservations were carved up into individual plots under the Dawes Act of 1887, with any leftover land reverting to the government for more settlement.

By the 20th century, fewer than 250,000 American Indians were left in North America. Government policies began to focus ever more on assimilation into the mainstream culture. Children were removed from their families and sent to boarding schools, sometimes forcibly. They were punished for speaking their native languages, sometimes by physical cruelty, and denied ties to their home cultures. In the 1960s and 1970s, a time of upheaval nationally, American Indians across the United States began to demand the return of federal surplus land and the rights given to them by long-dishonored treaties. Such events as the occupation of Alcatraz Island and the takeover of the Bureau of Indian Affairs in Washington, DC, drew attention to the continuing plight of American Indians. Some reforms began to be implemented and included the Indian Health Care Improvement Act of 1976 and the Indian Child Welfare Act of 1978. The former provided extra resources for improving American Indian health both on and off the reservation; the latter gave tribes greater power over placement of children put up for adoption.

Today, children are no longer forced to leave home for boarding schools. They may attend public schools or those provided on their reservations. Too often, reservation schools do not have the resources of local public schools, but children attending public schools have not been treated well. Even when much energy is devoted to making school a welcoming place, parents may be reluctant to participate in any way, recalling all too well the pain of their own experiences.

As you think about interacting with American Indian families, consider the cultural values discussed next. Keep in mind that they will be held to different degrees by people who live on reservations or in urban settings and will be somewhat different from tribe to tribe.

- *Group orientation.* Tribal affiliation is an important aspect of identity. Some American Indian languages do not include a word for *I*. Group consensus is important in decision-making, and everyone involved is permitted to speak. Decisions may not be made on the spot but are deferred until everyone has had time to think things over. Aggressive and competitive individualism are usually rejected; children who develop these qualities from the mainstream culture may be taunted by their peers (Joe & Malach, 1998). Mainstream teachers may mistake the more typical quiet, self-effacing behavior as evidence of passivity or laziness, rather than the thoughtful and respectful demeanor valued by the American Indian culture.

- *Acceptance of events.* Members of the mainstream culture tend to focus on taking charge of, or doing something about, negative events or natural disasters. The American Indian approach tends more toward acceptance of the situation "as part of the nature of life and that one must learn to live with life and accept what comes, both the good and the bad" (Joe & Malach, 1998, pp. 140–141).

- *Self-reliance.* Parent-to-child teaching style occurs largely through modeling and direct telling. As children observe their parents in action, they learn quickly about expectations of the adult world. One cross-cultural study (Miller, cited in Joe & Malach, 1998) showed that whereas White and Black children were expected to do regular chores after they reached age 6, American Indian children did so at less than age 5½. American Indian children learned to dress themselves earlier as well, at 2.8 years old as opposed to almost 4 years old for White and Black children.
- *Time orientation.* Time for many American Indians is a more flexible and fluid concept than for people in the mainstream culture. Keeping to the dictates of the clock is not nearly so important as the activity and interactions underway, for example making sure that a meeting or conference is finished satisfactorily for all parties.
- *Language.* During the years that assimilation was emphasized, tribal languages began to disappear. Today, there is a widespread effort to reclaim nearly dead ancient languages. Some schools, including Head Start centers, begin early to teach children both the native culture and language as well as mainstream culture and English.
- *The family.* The extended family is frequently important for American Indians living on reservations, but the nuclear family is more commonly found in urban areas. In extended families, grandparents or other relatives may take a major role in raising young children if the parents are working. It is important for a teacher or caregiver to understand each family's situation before conferring about the welfare of their child.
- *Childrearing.* The extended family may assign different roles to different members. In some tribes, grandparents may provide spiritual and cultural guidance and uncles may handle discipline (Joe & Malach, 1998).
- Traditionally, American Indian children were not disciplined with corporal punishment. They were generally introduced to this approach during the often-abusive years in boarding schools run by the mainstream culture. Their years away from home kept American Indian children from learning parenting skills either from their own culture or from the mainstream culture, whose homes they rarely observed. There are attempts during this generation to heal the wounds of the past and to return to more traditional ways.
- *Views of illness and disability.* Although American Indian families may accept a scientific explanation and treatment of children's sickness and disabilities, they may also turn to their culture to explain the reasons for the problems as well as for additional treatment ideas. Causes such as witchcraft, spirit loss or intrusion, or spells may be considered important influences. Parents may wish to consult with a tribal healer before or during mainstream treatment (Joe & Malach, 1998). In addition, there may be an emphasis on the role of a child with a disability or delay in the family and community that has little apparent relationship to the characteristics of the disability.

Interactions Between School or Center and Families

Remembering again that acculturation varies across families and situations, a number of suggestions can still be made for school–family interactions based on American Indian history, traditions, and present-day culture (Joe & Malach, 1998; Krogh, 1994):

■ Before a conference, ask parents which family members should be included. They may or may not wish to bring others. If several people do come, be sure to address and listen to them all.

■ Avoid intimidating family members; listen to their ideas and ask questions rather than lecturing to them. Ask them what they see as their child's special talents and gifts.

■ Visit the children's homes or reservation. Be a part of the community from time to time by being knowledgeable about holidays and perhaps participating in special events.

■ Respect the family's preference for bicultural or bilingual education for their child.

■ Take time to learn about the communication style of the American Indian culture in your area. You may need to become more reserved and quiet during meetings than you typically are, and do more listening than talking (another good piece of general advice).

Latin-American or Latino Culture

Today there is concern in much of the United States about illegal immigrants crossing the border from Mexico, but a century and a half ago the situation was reversed. Then, California, Texas, New Mexico, Arizona, and Colorado belonged to Mexico. But, as one Mexican of the time complained, Americans had "formed for themselves" the idea "that God made the world and them also, therefore what there is in the world belongs to them as sons of God" (Takaki, 1993, pp. 172–173). This view was corroborated by the statements and actions of Americans, from presidents to ordinary citizens, many of whom simply moved illegally into Mexican territory. Americans declared it their *manifest destiny* to control the major portion of the North American continent and, by the end of the Mexican War of the 1830s and 1840s, did just that. Suddenly, the northern half of Mexico belonged to the United States, and the area's residents found themselves with a choice of heading south or remaining as potential U.S. citizens. Most chose to stay and before long found they were facing increasing antagonism toward their language and culture on the part of the growing Anglo-European population. The hunger for ever more land also ensured that eventually even the richest Mexican-Californian landholders were stripped of everything they owned.

Many in the United States today have chosen to forget this past, but those of Mexican heritage have, not surprisingly, retained the history as part of their cultural heritage. Similarly, there is a general tendency in the U.S. to regard most Mexican Americans as immigrants although many can trace their ancestry in the area to the 1700s or earlier.

Although less noticeable than immigrant communities from Mexico, because they have not settled in an easily identifiable area, immigrants from other countries in Central America have also been changing the face of the United States in the past generation. The teacher or caregiver involved with families from the various Latino cultures needs to realize that there are a number of differences among them, just as there are within each of the cultures we discussed previously. It is not only geographical difference that must be taken into account but class differences as well. To a great extent, the Latin-American tradition has included notable separation of the classes. At the top are those who claim Spanish ancestry; far below are the *Mestizo* (mixed), Black, and Native classes. A middle-class immigrant family from Mexico City, for example, might well have more in common with the U.S. mainstream culture than with a U.S.-born Mexican family of low-socioeconomic status (Zuniga, 1998). Often, immigrants remain more conscious of their class status than people of the mainstream culture realize.

In the Southeast, particularly in Florida, immigration of Spanish speaking peoples has come primarily from Cuba, the Caribbean island the United States attempted to buy from Spain in the 1850s, then fought over five decades later. Making Cuba a U.S. colony was, at times, on the political agenda but, in the end, it retained its independence.

At the very end of the Spanish-American War, even as the final treaty was being delivered for signature, the United States managed to overtake Puerto Rico and keep it for its own territory. Today, immigration comes from both Cuba and Puerto Rico, but in very different fashions. Because Puerto Ricans have U.S. citizenship, they may travel as they please, usually to find more economically satisfying work, then return home, just as any other citizen might do. Cubans, on the other hand, have arrived as refugees in periodic waves since Fidel Castro's revolutionary takeover in 1959. Because the first wave of refugees came from the educated upper classes, the Cuban story has been one of greater economic success than has generally been true for Puerto Rican and Mexican immigrants. The development of Miami as an international trading center has been, to a great extent, the result of the efforts of Cuban exiles.

Although it is difficult to assign a single set of values to a cultural group with so many variations in its subcultures and such divergent geographical origins, several attributes can be listed for teachers and caregivers to consider (Zuniga, 1998):

- *Machismo and a changing patriarchy.* Traditionally, Latino culture has valued strong leadership on the part of the father. In the past generation, this has been changing, as more women enter the workforce and become more highly educated. The tradition remains in many ways and in many families, however, and it is most courteous to speak to the father first if both parents are present at a conference or meeting.
- *Personalismo.* Warm interpersonal interactions are valued over the task orientation of the mainstream culture. Beginning any encounter with some informal chatting helps establish a good working atmosphere and may go a long way toward establishing trust of the teacher or caregiver.
- *Time.* Interpersonal relationships are more important than retaining an inflexible timetable. It is important to avoid giving parents the feeling that you are impatient or always in a rush, connoting that you don't care about them.
- *Language.* It should not be assumed that Spanish is the first language of all immigrant families. A growing number of them come from areas where indigenous languages are prevalent, and they may not be completely fluent in Spanish.
- Communication is generally high context, making body language and attitude as important as the words spoken. Teachers should take care to communicate in all ways their acceptance and respect.
- *The family.* Although the urban family headed by a single mother is a growing phenomenon, Latino families have maintained a far lower divorce rate than have other cultures, a fact that may well be related to the continuing influence of the Roman Catholic religion. Extended families traditionally have predominated.
- *Childrearing.* In general, children are viewed as the prime reason for marriage and as the validation of it. A relaxed attitude is taken toward early achievement, with more focus on nurturing and indulging a young child. Both physical and emotional

closeness prevail among all members. Identity with the family rather than independence is nurtured throughout the child's growing up years. Cooperation rather than individualism is generally valued. In poorer families, children may be expected to pitch in by taking on work roles fairly early. Young children are highly valued and babies often garner the attention of unrelated adults and strangers in public places.

■ *Views of illness and disability*. Middle-class, acculturated families may well have adopted the Anglo-European scientific views described previously. Others may bring with them a folk tradition as well as influences from the Latino Catholic church, which also incorporates many folk traditions. Thus, a disability may be seen as a curse from some present evil force. Belief in a punishing God and in the inevitable tragedy of life may lead to an accepting and fatalistic view of a disability or chronic illness.

Interactions Between School or Center and Families

Some suggestions that may be helpful across the various Latino cultures include:

■ Always begin interactions with some informal conversation; avoid the temptation to get right down to business.
■ Tone of voice and body language are important. Avoid coming across as authoritarian, tough, and harsh.
■ Try not to appear hurried and impatient. Let the parents know that you are listening and that you care.
■ If both husband and wife are present, speak to the husband first. Unless it becomes apparent that they have adopted a more mainstream family structure, continue to defer to the husband as the family leader.
■ Communicate your delight in and affection for their children as a centerpiece of, rather than a sideline to, the discussion.

Asian-American Cultures

The fastest growing ethnic minority group in the United States in recent years has been Asian, with a population of about 3.5 million in 1980 expanding to over 8 million in 2000 (U.S. Census Bureau, 2003). Of the cultural groups discussed in this chapter, those of Asian influence are, perhaps, the most varied. The inability of many Americans to tell Chinese from Japanese or Thais from Vietnamese indicates a need to become more knowledgeable rather than any actual lack of difference between the nationalities. As one Chinese immigrant's son argues, the perception that Asian immigrants are all much the same or, at least, mysterious, "serves to disguise the reality of unique customs, traditions, values, beliefs, and familial systems based on political and religious foundations that are thousands of years old" (Chan, 1998, pp. 252–253). Most pertinent for our purposes, a lack of knowledge may lead a teacher or caregiver to misunderstand the feelings that children's families have toward one another—feelings that may be based on centuries of conflict or friendship.

Over the years, immigration from Asian countries to the United States has been affected by two general influences: changing U.S. immigration policies and difficulties in various Asian countries, such as economic hardship and wars. This section discusses these influences on immigrants from two countries. Further research into the experiences of other peoples will broaden a teacher's ability to work well with families from other cultures as well.

Chinese-American History

Widespread famine, economic depression, and civil wars in mid-19th-century China, coupled with the news of recently discovered gold in California, caused the first major influx of Chinese people to the United States. The plan for most of these men, who came by the tens of thousands, was to mine for three to five years, then return home with enough money to retire on. A very few were able to do just that, and so the legend of *Gam Saan* (Gold Mountain) continued to grow, despite the fact that most of the Chinese did not do well and had to find more menial jobs to survive. Soon, many of them were hired by private companies contracted to extend the national railroad system to the West Coast. The Chinese proved to be excellent workers who cost less than U.S. citizens, a situation almost guaranteed to lead eventually to resentments and disputes.

The result was the Chinese Exclusion Act of 1882, the first federal law that banned an entire nationality from entering the United States. It was not repealed until 1943. The years between found some Chinese returning home but many others remaining to face institutional and violent racism. To avoid deportation, it was generally necessary to change one's status from laborer to businessman. The creation of urban Chinatowns provided some cultural security, safety from racism, and business opportunities, and many of these cities within cities remain today.

Due to a rigid quota system, it was not until 1965, with the passage of the Immigration and Nationality Act Amendments, that a second wave of Chinese could enter the United States. Since preferred status was given to educated, professional, and skilled workers, this second group provided a new stereotype of Asians as overachievers. Their children and grandchildren are still labeled today with the expectation that they all will be the best performers in their classes.

Chinese-American Language

The Chinese are connected by a single written language, but the pronunciation of its pictographic characters varies widely across dialects. Chinese contains many monosyllabic words that are often differentiated by the pitch, or tone, of pronunciation. Word order is different from that of English, and there are no tenses, plural endings, or verb conjugations. Imagine the total reorientation to language that every Chinese immigrant child and parent must undergo when learning English!

Vietnamese-American History

Although Vietnam's northern border touches China, and many of its original inhabitants are thought to have come from southern China, the country's culture and language have evolved quite differently in many ways. China ruled the country for about a thousand years, but beginning in 111 B.C., numerous rebellions led to independence that lasted until the French colonized Vietnam, from 1883 to 1954. During World War II, the Japanese occupied the country and, this time, rebels adopted Communism. After the war, the French tried to regain control but managed only to retake the south while the

Communists controlled the north. With the French finally repelled from the south as well, the country was officially divided between North and South, both sides claiming exclusive power over the entire country. By 1960, war was in full swing, with the Soviet Union and China aiding the North and the United States supporting the South.

During the 20 years of the Vietnam War, many South Vietnamese put themselves at risk to aid the U.S. troops. As the South and its U.S. allies lost the war, many South Vietnamese were forced to flee. Over time, more than 1 million became refugees in both Asian and Western countries, primarily in France and in the United States. These ranged from educated professionals to Hmong people from remote mountain areas and to "boat people" who had survived extraordinarily horrific conditions. Immigration policy has been to disperse the Vietnamese throughout the United States rather than permitting "Vietnam-towns" to develop. Thus, in almost any area of the country, teachers and caregivers may encounter second- or even first-generation Vietnamese immigrants.

Vietnamese-American Language

Like Chinese, Vietnamese is tonal, contains many monosyllabic words, and has no plurals, tenses, or verb conjugations. Originally, written Vietnamese was based on the Chinese system but, since World War I, the Roman alphabet, with several additional tone marks, has been adopted.

Shared Values

Although their societies have developed in some differing ways, Chinese and Vietnamese also share values that are similar, with roots that go back thousands of years. Thus, the following cultural traits can generally be applied to both:

■ *Family.* The Asian family as the central focus of the individual's life "engenders primary loyalty, obligation, cooperation, interdependence, and reciprocity" (Chan, 1998, p. 292). In Asian cultures, the individual is believed to be today's extension of a family that goes back to the beginning of time. Thus, there is as much thought for the past as for the present. Both the Chinese and the Vietnamese adhere to the ancient Confucian hierarchical system in which the father has primary leadership within the nuclear family but living grandparents are at the top of the extended family.

■ *Harmony.* "The keynote of existence is to reconcile divergent forces, principles, and points of view in an effort to maintain harmony. The individual must strive to achieve intrapsychic harmony, interpersonal harmony, and harmony with nature as well as time" (Chan, 1998, p. 293). Asian Americans guided by the tradition of harmony avoid confrontation; demonstrate constraint in verbal, social, and emotional interactions; help others save face by showing respect; and value politeness and tact. A teacher or caregiver with a tendency toward extreme directness should keep these characteristics in mind in order to help interactions with more traditional Asian Americans to succeed.

■ *Patience and endurance.* Along with patience and endurance, industriousness and tolerance have provided strength to Vietnamese and other southeast Asians who have lived through subjugation, war, and great loss. For the Chinese, it has been important to persevere quietly, without complaint. For many Asian Americans, it is bad form to share problems with someone such as the teacher. They may even smile and assure everyone that everything is just fine, thus politely sparing others the need to share their pain.

- *Childrearing.* Having children is the cement of marriage, more important than the relationship between husband and wife. During a child's infancy, loving parents are permissive, tolerant, and ready to answer every discomfort. Breast feeding may last two years or longer, but toilet training may begin after just a few months, although it is not coercive. The indulgence of the early years is replaced, once school age is reached, with an expectation of self-discipline, responsibility, and a better understanding of adult mores and roles. Whereas the early years are characterized by guidance from the mother, the father now participates in childrearing as well, and disciplinary expectations are increased.
- *Views of illness and disability.* Families that have recently immigrated may well retain traditional views that conflict with the Anglo-European scientific model. A child's good behavior and success in school are viewed as the family's responsibility. Thus, a child with a behavior disorder or mental retardation can become a source of embarrassment for the family, someone who just needs more support from home. A mother's behavior during pregnancy may be seen as the cause of a disability, including such things as eating taboo foods, engaging in reckless or inappropriate activities, or using tools, particularly scissors or knives.

Interactions Between School or Center and Families

Asian cultures can vary widely, but some suggestions may prove helpful in your interactions:

- In communication, body language is much more subdued than in other cultures, e.g., Anglo-European, African American, and Latino. Speaking with great animation may be overwhelming and turn off useful exchanges. Emotional restraint and general reserve will be received with more comfort.
- Sustained eye-to-eye contact is considered rude and should be avoided.
- Until you know the parents well, avoid asking personal questions about their lives. This even includes asking their opinions on politics, which for many Asian cultures is akin to asking pointed questions in the mainstream culture about religious preference.

Some General Conclusions

There are in the United States today numerous ethnicities, cultures, and nations of origin. It is impossible within the confines of this single chapter to do more than touch on a few. We hope, however, that the descriptions provided here may give the reader two directions for further learning: a better realization that knowledge of child and family background can go far toward positive family interactions and progress in learning; and a better understanding of one's own culture. If your culture was represented in one or more of the descriptions, were there items that surprised you but rang true? Were there some that did not seem quite right? Should others be added? As we delve further into the attributes of our own and others' cultures, we gain appreciation of our common humanity as well as greater skill in providing the most positive atmosphere for the intellectual, emotional, and social growth of all the children entrusted to us.

It is important to learn about and respect other cultures, abilities, and viewpoints; yet doing so is not sufficient to move our society forward. It is also important to realize that biases develop very early in children's lives, thus making it a clear responsibility of early childhood educators to be proactive in their classroom responsibilities.

Being Proactive in the Classroom or Center: An Overview

Early childhood educators have a responsibility to avoid harm and provide an atmosphere that equips young children with tools and strategies to stand up against bias and prejudice, for the benefit of themselves, other adults, young children, and the adults the children will become. There is a large body of information and resources to support teachers in their efforts, most notably:

- *Anti-bias Education for Young Children and Ourselves*, by Louise Derman-Sparks and Julie Olsen Edwards.
- *Roots and Wings: Affirming culture in early childhood programs*, by Stacey York.
- *Teaching and Learning in a Diverse World*, by Patricia Ramsey.

Each of these resources provides philosophical, theoretical, and empirical information, as well as a multitude of practical strategies for addressing diversity in all its forms in early childhood programs. A hallmark of the materials available to support anti-bias and multi-cultural early education is that teachers are supported and encouraged to go beyond knowledge to take action, investigate their own beliefs, challenge existing practices, and make things better for children. Anti-bias education (ABE) has a very ambitious agenda, as illustrated by the four ABE goals:

1. Each child will demonstrate self-awareness, confidence, family pride, and positive social identities.
2. Each child will express comfort and joy with human diversity; accurate language for human differences; and deep, caring human connections.
3. Each child will increasingly recognize unfairness, have language to describe unfairness, and understand that unfairness hurts.
4. Each child will demonstrate empowerment and the skills to act, with others or alone, against prejudice and/or discriminatory actions.
                                    (Derman-Sparks & Olsen Edwards, 2010, p. xx)

Our goal in this chapter has been to provide some introductory considerations for the reader who is beginning to interact with children and families from a variety of backgrounds. We hope that an atmosphere of acceptance, caring, and concern for all children will imbue our readers' teaching practices and that you will adopt the four ABE goals above as your own. As you think about ways to make all children feel welcome and valued, it is essential to have some more specific guidelines to frame your everyday interactions. The following list is adapted from the three books listed above (Derman-Sparks & Olsen Edwards, 2010; Ramsey, 2004; and York, 2003).

Teachers should:
- Recognize the beauty, value, and contribution of each child.

- Provide children with accurate, developmentally appropriate information about race, language, culture, ability, gender anatomy and identity, and social class.
- Encourage young children's openness and interest in others, willingness to include others, and desire to cooperate.
- Promote effective and collaborative relationships with children's families.

Children should:
- Develop positive gender, racial, cultural, class, and individual identities.
- See themselves as part of the larger society, identifying with and relating to members of all groups, as well as with their own family and heritage.
- Learn to respect and appreciate the diverse ways in which other people live.
- Feel pride but not superiority in their racial identity.
- Feel free to ask about their own and others' physical characteristics; about issues of racism, ability, culture, gender; and about current events.
- Experience discussions and activities in early childhood programs that promote engagement with concepts related to diversity and interactions with people from a variety of backgrounds.

Families should:
- Feel welcome and comfortable in the early childhood program.
- Participate as active partners in their young children's educations to the extent they desire.
- Be confident about sharing information and making suggestions about their children and/or the program.
- Expect that their perspectives and opinions will be acknowledged and considered.

Suggestions to teachers for achieving these goals include:
- Post welcoming signs in each home language of the children in your classroom.
- Make anti-bias education a priority every day and include anti-bias updates as a standing feature of newsletters and conferences.
- Learn basic teaching and learning vocabulary in children's home languages.
- Invite visits from local community leaders and participate in community celebrations.
- Use words like "a few," "some," "usually," "sometimes," "many," and "most" to describe family structure, gender concepts, and SES. For example, "Many families have two parents, and some families have just one parent." "Some families have a Mom AND a Dad; sometimes there is a Mom OR a Dad; and sometimes there are two Mommies OR two Daddys." "In many families there are brothers and sisters, and many children are the only one; often children are the only one for a while and then there is a new baby."
- Look carefully at the room's materials for play. Do they respect and reflect the cultures of all your children? Are there chopsticks and a tortilla press in the housekeeping area? Commercial tools for the housekeeping corner, for example, typically reflect middle-class, Anglo-European values.
- Scan all books to see if pictures represent varying ethnicities, ages, family structures, and abilities. Are both genders engaged in nontraditional as well as traditional roles?

Are there pictures of same-sex parents, children of ambiguous gender, wheelchairs, eyeglasses, walkers, hearing aids, and so forth?

- Decorate the walls with photographs of people from various cultures, ethnicities, and abilities. Discuss them informally with the children.
- Balance individually oriented activities with cooperative learning experiences.
- Display alphabets, labels, and quotes from different writing systems. Teach a few words or numbers in different languages, particularly those represented by cultures in the classroom.
- Avoid pictures, dolls, and activities that stereotype or misrepresent other cultures: festival clothes presented as though they are worn all the time; historical representations presented as if they were current; teaching about a country of origin to explain about their U.S. descendants (e.g., Japan to learn about Japanese Americans).
- Avoid token studying of ethnic or cultural groups only at high-visibility times (e.g., Blacks for Martin Luther King's birthday, American Indians at Thanksgiving).
- Do not ignore children's discriminatory comments or behavior—they will not go away. Rather, make rules about the treatment of others, then intervene immediately if necessary, just as you do with any misbehavior. Teach about feelings, friendship, respect, citizenship, stereotypes, and differences.
- Listen to your own speech and observe your own interactions. Do you speak with a harsher tone of voice for some children than for others? Do you touch some children less than others? Are you more inclined to take disciplinary action toward some?

In this chapter we have discussed the need for all children and their families to feel welcomed and valued in our classrooms and centers. We described several cultures commonly seen in the United States today and the ways in which their members might look at their experiences in and out of the classroom environment. We also considered a few practical ways to incorporate a respect for diversity in the classroom or center. Finally, we should point out that given the multi-cultural nature of today's world, diversity is an important issue for all teachers, not just for those who teach in a diverse classroom. All children deserve opportunities to learn about the complex world around them.

EXTENDING YOUR LEARNING

As in the previous chapters, Suggestions 1 and 2 focus on your developing philosophy of teaching and learning.

1 After reading this chapter, do you find that your thinking has changed, or perhaps been solidified, pertaining to diversity issues and your teaching? Reflect on the feelings you had as you read this chapter and what those feelings will mean to your teaching. Add these ideas to your personal philosophy notes.

2 Look over the picture you drew. Now that you have read this chapter, does it appear that there are children who are missing from your classroom? How do you feel about your placement in relation to the children and to the physical environment? If you have used colored artwork and avoided stick figures, you should be able to answer these questions. Either redraw as appropriate or add commentary to the back of your picture.

3 Visit a school or center with several languages represented. Interview teachers and observe the ways in which non-English-speaking children are introduced to their new language. Find out how children's needs are met while they are learning to communicate using English.

4 Recall your first introduction to differences in gender, race and ethnicity, ability, and social status. How did you respond to your new knowledge: Was the experience positive, negative, or mixed? Do you have uncomfortable memories of your own actions or of those of others to children who were different in these ways? Have you experienced prejudice or discrimination yourself?

5 Think about the views of your family members concerning differences in gender, race, ability, and economic status. Do you generally accept them? Reject them? Can you explain why?

6 Choose a country about which you know little, one that has children registered in schools and centers in your area. First, do some library research about that country's history, geography, and culture. Then interview two or more parents (or grandparents) from that country about their views of education. Consider how you could adapt your curriculum or methodology to meet their children's needs from the family's cultural point of view while still providing the skills the children will need to survive well in the mainstream culture.

7 Start a file box of ideas for your classroom that incorporate ways to handle diversity issues. You might have a section for each area of the curriculum, another for parents, and another for the environment.

8 During your student-teaching experience, invite all parents to participate and share in classroom activities and outings. Have parents teach songs or read picture books in their native languages.

9 Has your thinking changed, or perhaps been solidified, pertaining to cultural issues and your teaching? Reflect on your feelings as you read this chapter and what they will mean to you in your teaching. Add these ideas to your personal philosophy notes.

10 Take advantage of opportunities to attend and participate in public events sponsored by cultural groups other than your own. Accompany families, if invited, to traditional healers, holiday celebrations, family gatherings. Note the aspects of each event that are familiar and comfortable as well as those that are unfamiliar and uncomfortable for you.

Internet Resources

Web sites provide much useful information for educators and we list some here that pertain to the topics covered in this chapter. The addresses of Web sites can also change, however, and new ones are continually added. Thus, this list should be considered as a first step in your acquisition of a larger and ever-changing collection.

Center for Language Minority Education and Research
www.clmer.csulb.edu/

Culturally & Linguistically Appropriate Services Early Childhood Research Institute
http://clas.uiuc.edu

Global Classroom
www.global-classroom.com

The Global Schoolhouse
www.gsh.org

Immigration and Naturalization Service
www.uscis.gov/portal/site/uscis

Multicultural Book Review Homepage
www.isomedia.com/homes/jmele/homepage.html

Multicultural Pavilion
www.edchange.org/multicultural/

National Black Child Development Institute
www.nbcdi.org/

National Latino Children's Institute
www.nlci.org/common/index2.htm

Viet Nam Online Community
www.php.com/

Vocabulary

Achievement gap. Systematic differences in educational performance across groups of students, usually defined by gender, race/ethnicity, and/or social-economic status (SES).

Affirmative action. Policies that attempt to promote equal opportunity members of minority groups and promote diversity, primarily in the workplace.

High context communication. Communication between people that emphasizes non-verbal signals such as body language.

Indentured servant. A person under contract binding him or her, as a laborer, to another for a given length of time. In the early American colonies, an immigrant so bound.

Institutionalized racism. Differential access to the goods, services, and opportunities of society; inherent limitations of opportunities that disadvantage members of minority racial groups.

Low context communication. Communication between people that emphasizes verbal language at the expense of non-verbal signals.

Manifest Destiny. A U.S. doctrine of the 19th century in which the country's continued territorial expansions was postulated to be obvious and necessary.

Mestizo. A colonial term used to refer to people of mixed European and Amerindian ancestry.

Monolingual. Proficiency in a single language.

Multi-cultural. Containing many cultures. In education, the focus is on appreciating the contributions of all cultures.

Nuclear family. Parents and their children who share living quarters.

Separate but Equal. Until 1954, when overturned by the U.S. Supreme Court, a doctrine that racial segregation in schools and other facilities was constitutional as long as the facilities were about equal for both Blacks and Whites.

SES. Abbreviation for *social economic status*, a descriptor that combines income, education, and occupation into a measure that describes social status.

Taken for granted realities. Elements of a culture that are so embedded as to be invisible to the members of the culture as anything other than realities that are believed to pertain to all humans.

References

Althen, G. (1988). *American ways: A guide for foreigners in the United States*. Yarmouth, ME: Intercultural Press.

Barnett, W. S., & Yarosz, D. J. (2007). Who goes to preschool and why does it matter? *Preschool Policy Brief*, Issue 15. New Brunswick, NJ: National Institute for Early Education Research.

Boutte, G. S. (2008). Beyond the illusion of diversity: How early childhood teachers can promote social justice. *The Social Studies*, 99(4), 165–173.

Bredekamp, S. (Ed.) (1987). *Developmentally appropriate practice in early childhood programs serving children from birth through age 8*. Washington, DC: National Association for the Education of Young Children.

Bredekamp, S., & Copple, C. (Eds.) (1997). *Developmentally appropriate practice in early childhood programs* (2nd ed.). Washington, DC: National Association for the Education of Young Children.

Bredekamp, S., & Copple, C. (Eds.) (2009). *Developmentally appropriate practice in early childhood programs: Serving children from birth to age 8* (3rd ed.). Washington, DC: National Association for the Education of Young Children.

Brill, S., & Pepper, R. (2008). *The transgender child: A handbook for families and professionals*. San Francisco: Cleis Press.

Burkam, D. T., & Lee, V. E. (2002). *Inequity at the starting gate*. Washington, DC: Economic Policy Institute.

Burt, T., Gelnaw, A., & Lesser, L. K. (2010). Do no harm: Creating welcoming and inclusive environments for lesbian, gay, bisexual, and transgender families in early childhood settings. *Young Children*, 65(1).

Chan, S. (1998). Families with Asian roots. In E. Lynch & M. Hanson (Eds.), *Developing cross-cultural competence* (2nd ed.). Baltimore, MD: Paul H. Brookes.

Children's Defense Fund (2008). *The state of America's children 2008: Highlights*. Washington, DC: Author.

Demmert, W. (2005). Personal communication.

Derman-Sparks, L. (1993). *Anti-bias curriculum: Tools for empowering young children*. Washington, DC: National Association for the Education of Young Children.

Derman-Sparks, L., & Olsen Edwards, J. (2010). *Anti-bias education for young children and ourselves*. Washington, DC: National Association for the Education of Young Children.

Dillard, J. (1972). *Black English: Its history and usage in the United States*. New York: Random House.

Joe, J., & Malach, R. (1998). Families with Native American roots. In E. Lynch & M. Hanson (Eds.), *Developing cross-cultural competence* (2nd ed.). Baltimore, MD: Paul H. Brookes.

Krogh, S. (1994). *Educating young children: Infancy to grade three*. New York: McGraw-Hill.

Lynch, E., & Hanson, M. (2004). *Developing cross-cultural competence: A guide for working with young children and their families* (3rd ed.). Baltimore, MD: Paul Brookes Publishing Company.

NAEYC (2005). Position statement. *NAEYC code of ethical conduct and statement of commitment*, rev. ed. Brochure. Washington, DC: Author.

Ramsey, P. (2004). *Teaching and learning in a diverse world: Multicultural education for young children* (3rd ed.). New York: Teachers College Press.

Swiniarski, L., Breitborde, M., & Murphy, J. (1999). *Educating the global village: Including the young child in the world*. Upper Saddle River, NJ: Merrill.

Takaki, R. (1993). *A different mirror*. Boston, MA: Little, Brown.

U.S. Census Bureau (2003). *The foreign-born population: 2000. Census 2000 brief*. U.S. Department of Commerce.

U.S. Department of Education, National Center for Education Statistics, Digest of Education Statistics, 2003.

U.S. Department of Health and Human Services: Commissioner's Office of Research and Evaluation and the Head Start Bureau, Administration on Children, Youth, and Families. (2008). *Dual language learners: What does it take?* Washington, DC: Author.

Willis, W. (1998). Families with African American roots. In E. Lynch & M. Hanson (Eds.), *Developing cross-cultural competence* (2nd ed.). Baltimore, MD: Paul H. Brookes.

York, S. (1991). *Roots and wings: Affirming culture in early childhood programs.* St. Paul, MN: Redleaf Press.

York, S. (2003). *Roots and wings: Affirming culture in early childhood programs* (Revised ed.). St. Paul, MN: Redleaf Press.

Zuniga, M. (1998). Families with Latino roots. In E. Lynch & M. Hanson (Eds.), *Developing cross-cultural competence* (2nd ed.). Baltimore, MD: Paul H. Brookes.

part three
Tomorrow

In this final section, you will be asked to consider some of today's unresolved issues in the field, and their potential impact for your future as an early childhood educator. Each issue is presented with some current context, arguments from at least two perspectives, and supporting evidence from research, theory, and/or well-considered opinions. Thus, while there may be no one "right" answer for these issues, our goal is that you understand differing background and opinions. As you discuss the issues with classmates, your instructor, and other early childhood professionals, remember this point and treat opposing viewpoints with the utmost respect, whether you agree with them or not.

five
Issues That Will Shape the Future

In an educational experience that is truly shared, choices and decisions have to be made with the widest possible consensus, and with a deep respect for a plurality of ideas and viewpoints.

Sergio Spaggiari

Chapter Objectives

After reading this chapter, you should be able to:

- Describe differing perspectives of some of today's more perplexing issues related to young children and their education.
- Begin to evaluate unresolved issues by reviewing and investigating all viewpoints.
- Draw conclusions based on available evidence from multiple sources.

As you think about and apply chapter content on your own, you should be able to:

- Analyze each of the chapter's issues in greater depth via discussion and further reading.
- Add issues of your own to discussions of early childhood and perhaps, research them more fully.
- Take your own stand on the issues and add this thinking to your growing philosophy of early education; consider writing a first-draft philosophy statement.

Numerous and complex issues face today's early childhood professionals, and sometimes it seems that as soon as we resolve one issue, another arises. Each of these topics reflects values of the society we now live in and all will influence the course of your professional life as you enter the world of teaching. This chapter presents several issues, all of which have more than one perspective. Some issues, such as the age of school entry, relate directly to early childhood program operations. Others, such as pluralism or roles of early educators, might occasion personal problem-solving and inform personal decision-making and, thus, have a more indirect impact on everyday teaching.

The issues presented here are frequently the subject of research, opinion writing, position papers, and legislative action. Rarely is there agreement on all sides as to the best course of action for resolving the various views or to apply the information from conflicting perspectives to decision-making. Decisions are often made for political or financial reasons or because of convenience, perceived needs of children, or preferred philosophies. You may want to take a moment to reflect on your reading of the previous chapters before trying to reach your own conclusions about this chapter's issues.

Think about how your own viewpoint has developed, by turning back to Chapter One and reviewing the ideas and approaches of the field's early thinkers. Then, as you consider each of the issues, think how you might respond from each of the theoretical or philosophical points of view. Such an exercise might not only help you see how to deal with issues in your own future classroom but may lead you toward the development of a more fully realized philosophy of early education.

As the varying sides of each issue are presented, we include expert opinions for you to contemplate as well as examples of research. At times the research focuses on toddlers or preschoolers and at other times on children in the primary grades. These are only samples of available studies, and we encourage you to expand your knowledge through your own library research.

Issue 1: Schooling From What Age?

School-entry age is an issue peculiar to educators involved in the early years, one that has given rise to philosophical and practical arguments over many centuries, with the most recent battle having begun some five decades ago with the initiation of Head Start. As you read in Chapter Three, it was believed by many at the time that children from economically disadvantaged families might well benefit from earlier entry into formal school learning. It was during this time, as well, that middle-class U.S. society seemed increasingly inclined to push children to be more competitive in academics and after-school activities. For the youngest children, even infants, materials to teach letters and numbers became popular with some eager parents. In many schools both public and private, the elementary curriculum was pushed down to kindergarten, and upper-grade material was similarly expected to be mastered in the primary grades. Programs were established for gifted and talented students, and for a while in the 1960s and 1970s, young children nationwide were encouraged to begin mastering academic content as early as possible.

During this era, many professionals and parents who chose not to push their children expressed concerns. One of the best-known publications of the time was *Better Late Than Early*, by Raymond Moore and Dorothy Moore (1975). Agreeing that early care and education might be advantageous for the children of working parents or for those with special needs, the Moores argued, however, that the home should be the primary institution for young children, that preschool probably is not needed for the larger population, that effective government-run preschool programs would be too costly to maintain well, and that planners of programs for younger children might well move too far too fast, with little or no regard to what research could tell them.

Even more widely read was David Elkind's (1981) *The Hurried Child*, a book that provided eloquently quotable arguments against the push to have young children learn more quickly and grow up faster. Elkind pointed with concern not only to pressured

FIGURE 5.1a and 5.1b Should children enroll in education experiences from an early age, or is their growth better fostered by remaining at home? Experts disagree.

academics but to summer camps that were moving from traditional outdoor sports and campfire routines to specialized training in foreign languages, computers, tennis, and so on. Elkind has continued to write and present on this theme, and recently argued that an ever decreasing amount of unstructured play in the lives of American children is detrimental to early cognitive and academic development: "Years of research has confirmed the value of play. In early childhood, play helps children develop skills they cannot get in any other way" (Elkind, 2008, p. 1).

Another view on when children should enter school essentially holds that it is best to educate youngsters entirely at home. Of course, home schooling, especially for younger children, is historically quite commonplace. Yet, the move toward school-based early education has been so pervasive in recent decades that a parental decision to educate children at home remains noteworthy. According to a review of research, the three most frequent reasons parents gave for deciding to home-school their children are: concerns about the school environment; beliefs that parents can provide a better education than schools can; and the desire to transmit family religious values within the context of the children's education. The same review showed that in 2007 there were 1.5 million children being home-schooled in the United States, a number that has been increasing steadily for a decade (National Center for Educational Statistics, 2008). As of early 2010, there was insufficient high-quality research to compare academic outcomes of home-schooled children to those educated in public or private schools.

We are left, then, with questions: When is the right time to begin a child's formal, school-based education? Is there a best time? In the next sections we look at two sides of this question more closely.

Early Education Experiences Give Children More Benefits

The 1990s were marked by a great increase in knowledge about the importance of the earliest years in children's lives. Biological and psychological research continually uncovered new data pointing to the influence that environment and experience have on cognitive, social, emotional, and physical development. In 2001, the National Research Council published a book entitled *Eager to Learn: Educating our preschoolers*. An impressive group of researchers collected, synthesized, and analyzed results of research in out-of-home education and care settings for children between age 2 and 5. They concluded that early childhood professionals and a growing number of parents supported early educational experiences, and that high-quality early education supported success in school. They also concluded, on the first page of their Executive Summary, that "voluntary universal early childhood education, a feature of other wealthy industrialized nations, is also on the horizon here" (p. 1), and recommended publicly funded preschool programs with highly trained teachers for young children at risk for school failure.

Another review of research (Marshall, 2003) found that children who were held back from school entry, not because of potential problems but because of parental choice, often had poor attitudes toward school and were less likely to graduate from high school.

In general, research on school readiness programs has focused on children at risk for school failure participating in Head Start and similar state-funded programs. The body of research provides evidence that high-quality early education programs are associated with positive outcomes on measures of academic performance and social success later in life. Proponents of universal publicly funded preschool and other school readiness initiatives emphasize not only the benefits of improved early academic performance, but also the importance of reducing disparities between more and less affluent children at school entry, and prevention of mental health and social-behavioral problems (National Research Council, 2000).

Children Benefit From Remaining at Home Longer

The same biological and psychological research from the 1990s has been used to support the belief that schooling is better delayed than rushed. Early experiences have been found to frame an important interplay between biology and experience, setting the stage for continuing vulnerability to risk and/or the positive influences of protective factors (National Research Council, 2000). Those who support keeping young children out of structured educational settings emphasize the nurturing aspects of home-based early environments over preparation for school:

> So sensitive are these first years of life to environmental conditions, it is argued, that only the parents, within the security of the home, should educate the young. Providing early care and education is not only the parents' responsibility, but early separation of parents and child could be detrimental.
>
> (Seefeldt, 1990, pp. 58–59)

Arguments against early education include the importance of self-directed learning for young children, and the inherent dangers in stifling children's natural initiative and curiosity with a school framework of right/wrong, correct/incorrect (Meyers, 1993). Additional concerns include the developmental inappropriateness for youngsters in group settings to be deprived of individual adult attention, to be required to follow rigid schedules, and to get along with many other children, difficult tasks in the very early stages of social development.

Additionally, large numbers of poor children in group programs experience low quality or mediocre care, bolstering arguments that home environments or care by relatives provide healthier environments for very young children. In addition, even mediocre child care can tax the financial resources of poor families, causing additional stress for parents who often pay an inordinately large proportion of their income for care. Those who argue for longer periods of home care and parental teaching would ideally like to see children defer formal schooling until 5 or even 8 years of age (Meyers, 1993).

Finally, many parents who keep their children home until they are older often have well-founded concerns about the increased academic orientation of their local preschools and kindergartens. They believe that it is more developmentally appropriate to provide children more playful experiences when they are young (Marshall, 2003).

What Do You Think?

Although you are most likely in your teacher education program to prepare for a position in a school or center, it is important to consider positions taken by those on all sides of this argument. You may, in fact, find yourself in conversation or negotiations with home-schooling parents. What do you think are the positive points and the dangers of early education? Of staying home longer? Is early formal education more advantageous for some children than for others? As you consider the pros and cons of early education, think about the concept of voluntary universal preschool. Do you support the idea that all preschoolers could go to a group program without cost to their parents? And if so, at age 3 or 4, or even earlier? Even the possibility of universal publicly funded preschool does not completely answer the question of what age is the best age to begin schooling.

Issue 2: Incorporating Pluralism in the Early Childhood Curriculum

In Chapter Four we addressed the many types of diversity that you may encounter working with young children and their families as an early childhood professional. Issue 2 is related to diversity and the three-way interactions that occur between parents, early educators, and young children.

As described in Chapter Four, early care and education programs are enrolling increasing numbers of children whose families have come from other countries. The United States has always been a nation of immigrants, with the vast majority coming from European countries from the early 1800s through the mid-1900s. However, as was pointed out in Chapter Four, in the early 21st century over half of all people living in America who were not born as citizens have come from Latin America, primarily from Central American countries, but also from the Caribbean and South America. Over 25% of immigrants to the United States now come from Asia, and only 16% hail from Europe (U.S. Census Bureau, 2003). These statistics reflect the multitude of different family traditions and customs, physical appearances, personal histories, and languages other than English that children bring with them to early childhood centers and classrooms.

Another important aspect of diversity in early childhood settings is social-economic status. Some entitlement programs, such as special education for infants, toddlers, and preschoolers, serve eligible children without regard to family income. By comparison, Head Start and Early Head Start programs provide services based on family income. Private preschool and primary programs often charge tuition that is only affordable for more affluent families, and public schools serve everyone in a certain geographic area. So you may work in early childhood programs that serve affluent families, low-income families, or a mixed group of families across income levels.

In our country, being young and belonging to a minority culture and/or language group are risk factors for poverty. Children are more likely to be poor than are adults, and the child poverty rate increased nationwide between 2000 and 2008 to the highest levels since 1997 (U.S. Census Bureau, 2008). According to the Children's Defense Fund (2009), over 13 million American children live in poverty, and almost half of them live in extreme poverty. Over 12 million children are going hungry, and the majority of poor children have no health insurance. Black, Hispanic, and American Indian children are more likely to be poor than their White peers. Various levels of poverty and affluence are a fact of life for young children and you may have any or all levels represented in your classroom.

Issues related to individual characteristics of children can be even more sensitive for early educators than issues surrounding family income. Some parents of young children with disabilities may ask that their daughters and sons be treated as much as possible as all children are, while others may ask if they can explain a child's disability to the class. Some children with special needs take longer than their peers to learn to share, take turns, control their behavior, and express themselves appropriately. Others have disabilities that involve difficulty in communication and movement.

Parents of *English language learners (ELLs)* may want their young children to retain their home languages as they learn English. But some parents with home languages other than English believe that they should speak English as much as possible to help their children succeed in American schools. Parents of monolingual English-speaking children might worry that their youngsters will not learn appropriate oral language or early literacy skills if teaching has to include languages other than English.

Some of the most sensitive aspects of teaching other people's children are associated with topics related to sex and gender. Adults tend to have strong opinions and values about topics related to sexual orientation, gender identity, and terminology related to body parts.

Young children are naturally curious about themselves and about their peers. They ask questions about differences and make blunt, sometimes hurtful comments. Parents are naturally supportive and protective of their young sons and daughters, and want what is best based on their own families' values and beliefs. Early educators encounter many different life styles, beliefs about childrearing, and family traditions among the parents of children in early childhood programs. The NAEYC Code of Ethical Conduct holds primary a principle of doing no harm (NAEYC, 2005), but there is more than one interpretation of the NAEYC Code relative to the role of pluralism in the early childhood curriculum.

Questions Teachers Need to Ask Themselves

The topic of diversity is an extraordinarily complex one. Before debating a pro-and-con question related to it, it would be good to take some time to ask yourself the following questions related to the above section:

- Will the metaphor for diversity in your classroom be a melting pot (focus on similarities) or a stew (emphasis on differences)?
- How important is anti-bias and multi-cultural education to you as you plan curricula?
- How will you address the discomfort children and families may express about each other's characteristics, lifestyles, backgrounds, and behaviors?
- How much will you share with children and families when a child has a chronic illness or disability, has identified as transgender, or is just beginning to learn English?
- To what extent will you teach children about one another in general and incorporate their differences into your teaching?
- How important do you think it is for young children to know about race, language, and social-economic status?
- How would you ensure in an inclusive setting that children with special needs are active and engaged participants, without putting undue emphasis on their disabilities or delays?

- How will you respond to parents of typically developing youngsters who are worried their children will have less fun, learn more slowly, or imitate inappropriate behavior in an inclusive center or classroom?
- How would you respond to parents who ask you to separate English and Spanish speaking children, or to hire a Russian-speaking teaching assistant to support their child's learning?
- How would you respond to parents who ask that you avoid discussing where babies come from?
- What would your approach be if parents asked you to let their biological daughter be treated in all respects as a boy?

It is likely that, in your teaching career, you won't have to answer every one of these questions, but you should be prepared for all of them. We now ask you to consider the pros and cons of two very different teaching approaches.

Early Educators Should Teach Multi-cultural and Anti-bias Education

Advocates of anti-bias and multi-cultural education argue that diversity should pervade the early childhood curriculum, so that all children see themselves represented in teaching materials, illustrations, and topics. This position seeks to instill attitudes about fairness and curiosity about individual differences among young children, with long-term goals for an equitable and just society.

Multi-cultural education includes teaching about different cultures, and emphasizes the backgrounds of children in the program. Teaching multi-cultural education includes creative and academic materials that represent the full range of physical appearance, life ways, families, and events in children's lives. Appropriate art materials would include crayons, paints, and markers in skin tone shades from very pale to very dark brown. Books, songs, puzzles, dolls, dollhouses, and games that represent similarities and differences among children and families are also recommended. The goal of multi-cultural education for young children is that as they learn about themselves, other children, and families, they explicitly explore similarities and differences across a continuum, rather than implicitly learning about "us" and "them." Explorations include teacher-facilitated discussions and activities, as well as content lessons about physical appearance, language, and heritage, and all types of family lifestyles and structures (two parents, single male or female parents, extended families under one roof, same-sex parents) (Lee, Ramsey, & Sweeney, 2008).

An even more pluralistic approach is anti-bias education, which aims to help children recognize and combat bias and prejudice from any source (TV, jokes, teasing, books, pictures, and stories). Anti-bias education goes beyond multi-cultural education by emphasizing that White children are damaged by a false sense of superiority and entitlement. The intent is to teach them to become allies by resisting prejudice, exclusion, and discrimination (Derman-Sparks & Ramsey, 2005). Some authors even suggest the use of the term *allophilia* to connote an approach that goes beyond reducing prejudice to promote positive feelings of affection, engagement, kinship, comfort, and enthusiasm among children and those they perceive as "different" or "other" (Pittinsky, Rosenthal, & Montoya, 2009).

Teachers Should Teach About Commonalities in School, and Parents Should Teach About Diversity Within the Family Context

Not all teachers and parents agree that differences among children and families should be addressed in early childhood programs. Some professionals cite a knowledge base about development of racial and ethnic identity that has remained consistent for decades (Katz, 1976; Aboud & Doyle, 1993), which argues that a mature personal identity does not solidify until later in elementary school. From this perspective, it is considered irresponsible and developmentally inappropriate to expect young children to take others' perspectives and develop understanding of experiences they do not share.

There are also those who feel that it is the job of schools to emphasize the commonalities among people in order to build a uniquely U.S. culture. This approach has worked in the past, they argue, and it should serve us well now and in the future despite the introduction of many new cultural and ethnic backgrounds to our schools and communities. Some early childhood professionals may feel more comfortable teaching about similarities and avoiding potential social justice connotations of multi-cultural and anti-bias education curricula.

Another criticism of multi-cultural and anti-bias curricula comes from the point of view that discussion of sensitive, personal topics is the responsibility of parents and families, rather than teachers and schools. Some parents prefer that topics related to culture, race, and especially gender are reserved for discussion and learning within the

FIGURE 5.2 Today's multi-cultural education must take into account such modern-day commonplaces as transracial adoptions.

family context, rather than being topics of public discussion at schools or centers. In other families sensitive topics are not discussed or addressed directly (Derman-Sparks & Edwards, 2010). For some teachers, this is reason enough to avoid topics such as race, language, culture, and gender in the classroom, especially if their teacher preparation programs did not include a strong foundation in cross-cultural competence. Early educators may fear inadvertently stereotyping or leaving children out in their discussions, making things worse instead of better by trying to incorporate the complexities of multi-cultural or anti-bias education in early childhood programs.

What Do You Think?

Never before in our history have we had to contend with so many cultures, languages, and competing value systems as we do now. We cannot simply ignore these differences. They affect the children in our centers and classrooms, sometimes profoundly. You have read about two very different views on addressing pluralism in your teaching site. Should early childhood professionals directly address diversity in all its forms in their centers and classrooms, including parents and colleagues in the effort? Or is it wiser to leave issues of diversity for parents and families to address with their own children at home?

FIGURE 5.3 Should early childhood teachers emphasize similarities or differences among children?

How will you resolve tension between your own values, attitudes, and beliefs, and the characteristics of children and parents? Will you challenge yourself to interact equitably with all children if you are uncomfortable with children whose disabilities require you to change diapers in preschool or to manage disruptive behavior? If you find children from families more affluent than your own to be overly privileged and sheltered, how will you ensure that they are treated fairly? How will you provide a welcoming environment for same-sex parents if you believe homosexuality is morally wrong? Perhaps you can explore the many available materials to identify resources and strategies that allow for family individuality while building your confidence and competence at bringing sensitive topics into classrooms and centers.

Issue 3: Television and the Violence That Pervades Today's Culture

The culture of the United States seems to be an increasingly violent one, with repercussions for even the very youngest of our citizens. At least some of the blame can be traced directly to the powerful influence of television and to the products that are marketed in conjunction with violent child-oriented programs.

Quite significantly, more than 30 years of research have verified that television promotes aggression in young children for several reasons: observation of real-life aggression leads to increased aggressiveness in behavior; observation of TV aggression leads to desensitization toward and acceptance of violence in real life; the more children see violence on TV, the more likely they are to imitate it, particularly in their dramatic play; and, finally, violent TV provides young children with "scripts" that they then use both in their dramatic play and in real-life interactions (Boyatzis, 1997; NAEYC, 1990). And longitudinal research indicates that TV-related violent behavior in young children translates into aggressive behavior in the same people as they become adults (Huesmann, Moise-Titus, Podolski, & Eron, 2003).

If television were the only villain promoting a culture of violence, a concerted nationwide effort might actually wipe out the problem. The situation becomes more complex, however, when the influence of movies, computer games, videos, and an increasingly diverse collection of toy weapons is considered. Add to all these influences some observations of the wider culture, where statistics demonstrate that a view of American society as violent is not just in the imagination. For example, in 2008 the intentional homicide rate in this country was six times that of Germany, 12 times that of Japan, almost five times that of Australia. Some of the causes of our violent society have been listed as "poverty, racism, unemployment, illegal drugs, inadequate or abusive parenting practices, and real-life adult models of violent problem-solving behavior" (NAEYC, 1990, p. 18), but any number of other countries have similar difficulties multiplied many times over, without the same violence levels. It is, perhaps, the young children who suffer most; at the time of their lives when they are most in need of protection, security, and safety, they are bombarded with the anxiety, threat, and insecurity inherent in the violence of the culture around them.

What can teachers of young children do? Much has been written about the problem of young children in a violent society, particularly as reflected in increasingly violent behaviors in early childhood centers and classrooms. Most researchers are in agreement that there is no single, best solution, but experts tend to favor either total abolition of violent dramatic play in the classroom or acceptance of it within limits. Here are their views and supporting arguments.

Aggression of All Sorts Should be Abolished in Centers and Classrooms

One writer has argued that for at least a few hours each day children should "not be subjected to chaos, confusion, and wild, aggressive play" and that if teachers permit such play, they are sending children a message that "powerful positions are important, and if you make a lot of noise and disrupt the work of a lot of people, you are more important, because you get more attention" (Kuykendall, 1995, p. 58). This long-time director of early education programs also points out that children can work out their feelings in activity centers such as those related to construction or art; that there is often little time for teachers to sit down and sufficiently discuss the negative aspects of aggressive play; that young children often confuse fantasy and reality, leading to unfortunate behaviors; and that nonaggressive children may actually be inspired by their more aggressive playmates to imitate their behavior.

There are other arguments as well for abolishing any sort of aggression or rough play in centers and schools. A society that is not only violent but litigious creates concerns for principals and directors about potential lawsuits should any child be harmed in any way. In addition, teachers who hope to create an environment that feels safe to children often feel that the only way to do this is to deny them any sort of roughness or even argumentation.

Aggressive Play Can be Channeled in Positive and Beneficial Ways

At its best, say advocates of this view, such activities as war play help children "work on their understanding of the boundaries between pretend and reality, build basic cognitive concepts, develop a beginning understanding of political and moral ideas, and even learn about cooperation and the needs of others." Furthermore, such play "can serve as an important vehicle through which children can work on the thoughts and feelings they have about the violence they see around them" (Carlsson-Paige & Levin, 1990, p. 31). Close to 80 years ago Piaget (1932) wrote about the advantages of snowball fights (mostly engaged in by boys) over jump rope and jacks (primarily played by girls) as a training ground for adult negotiations and interactions.

What many teachers see as aggressive play may actually be a friendlier version of physicality typically referred to as "rough and tumble" play. A position of the National Institute for Play states that:

> The importance of R&T play in animals and humans, has been shown to be necessary for the development and maintenance of social awareness, cooperation, fairness and altruism. ... Lack of experience with this pattern of play hampers the normal give and take necessary for social mastery, and has been linked to poor control of violent impulses in later life.

In recent years, increasing numbers of educators and psychologists worry that taking away opportunities for rough and tumble play does a disservice to boys in particular.

Rough and tumble play is primarily engaged in by boys but most teachers of young children are female. This most likely leads to a lack of connection between the comfort zone of teachers and the needs of young boys, and some girls as well.

What Do You Think?

There seems to be little agreement about what should be done about this issue, with experts on both sides weighing in. You, too, will need to decide how to deal with the violence that seems to seep into many U.S. centers and classrooms today. You will also need to determine if what appears as violence is actually a potentially harmless form of play. Do you think of your future center or classroom as a safe haven where no violence or roughness is permitted, or do you see it as a place where children can learn to work out their conflicts in a protected environment? Is there a middle road?

Issue 4: Young Children in a Technological Age

The use of technology, in particular computers, by young children has become generally accepted by the educational community. It was not many years ago that the question of developmental appropriateness created a fierce debate among those who believed no age was too young to introduce children to the technology that was beginning to pervade most of society, and those who feared that the use of computers would deny children the access they need to hands-on manipulative materials. Each year it becomes more obvious that the former group is winning this argument on all fronts.

In fact, as early as 1996 the National Association for the Education of Young Children formally adopted a position statement regarding technology that remains in place today. It demonstrates this evolution of opinion:

> The potential benefits of technology for young children's learning and development are well documented. … the research indicates that, in practice, computers supplement and do not replace highly valued early childhood activities and materials, such as art, blocks, sand, water, books, explorations with writing materials, and dramatic play.
>
> (1996, p. 11)

As acceptance of technology for young children increased, however, another problem arose in terms of equity in ownership. Most frequently known as the *digital divide*, the problem can refer to the division between rich and poor families and their differing abilities to have computers and other technologies at home; or, it can refer to the differing abilities of schools and centers to make such purchases based on their budgets.

For example, arguments have been made that even very young children can benefit from the use of such equipment as digital cameras, document cameras, digital microscopes, interactive whiteboards, and internet access (Wang et al., 2008). Yet, however beneficial these materials might be for children's learning, access to the necessary funds for them remains a problem for many schools and centers.

As a second example, lower-income families may not have a home computer, thus making email communication with their children's schools or centers impossible. Sensitive institutions will arrange to have multiple options available for communication. At

FIGURE 5.4 The use of computers by even very young children has become accepted by most early educators. How they can best be used remains an issue.

the same time, however, children who have technology opportunities at home from an early age will, no doubt, feel more comfortable with technology in school, just as children with more books at home will feel more at ease with a school's focus on literacy.

Over time the digital divide may become less of an issue as the price of technology goes down and grants make purchases possible. Another issue remains however, one related to philosophy of use. Curriculum and teaching methodologies provided by an ever-expanding supply of software seem to fall into two competing groups. Read about them both and then decide what your own approach should be.

Computers Are Most Useful for Enhancing Skills

In its earliest days, the classroom computer was used largely for the purpose of skill enhancement. In the mid-1990s, software for tutorial purposes was still dominating the marketplace (Shade, 1996). Software companies continue to promote materials that include applications for such practice in both language arts and mathematics, providing teachers with ready-made, easy-to-use drills that require little teacher–child interaction time.

An additional attraction is that programming of this software requires little time, thus keeping costs low. Research has shown that this type of software can be useful in promoting reading readiness skills, including those that are most difficult for children to grasp (Clements & Swaminathan, 1995).

In a review of research, Doug Clements concluded that "technology can support either drill or the highest-order thinking and creativity" (2002, p. 174). On behalf of using Computer Assisted Instruction (CAI) for the former, Clements found that "Drill and practice software can help young children develop competence in such skills as counting and sorting" (p. 162). In answer to the question, "How young can children be and still find CAI useful?" Clements found that "Three-year-olds learned sorting from a computer task as easily as from a concrete doll task" (p. 162). As recently popular, more creative mathematics programs demonstrate their ability to promote children's skills, it may be that the use of computers will be increasingly important. As Clements found from several studies, "the largest gains in the use of CAI have been in mathematics for *primary* grade children, especially in compensatory education" (p. 162).

Using the Computer for Open-ended Exploration

Drill-and-practice software provides children with the correct answers to their questions and problems. On the other hand, there is software that offers quite the opposite benefit, engaging children in creative play and open-ended problem solving. Although drill software has long been used to improve children's abilities in reading and math, educators at all levels have, given the ever-increasing sophistication of software, looked more and more at creative applications of technology.

Arguing for the more open-ended approach, the NAEYC *Position Statement* of 1996 notes that such software enables the child "to find new challenges as she becomes more proficient. Appropriate visual and verbal prompts designed in the software expand play themes and opportunities while leaving the child in control" (p. 12).

A number of writers have observed that drill software tends to be associated with computers that have been placed in special labs rather than in classrooms. Those who favor open-ended software also prefer classroom-based hardware, believing that technology-based education is most effective when easily integrated into the ongoing curriculum and with everyday classroom materials.

What Do You Think?

Publishers and school systems have a long history of favoring the use of computer software that provides skill enhancement through drill and practice. Meanwhile, early childhood organizations such as the NAEYC and educators who prefer constructivist approaches look more toward open exploration. The costs of technology, although lessening over time, remain high for those on prescribed budgets (and that is, of course, most of us). Thus, careful decisions about the type of software purchased must be made. Is there a direction that feels right to you? Finally, we have said that computers are generally accepted for early childhood, but this is not the case for everyone, as you saw in Chapter Three during a visit to the Waldorf School in Vancouver, British Columbia. Perhaps you are in agreement with this school's view, and there is no software at all that seems right to you.

Issue 5: Privately Designing Early Childhood Environments or Taking Early Education into the Community?

Thus far you have been asked to consider four issues of importance to early educators: the appropriate age for school entry, dealing with aggressive behavior, attitudes toward diversity of various kinds, and the uses of technology. By now you will, no doubt, have a good idea about where you stand on these issues as well as about the opinions of your peers. That, however, leads to yet another issue: How can and should you present your opinions to other professionals, your children's parents, and to the public at large?

Perhaps you are someone who ordinarily keeps your opinions to yourself, but would be willing to go public if the right situation presented itself. Alternatively, you might be a natural advocate who willingly puts your opinions on the public line. And there are, of course, many variations on these two positions. As you read further, think through the pros and cons of privately and publicly living and defending your beliefs about early education. Consider whether your original view calls for alteration or whether you are already on the track that is right for you.

Early Educators Should Focus on Creating the Best Possible Classroom or Center Environments

One perspective on the primary role of early educators is that they should strive to create a safe, consistent, and predictable environment with a well-defined curriculum that is delivered equitably to all children. From this viewpoint, you will concentrate on developing and refining all aspects of your classroom or center:

- Designing a physical environment that is safe, beautiful, developmentally appropriate, well-stocked with supplies and equipment, and accessible to all children.
- Selecting and updating curricula that guide your teaching in all areas, including social-emotional, early academic, physical and health, and communication.
- Arranging learning centers and movement areas that promote self-initiated exploration and peer interaction.
- Collaborating with parents and other family members, providing parent education materials and activities, and opportunities for parents to volunteer in the classroom.
- Organizing and developing administrative and fiscal procedures to support center or classroom operations.

Your primary focus will be on supporting the development and learning of the children in your care, through provision of an ideal environment where they can learn through play and develop their individual identities and skill sets. All children in the group will have a consistent, high-quality experience while they are in your center or classroom. The classroom or center, from this viewpoint, is a safe haven for learning that provides the point of departure for children to venture out into the larger world.

Early Educators Should Advocate for Changes That Will Benefit Young Children and Families

Early educators are in a unique position, by virtue of their training and relationships with children and families, to make meaningful contributions beyond the classroom. From this perspective, early educators are encouraged to teach beyond the classroom, get out into the communities where children and families live, and advocate for change in areas relevant to young children.

Such teachers partner with families to become advocates, and even activists, on behalf of children and families. Professionals who subscribe to this perspective on early education believe that it is incumbent on teachers to speak out publicly, share information to educate the public about issues, and work through the political process to promote policy changes (Dykstra, 2005).

Examples of the sorts of activities you could undertake as an advocate or activist for young children might include:

- Writing improved anti-bias statements for your school or center, to achieve better inclusion of all children.
- Advocating for gender-neutral bathrooms for transgender children.
- Collecting signatures on petitions and working on political campaigns to support policies and candidates who are allies for early childhood education.
- Working at the state level to promote full-day kindergarten or universal preschool.

What Do You Think?

Of course, creating the ideal early childhood environment and becoming an advocate are not mutually exclusive goals. The relative importance of each to you as a professional is a highly personal preference that may well shift over the course of your career. At this point it is a good idea to think about which approach is more natural and comfortable to you. Then think about and discuss what it would take for you to move more into the other approach.

Issue 6: Young Children, and You, in the 21st Century

This final section is shaped differently than the previous ones. Instead of asking you to consider conflicting sides of a single issue, it presents 20th-century predictions for the new century currently underway and evaluates their accuracy. It also asks you to consider the qualities that are important for you to possess and demonstrate as a 21st-century teacher. Of course, the children you teach will need to grow into such qualities and we will provide an opportunity for you to consider how to help make that happen.

The first widely read author to predict the place of children and learning in the 21st century published his views 30 years before its beginning. In *Future Shock* (1970), *Learning for Tomorrow* (1974), and *The Third Wave* (1980), Alvin Toffler argued that the world was beginning to change so fast that all the traditional ways of learning and knowing would necessarily need to change as well. Education must be lifelong and its prime objective, he said, "must be to increase the individual's 'cope-ability'—the speed and economy with which he can adapt to continual change" (1970, p. 403).

Three societal skills, Toffler (1970) said, would be necessary for survival, but each would present its own challenges: learning, relating, and choosing. As applied to the teacher's role, these three would include such considerations as:

- Today's facts become tomorrow's misinformation. So, children must learn how to discard old ideas and grasp new ones. They must, in other words, learn how to learn.
- With increased technology and change in all walks of life, relating to others will

become a greater challenge. More imaginative grouping of children for learning may teach new lessons in making and maintaining rewarding human ties.

■ Increasing options of all kinds present the increasing challenge of "overchoice." Children need to be taught what values are and how to define their own. Schools must stop shying away from teaching about values and embrace the subject.

In the 1990s, thinkers began to focus with increasing seriousness on the changes and continuities that the 21st century might bring and the kinds of people who could live most successfully in it. To a great extent, this thinking was influenced by the onset of just what Toffler predicted: a new, postindustrial, global, information age with its overlay of quickly expanding and radically changing technological capabilities. The qualities needed for success in the world of work, for example, are quite different than those historically valued. For example, one business writer (Pritchett, n.d.) suggested such practices as:

■ Learning not to resist change while adapting—quickly—to new ways of working.
■ Working with a strong sense of urgency, emphasizing action.
■ Accepting ambiguity and uncertainty.
■ Becoming a lifelong learner.
■ Managing one's own morale rather than expecting management to do it.
■ Continuing to stretch oneself to be better than yesterday.

There is nothing in this list that would predict long-term stability in any aspect of one's work life. Instead, there is a predicted need to be flexible and ready for constant change. Another author, looking more holistically at the 21st-century mind that we all need to possess, suggested similar and complementary qualities (Sinetar, 1991). She wrote that our 21st-century minds would need to:

■ Have a high tolerance for change, discontinuity, paradox.
■ Be willing to think independently.
■ Be non-entrenched and able to release unproductive beliefs.
■ Be able to experiment, always willing to look for better ways to do things.

These are all qualities necessary for survival in a world that had begun to change with unprecedented speed well before the turn of the new century. To predictions that the world would continue to move ever faster, another was added that the world would be more crowded as well. In 2000, the United States Census Bureau showed a nation of approximately 275 million, predicted 323 million by 2020, with perhaps 394 million by mid-century. By that same mid-century, the U.S. population was projected to be 25% Black, Asian, or American Indian, 25% Hispanic, and 50% Caucasian (2008).

It was expected that children born at the turn of the century would be about the same size as their parents, but that life expectancy would continue to grow, to about 73 years for males and 80 years for females. Mortality rates for newborns, which in the 1990s were about 8 per 1000, were predicted by the Center for Disease Control to fall dramatically, perhaps to as low as 1 per 1,000. Doctors would be able to cope more successfully with congenital defects and diseases, even before birth. Routine genetic screening would be able to identify risks to individual children, making treatment, family planning, and health advice individually applicable (Adler, 1998).

In the 1990s then, it appeared that U.S. children in the 21st century would be healthier, more likely to survive disabling conditions, and more ethnically diverse. They would need skills to cope with constant change, the increasing incursion of technology, and the need to live harmoniously in ever more crowded conditions. Indeed, by 2009 the infant mortality rate had improved from 8 per 1,000 to 6.3. However, much improvement would be needed before the United States could catch up with countries such as Japan and Sweden whose rates were less than 3 per 1,000.

Unfortunately, not all the positive predictions for the nation's health came to pass. Between 1980 and 2010 the percentage of overweight children tripled until a third of all American children were overweight or obese. The adult rate soared to two-thirds. By 2010, $150 billion was being spent annually on obesity-related diseases and the military was newly unable to admit many recruits because of their size.

Thus, as often happens, some predictions were made with a measure of accuracy and others fell victim to unexpected, or unnoticed, changes in culture or other influences. We have updated just two predictions—improved infant mortality rates and the obesity epidemic's influence on health. It is now your turn to consider other aspects of this new century and your place in it.

What Do You Think?

- Consider the positions presented by thinkers of the late 20th century. Do you agree with them?
- What qualities would you add as being essential to the 21st-century citizen?
- What qualities are important for the 21st-century early childhood professional?
- In what ways can teachers make their classrooms or centers most supportive of children, taking into account your views about 21st-century citizenship?
- What changes will, or should there be in the education of early childhood professionals? Think about both content knowledge and methodology.

EXTENDING YOUR LEARNING

As in the previous chapters, Suggestions 1 and 2 focus on your developing philosophy of teaching and learning.

 1 Reflect back on your readings, class discussions, field experiences, and the notes you have kept after each chapter. Write a position statement that uses all this input as your basis. Consider this your first-draft thinking and, as you progress through your coursework and experiences with children, add to and delete as you deem appropriate. You might even save this paper for five years or more to see how your thinking changes and develops and to remind yourself of good ideas that might have been temporarily shelved.

 2 Regard your drawing one last time along with the metaphors you chose for yourself, the children, and your classroom. Do your metaphors match philosophically with your drawing? Are the metaphors mixed but still within a similar philosophy? Or are there disparities all around? Research has

shown that successful teaching requires that metaphors and philosophies match!

3 Discover more controversial issues by interviewing teachers, center directors, principals, parents, school board members, and professors. Bring these, including arguments on various sides, to your class for discussion.

4 Research an issue—one discussed in this chapter or one you have discovered— through extended reading. Write a position paper that presents all sides as fairly and completely as possible, then presents your own opinion based on your reflections of what you have learned.

5 Stage a classroom debate around one or more issues discussed in this chapter. You can choose to follow the rules of formal debate or discuss more informally. You are encouraged to expand your reading and knowledge of the topic before you begin.

6 Be alert for newspaper articles, radio and TV broadcasts, and new magazine stories about the issues presented in this chapter, especially as related to early childhood. Keep a media journal for a month and then review the themes, issues, and trends you have collected.

7 Obtain a copy of the teacher certification standards for preschool and primary teachers in public schools in your state. Compare them to the requirements for a Child Development Associate or other types of training required for Head Start and child care licensure.

8 Visit the NAEYC and DEC Web sites to explore the full text of position papers on inclusion, diversity, technology, and other issues.

References

Aboud, R. & Doyle, A. B. (1993). The early development of ethnic identity and attitudes. In M. E. Bernal & G. P. Knight (Eds.), *Ethnic identity: 1. Formation and transmission among Hispanics and other minorities*, 46–59. Albany, NY: SUNY Press.

Adler, J. (1998, November 2). Tomorrow's child. *Newsweek*, 54–65.

Boyatzis, C. (1997). Of Power Rangers and V-chips. *Young Children, 52*(7), 74–79.

Carlsson-Paige, N., & Levin, D. (1990). *Who's calling the shots?* Philadelphia, PA: New Society.

Children's Defense Fund (2009). *Children in the states factsheets*. Washington, DC: Author.

Clements, D. (2002). Computers in early childhood mathematics. *Contemporary Issues in Early Childhood, 3*(2), 160–181.

Clements, F., & Swaminathan, S. (1995). Technology and school change: New lamps for old? *Childhood Education, 71*(5), 275–281.

Derman-Sparks, L., & Edwards, J. (2010). *Anti-bias education for young children and ourselves*. Washington, DC: NAEYC.

Derman-Sparks, L., & Ramsey, P. (2005). What if all the children in my class are White? Anti-bias multicultural education with White children. *Young Children, 60*(6), 20–27.

Dykstra, L. (2005). Trans-friendly preschool. *Journal of Gay & Lesbian Issues in Education, 3*(1), 7–13.

Elkind, D. (1981). *The hurried child: Growing up too fast too soon*. Reading, MA: Addison-Wesley.

Elkind, D. (2008). Can we play? *Greater Good Magazine, 4*(4), 1–3.

Huesmann, L., Moise-Titus, J., Podolski, C., & Eron, L. (2003). Longitudinal relations between children's exposure to TV violence and their aggressive and violent behavior in young adulthood: 1977–1992. *Developmental Psychology, 39*, 201–221.

Katz, P. (1976). The acquisition of racial attitudes in children. In *Towards the elimination of racism*. New York: Pergamon.

Kuykendall, J. (1995). Is gun play OK here??? *Young Children, 50*(5), 56–59.

Lee, R., Ramsey, P. G., & Sweeney, B. (2008). Engaging young children in activities and conversations about race and social class. *Young Children, 65*(3), 68–76.

Marshall, H. (2003). Opportunity deferred or opportunity taken? An updated look at delaying kindergarten entry. *Young Children, 58*(5), 84–93.

Meyers, M. (1993, spring). An argument against educating young children. *Education*. Retrieved from http://findarticles.com/p/articles/mi_qa3673/is_n3_v113/ai_n28626206/pg_3/?tag=content;col1, February 13, 2010.

Moore, R., & Moore, D. (1975). *Better late than early*. New York: Reader's Digest.

NAEYC (National Association for the Education of Young Children) (1990). NAEYC position statement on media violence in children's lives. *Young Children, 45*(5), 18–21.

NAEYC (National Association for the Education of Young Children) (1996). NAEYC position statement: Technology and young children—ages three through eight. *Young Children, 51*(6), 11–16.

NAEYC (National Association for the Education of Young Children) (2005). Position statement: *NAEYC code of ethical conduct and statement of commitment* (Revised ed.). Brochure, Washington, DC: Author.

National Center for Educational Statistics (2008). *1.5 Million homeschooled students in the United States in 2007*. Institute of Educational Sciences Brief, U.S. Department of Education.

National Institute for Play. *Play science—the patterns of play*. Retrieved from www.nifplay.org/states_play, February 13, 2010.

National Research Council (2001). *Eager to learn: Educating our preschoolers*. Committee on Early Childhood Pedagogy. B. T. Bowman, M. S. Donovan, & M. S. Burns (Eds.). Commission on Behavioral and Social Sciences and Education. Washington, DC: National Academy Press.

Piaget, J. (1932). *The moral judgment of the child*. London: Routledge & Kegan Paul.

Pittinsky, T. L., Rosenthal, S. A., & Montoya, R. M. (2009). Allophilia: Moving beyond tolerance in the classroom. *Childhood Education, 85*(4), 212–215.

Pritchett, P. (n.d.). *New work habits for a radically changing world*. Dallas, TX: Pritchett & Associates.

Seefeldt, C. (1990). *Continuing issues in early childhood education*. New York: Prentice Hall.

Shade, D. (1996). Software evaluation. *Young Children, 51*(6), 17–22.

Sinetar, M. (1991). *Developing a 21st century mind*. New York: Academic Press.

Toffler, A. (1970). *Future shock*. New York: Random House.

Toffler, A. (1974). *Learning for tomorrow*. New York: Random House.

Toffler, A. (1980). *The third wave*. New York: Morrow.

U.S. Census Bureau (2003). *The foreign-born population: 2000. Census 2000 brief*. U.S. Department of Commerce. Available from www.census.gov

U.S. Census Bureau (2008). *Income, expenditures, poverty & wealth*. Available from www.census.gov

Wang, C. et al. (2008). Meaningful technology integration in early learning environments. *Young Children, 63*(5), 48–50.

appendix A
NAEYC Code of Ethical Conduct and Statement of Commitment

POSITION STATEMENT

naeyc

Code of Ethical Conduct and Statement of Commitment

Revised April 2005

A position statement of the National Association for the Education of Young Children

Endorsed by the Association for Childhood Education International
Adopted by the National Association for Family Child Care

Preamble

NAEYC recognizes that those who work with young children face many daily decisions that have moral and ethical implications. The **NAEYC Code of Ethical Conduct** offers guidelines for responsible behavior and sets forth a common basis for resolving the principal ethical dilemmas encountered in early childhood care and education. The **Statement of Commitment** is not part of the Code but is a personal acknowledgement of an individual's willingness to embrace the distinctive values and moral obligations of the field of early childhood care and education.

The primary focus of the Code is on daily practice with children and their families in programs for children from birth through 8 years of age, such as infant/toddler programs, preschool and prekindergarten programs, child care centers, hospital and child life settings, family child care homes, kindergartens, and primary classrooms. When the issues involve young children, then these provisions also apply to specialists who do not work directly with children, including program administrators, parent educators, early childhood adult educators, and officials with responsibility for program monitoring and licensing. (Note: See also the "Code of Ethical Conduct: Supplement for Early Childhood Adult Educators," online at www.naeyc.org/about/positions/pdf/ethics04.pdf.)

Core values

Standards of ethical behavior in early childhood care and education are based on commitment to the following core values that are deeply rooted in the history of the field of early childhood care and education. We have made a commitment to

• Appreciate childhood as a unique and valuable stage of the human life cycle

• Base our work on knowledge of how children develop and learn

• Appreciate and support the bond between the child and family

• Recognize that children are best understood and supported in the context of family, culture,* community, and society

• Respect the dignity, worth, and uniqueness of each individual (child, family member, and colleague)

• Respect diversity in children, families, and colleagues

• Recognize that children and adults achieve their full potential in the context of relationships that are based on trust and respect

---

* The term *culture* includes ethnicity, racial identity, economic level, family structure, language, and religious and political beliefs, which profoundly influence each child's development and relationship to the world.

Conceptual framework

The Code sets forth a framework of professional responsibilities in four sections. Each section addresses an area of professional relationships: (1) with children, (2) with families, (3) among colleagues, and (4) with the community and society. Each section includes an introduction to the primary responsibilities of the early childhood practitioner in that context. The introduction is followed by a set of ideals (I) that reflect exemplary professional practice and by a set of principles (P) describing practices that are required, prohibited, or permitted.

The **ideals** reflect the aspirations of practitioners. The **principles** guide conduct and assist practitioners in resolving ethical dilemmas.* Both ideals and principles are intended to direct practitioners to those questions which, when responsibly answered, can provide the basis for conscientious decision making. While the Code provides specific direction for addressing some ethical dilemmas, many others will require the practitioner to combine the guidance of the Code with professional judgment.

The ideals and principles in this Code present a shared framework of professional responsibility that affirms our commitment to the core values of our field. The Code publicly acknowledges the responsibilities that we in the field have assumed, and in so doing supports ethical behavior in our work. Practitioners who face situations with ethical dimensions are urged to seek guidance in the applicable parts of this Code and in the spirit that informs the whole.

Often "the right answer"—the best ethical course of action to take—is not obvious. There may be no readily apparent, positive way to handle a situation. When one important value contradicts another, we face an ethical dilemma. When we face a dilemma, it is our professional responsibility to consult the Code and all relevant parties to find the most ethical resolution.

Section I

Ethical Responsibilities to Children

Childhood is a unique and valuable stage in the human life cycle. Our paramount responsibility is to provide care and education in settings that are safe,

_____
* There is not necessarily a corresponding principle for each ideal.

healthy, nurturing, and responsive for each child. We are committed to supporting children's development and learning; respecting individual differences; and helping children learn to live, play, and work cooperatively. We are also committed to promoting children's self-awareness, competence, self-worth, resiliency, and physical well-being.

Ideals

I-1.1—To be familiar with the knowledge base of early childhood care and education and to stay informed through continuing education and training.

I-1.2—To base program practices upon current knowledge and research in the field of early childhood education, child development, and related disciplines, as well as on particular knowledge of each child.

I-1.3—To recognize and respect the unique qualities, abilities, and potential of each child.

I-1.4—To appreciate the vulnerability of children and their dependence on adults.

I-1.5—To create and maintain safe and healthy settings that foster children's social, emotional, cognitive, and physical development and that respect their dignity and their contributions.

I-1.6—To use assessment instruments and strategies that are appropriate for the children to be assessed, that are used only for the purposes for which they were designed, and that have the potential to benefit children.

I-1.7—To use assessment information to understand and support children's development and learning, to support instruction, and to identify children who may need additional services.

I-1.8—To support the right of each child to play and learn in an inclusive environment that meets the needs of children with and without disabilities.

I-1.9—To advocate for and ensure that all children, including those with special needs, have access to the support services needed to be successful.

I-1.10—To ensure that each child's culture, language, ethnicity, and family structure are recognized and valued in the program.

I-1.11—To provide all children with experiences in a language that they know, as well as support children in maintaining the use of their home language and in learning English.

I-1.12—To work with families to provide a safe and smooth transition as children and families move from one program to the next.

3

Principles

P-1.1—Above all, we shall not harm children. We shall not participate in practices that are emotionally damaging, physically harmful, disrespectful, degrading, dangerous, exploitative, or intimidating to children. *This principle has precedence over all others in this Code.*

P-1.2—We shall care for and educate children in positive emotional and social environments that are cognitively stimulating and that support each child's culture, language, ethnicity, and family structure.

P-1.3—We shall not participate in practices that discriminate against children by denying benefits, giving special advantages, or excluding them from programs or activities on the basis of their sex, race, national origin, religious beliefs, medical condition, disability, or the marital status/family structure, sexual orientation, or religious beliefs or other affiliations of their families. (Aspects of this principle do not apply in programs that have a lawful mandate to provide services to a particular population of children.)

P-1.4—We shall involve all those with relevant knowledge (including families and staff) in decisions concerning a child, as appropriate, ensuring confidentiality of sensitive information.

P-1.5—We shall use appropriate assessment systems, which include multiple sources of information, to provide information on children's learning and development.

P-1.6—We shall strive to ensure that decisions such as those related to enrollment, retention, or assignment to special education services, will be based on multiple sources of information and will never be based on a single assessment, such as a test score or a single observation.

P-1.7—We shall strive to build individual relationships with each child; make individualized adaptations in teaching strategies, learning environments, and curricula; and consult with the family so that each child benefits from the program. If after such efforts have been exhausted, the current placement does not meet a child's needs, or the child is seriously jeopardizing the ability of other children to benefit from the program, we shall collaborate with the child's family and appropriate specialists to determine the additional services needed and/or the placement option(s) most likely to ensure the child's success. (Aspects of this principle may not apply in programs that have a lawful mandate to provide services to a particular population of children.)

P-1.8—We shall be familiar with the risk factors for and symptoms of child abuse and neglect, including physical, sexual, verbal, and emotional abuse and physical, emotional, educational, and medical neglect. We shall know and follow state laws and community procedures that protect children against abuse and neglect.

P-1.9—When we have reasonable cause to suspect child abuse or neglect, we shall report it to the appropriate community agency and follow up to ensure that appropriate action has been taken. When appropriate, parents or guardians will be informed that the referral will be or has been made.

P-1.10—When another person tells us of his or her suspicion that a child is being abused or neglected, we shall assist that person in taking appropriate action in order to protect the child.

P-1.11—When we become aware of a practice or situation that endangers the health, safety, or well-being of children, we have an ethical responsibility to protect children or inform parents and/or others who can.

Section II

Ethical Responsibilities to Families

Families* are of primary importance in children's development. Because the family and the early childhood practitioner have a common interest in the child's well-being, we acknowledge a primary responsibility to bring about communication, cooperation, and collaboration between the home and early childhood program in ways that enhance the child's development.

Ideals

I-2.1—To be familiar with the knowledge base related to working effectively with families and to stay informed through continuing education and training.

I-2.2—To develop relationships of mutual trust and create partnerships with the families we serve.

I-2.3—To welcome all family members and encourage them to participate in the program.

---

* The term *family* may include those adults, besides parents, with the responsibility of being involved in educating, nurturing, and advocating for the child.

I-2.4—To listen to families, acknowledge and build upon their strengths and competencies, and learn from families as we support them in their task of nurturing children.

I-2.5—To respect the dignity and preferences of each family and to make an effort to learn about its structure, culture, language, customs, and beliefs.

I-2.6—To acknowledge families' childrearing values and their right to make decisions for their children.

I-2.7—To share information about each child's education and development with families and to help them understand and appreciate the current knowledge base of the early childhood profession.

I-2.8—To help family members enhance their understanding of their children and support the continuing development of their skills as parents.

I-2.9—To participate in building support networks for families by providing them with opportunities to interact with program staff, other families, community resources, and professional services.

Principles

P-2.1—We shall not deny family members access to their child's classroom or program setting unless access is denied by court order or other legal restriction.

P-2.2—We shall inform families of program philosophy, policies, curriculum, assessment system, and personnel qualifications, and explain why we teach as we do—which should be in accordance with our ethical responsibilities to children (see Section I).

P-2.3—We shall inform families of and, when appropriate, involve them in policy decisions.

P-2.4—We shall involve the family in significant decisions affecting their child.

P-2.5—We shall make every effort to communicate effectively with all families in a language that they understand. We shall use community resources for translation and interpretation when we do not have sufficient resources in our own programs.

P-2.6—As families share information with us about their children and families, we shall consider this information to plan and implement the program.

P-2.7—We shall inform families about the nature and purpose of the program's child assessments and how data about their child will be used.

P-2.8—We shall treat child assessment information confidentially and share this information only when there is a legitimate need for it.

P-2.9—We shall inform the family of injuries and incidents involving their child, of risks such as exposures to communicable diseases that might result in infection, and of occurrences that might result in emotional stress.

P-2.10—Families shall be fully informed of any proposed research projects involving their children and shall have the opportunity to give or withhold consent without penalty. We shall not permit or participate in research that could in any way hinder the education, development, or well-being of children.

P-2.11—We shall not engage in or support exploitation of families. We shall not use our relationship with a family for private advantage or personal gain, or enter into relationships with family members that might impair our effectiveness working with their children.

P-2.12—We shall develop written policies for the protection of confidentiality and the disclosure of children's records. These policy documents shall be made available to all program personnel and families. Disclosure of children's records beyond family members, program personnel, and consultants having an obligation of confidentiality shall require familial consent (except in cases of abuse or neglect).

P-2.13—We shall maintain confidentiality and shall respect the family's right to privacy, refraining from disclosure of confidential information and intrusion into family life. However, when we have reason to believe that a child's welfare is at risk, it is permissible to share confidential information with agencies, as well as with individuals who have legal responsibility for intervening in the child's interest.

P-2.14—In cases where family members are in conflict with one another, we shall work openly, sharing our observations of the child, to help all parties involved make informed decisions. We shall refrain from becoming an advocate for one party.

P-2.15—We shall be familiar with and appropriately refer families to community resources and professional support services. After a referral has been made, we shall follow up to ensure that services have been appropriately provided.

Section III

Ethical Responsibilities to Colleagues

In a caring, cooperative workplace, human dignity is respected, professional satisfaction is promoted, and positive relationships are developed and sustained. Based upon our core values, our primary responsibility to colleagues is to establish and maintain settings and relationships that support productive work and meet professional needs. The same ideals that apply to children also apply as we interact with adults in the workplace.

A—Responsibilities to co-workers

Ideals

I-3A.1—To establish and maintain relationships of respect, trust, confidentiality, collaboration, and cooperation with co-workers.

I-3A.2—To share resources with co-workers, collaborating to ensure that the best possible early childhood care and education program is provided.

I-3A.3—To support co-workers in meeting their professional needs and in their professional development.

I-3A.4—To accord co-workers due recognition of professional achievement.

Principles

P-3A.1—We shall recognize the contributions of colleagues to our program and not participate in practices that diminish their reputations or impair their effectiveness in working with children and families.

P-3A.2—When we have concerns about the professional behavior of a co-worker, we shall first let that person know of our concern in a way that shows respect for personal dignity and for the diversity to be found among staff members, and then attempt to resolve the matter collegially and in a confidential manner.

P-3A.3—We shall exercise care in expressing views regarding the personal attributes or professional conduct of co-workers. Statements should be based on firsthand knowledge, not hearsay, and relevant to the interests of children and programs.

P-3A.4—We shall not participate in practices that discriminate against a co-worker because of sex, race, national origin, religious beliefs or other affiliations, age, marital status/family structure, disability, or sexual orientation.

B—Responsibilities to employers

Ideals

I-3B.1—To assist the program in providing the highest quality of service.

I-3B.2—To do nothing that diminishes the reputation of the program in which we work unless it is violating laws and regulations designed to protect children or is violating the provisions of this Code.

Principles

P-3B.1—We shall follow all program policies. When we do not agree with program policies, we shall attempt to effect change through constructive action within the organization.

P-3B.2—We shall speak or act on behalf of an organization only when authorized. We shall take care to acknowledge when we are speaking for the organization and when we are expressing a personal judgment.

P-3B.3—We shall not violate laws or regulations designed to protect children and shall take appropriate action consistent with this Code when aware of such violations.

P-3B.4—If we have concerns about a colleague's behavior, and children's well-being is not at risk, we may address the concern with that individual. If children are at risk or the situation does not improve after it has been brought to the colleague's attention, we shall report the colleague's unethical or incompetent behavior to an appropriate authority.

P-3B.5—When we have a concern about circumstances or conditions that impact the quality of care and education within the program, we shall inform the program's administration or, when necessary, other appropriate authorities.

C—Responsibilities to employees

Ideals

I-3C.1—To promote safe and healthy working conditions and policies that foster mutual respect, cooperation, collaboration, competence, well-being, confidentiality, and self-esteem in staff members.

I-3C.2—To create and maintain a climate of trust and candor that will enable staff to speak and act in the best interests of children, families, and the field of early childhood care and education.

I-3C.3—To strive to secure adequate and equitable compensation (salary and benefits) for those who work with or on behalf of young children.

I-3C.4—To encourage and support continual development of employees in becoming more skilled and knowledgeable practitioners.

Principles

P-3C.1—In decisions concerning children and programs, we shall draw upon the education, training, experience, and expertise of staff members.

P-3C.2—We shall provide staff members with safe and supportive working conditions that honor confidences and permit them to carry out their responsibilities through fair performance evaluation, written grievance procedures, constructive feedback, and opportunities for continuing professional development and advancement.

P-3C.3—We shall develop and maintain comprehensive written personnel policies that define program standards. These policies shall be given to new staff members and shall be available and easily accessible for review by all staff members.

P-3C.4—We shall inform employees whose performance does not meet program expectations of areas of concern and, when possible, assist in improving their performance.

P-3C.5—We shall conduct employee dismissals for just cause, in accordance with all applicable laws and regulations. We shall inform employees who are dismissed of the reasons for their termination. When a dismissal is for cause, justification must be based on evidence of inadequate or inappropriate behavior that is accurately documented, current, and available for the employee to review.

P-3C.6—In making evaluations and recommendations, we shall make judgments based on fact and relevant to the interests of children and programs.

P-3C.7—We shall make hiring, retention, termination, and promotion decisions based solely on a person's competence, record of accomplishment, ability to carry out the responsibilities of the position, and professional preparation specific to the developmental levels of children in his/her care.

P-3C.8—We shall not make hiring, retention, termination, and promotion decisions based on an individual's sex, race, national origin, religious beliefs or other affiliations, age, marital status/family structure, disability, or sexual orientation. We shall be familiar with and observe laws and regulations that pertain to employment discrimination. (Aspects of this principle do not apply to programs that have a lawful mandate to determine eligibility based on one or more of the criteria identified above.)

P-3C.9—We shall maintain confidentiality in dealing with issues related to an employee's job performance and shall respect an employee's right to privacy regarding personal issues.

Section IV

Ethical Responsibilities to Community and Society

Early childhood programs operate within the context of their immediate community made up of families and other institutions concerned with children's welfare. Our responsibilities to the community are to provide programs that meet the diverse needs of families, to cooperate with agencies and professions that share the responsibility for children, to assist families in gaining access to those agencies and allied professionals, and to assist in the development of community programs that are needed but not currently available.

As individuals, we acknowledge our responsibility to provide the best possible programs of care and education for children and to conduct ourselves with honesty and integrity. Because of our specialized expertise in early childhood development and education and because the larger society shares responsibility for the welfare and protection of young children, we acknowledge a collective obligation to advocate for the best interests of children within early childhood programs and in the larger community and to serve as a voice for young children everywhere.

The ideals and principles in this section are presented to distinguish between those that pertain to the work of the individual early childhood educator and those that more typically are engaged in collectively on behalf of the best interests of children—with the understanding that individual early childhood educators have a shared responsibility for addressing the ideals and principles that are identified as "collective."

Ideal (Individual)

I-4.1—To provide the community with high-quality early childhood care and education programs and services.

Ideals (Collective)

I-4.2—To promote cooperation among professionals and agencies and interdisciplinary collaboration among professions concerned with addressing issues in the health, education, and well-being of young children, their families, and their early childhood educators.

I-4.3—To work through education, research, and advocacy toward an environmentally safe world in which all children receive health care, food, and shelter; are nurtured; and live free from violence in their home and their communities.

I-4.4—To work through education, research, and advocacy toward a society in which all young children have access to high-quality early care and education programs.

I-4.5—To work to ensure that appropriate assessment systems, which include multiple sources of information, are used for purposes that benefit children.

I-4.6—To promote knowledge and understanding of young children and their needs. To work toward greater societal acknowledgment of children's rights and greater social acceptance of responsibility for the well-being of all children.

I-4.7—To support policies and laws that promote the well-being of children and families, and to work to change those that impair their well-being. To participate in developing policies and laws that are needed, and to cooperate with other individuals and groups in these efforts.

I-4.8—To further the professional development of the field of early childhood care and education and to strengthen its commitment to realizing its core values as reflected in this Code.

Principles (Individual)

P-4.1—We shall communicate openly and truthfully about the nature and extent of services that we provide.

P-4.2—We shall apply for, accept, and work in positions for which we are personally well-suited and professionally qualified. We shall not offer services that we

do not have the competence, qualifications, or resources to provide.

P-4.3—We shall carefully check references and shall not hire or recommend for employment any person whose competence, qualifications, or character makes him or her unsuited for the position.

P-4.4—We shall be objective and accurate in reporting the knowledge upon which we base our program practices.

P-4.5—We shall be knowledgeable about the appropriate use of assessment strategies and instruments and interpret results accurately to families.

P-4.6—We shall be familiar with laws and regulations that serve to protect the children in our programs and be vigilant in ensuring that these laws and regulations are followed.

P-4.7—When we become aware of a practice or situation that endangers the health, safety, or well-being of children, we have an ethical responsibility to protect children or inform parents and/or others who can.

P-4.8—We shall not participate in practices that are in violation of laws and regulations that protect the children in our programs.

P-4.9—When we have evidence that an early childhood program is violating laws or regulations protecting children, we shall report the violation to appropriate authorities who can be expected to remedy the situation.

P-4.10—When a program violates or requires its employees to violate this Code, it is permissible, after fair assessment of the evidence, to disclose the identity of that program.

Principles (Collective)

P-4.11—When policies are enacted for purposes that do not benefit children, we have a collective responsibility to work to change these practices.

P-4.12—When we have evidence that an agency that provides services intended to ensure children's well-being is failing to meet its obligations, we acknowledge a collective ethical responsibility to report the problem to appropriate authorities or to the public. We shall be vigilant in our follow-up until the situation is resolved.

P-4.13—When a child protection agency fails to provide adequate protection for abused or neglected children, we acknowledge a collective ethical responsibility to work toward the improvement of these services.

Glossary of Terms Related to Ethics

Code of Ethics. Defines the core values of the field and provides guidance for what professionals should do when they encounter conflicting obligations or responsibilities in their work.

Values. Qualities or principles that individuals believe to be desirable or worthwhile and that they prize for themselves, for others, and for the world in which they live.

Core Values. Commitments held by a profession that are consciously and knowingly embraced by its practitioners because they make a contribution to society. There is a difference between personal values and the core values of a profession.

Morality. Peoples' views of what is good, right, and proper; their beliefs about their obligations; and their ideas about how they should behave.

Ethics. The study of right and wrong, or duty and obligation, that involves critical reflection on morality and the ability to make choices between values and the examination of the moral dimensions of relationships.

Professional Ethics. The moral commitments of a profession that involve moral reflection that extends and enhances the personal morality practitioners bring to their work, that concern actions of right and wrong in the workplace, and that help individuals resolve moral dilemmas they encounter in their work.

Ethical Responsibilities. Behaviors that one must or must not engage in. Ethical responsibilities are clear-cut and are spelled out in the Code of Ethical Conduct (for example, early childhood educators should never share confidential information about a child or family with a person who has no legitimate need for knowing).

Ethical Dilemma. A moral conflict that involves determining appropriate conduct when an individual faces conflicting professional values and responsibilities.

Sources for glossary terms and definitions

Feeney, S., & N. Freeman. 1999. *Ethics and the early childhood educator: Using the NAEYC code.* Washington, DC: NAEYC.
Kidder, R.M. 1995. *How good people make tough choices: Resolving the dilemmas of ethical living.* New York: Fireside.
Kipnis, K. 1987. How to discuss professional ethics. *Young Children* 42 (4): 26–30.

The National Association for the Education of Young Children (NAEYC) is a nonprofit corporation, tax exempt under Section 501(c)(3) of the Internal Revenue Code, dedicated to acting on behalf of the needs and interests of young children. The NAEYC Code of Ethical Conduct (Code) has been developed in furtherance of NAEYC's nonprofit and tax exempt purposes. The information contained in the Code is intended to provide early childhood educators with guidelines for working with children from birth through age 8.

An individual's or program's use, reference to, or review of the Code does not guarantee compliance with NAEYC Early Childhood Program Standards and Accreditation Performance Criteria and program accreditation procedures. It is recommended that the Code be used as guidance in connection with implementation of the NAEYC Program Standards, but such use is not a substitute for diligent review and application of the NAEYC Program Standards.

NAEYC has taken reasonable measures to develop the Code in a fair, reasonable, open, unbiased, and objective manner, based on currently available data. However, further research or developments may change the current state of knowledge. Neither NAEYC nor its officers, directors, members, employees, or agents will be liable for any loss, damage, or claim with respect to any liabilities, including direct, special, indirect, or consequential damages incurred in connection with the Code or reliance on the information presented.

NAEYC Code of Ethical Conduct Revisions Workgroup

Mary Ambery, Ruth Ann Ball, James Clay, Julie Olsen Edwards, Harriet Egertson, Anthony Fair, Stephanie Feeney, Jana Fleming, Nancy Freeman, Marla Israel, Allison McKinnon, Evelyn Wright Moore, Eva Moravcik, Christina Lopez Morgan, Sarah Mulligan, Nila Rinehart, Betty Holston Smith, and Peter Pizzolongo, *NAEYC Staff*

Statement of Commitment*

As an individual who works with young children, I commit myself to furthering the values of early childhood education as they are reflected in the ideals and principles of the NAEYC Code of Ethical Conduct. To the best of my ability I will

- Never harm children.
- Ensure that programs for young children are based on current knowledge and research of child development and early childhood education.
- Respect and support families in their task of nurturing children.
- Respect colleagues in early childhood care and education and support them in maintaining the NAEYC Code of Ethical Conduct.
- Serve as an advocate for children, their families, and their teachers in community and society.
- Stay informed of and maintain high standards of professional conduct.
- Engage in an ongoing process of self-reflection, realizing that personal characteristics, biases, and beliefs have an impact on children and families.
- Be open to new ideas and be willing to learn from the suggestions of others.
- Continue to learn, grow, and contribute as a professional.
- Honor the ideals and principles of the NAEYC Code of Ethical Conduct.

---

* This Statement of Commitment is not part of the Code but is a personal acknowledgment of the individual's willingness to embrace the distinctive values and moral obligations of the field of early childhood care and education. It is recognition of the moral obligations that lead to an individual becoming part of the profession.

appendix B
DEC Code of Ethics

CODE OF ETHICS

August 2009

The Code of Ethics of the Division for Early Childhood (DEC) of the Council for Exceptional Children is a public statement of principles and practice guidelines supported by the mission of DEC.

The foundation of this Code is based on sound ethical reasoning related to professional practice with young children with disabilities and their families and with interdisciplinary colleagues. Foremost, is our value of respecting the autonomy of families as they make decisions for their young children with disabilities while also practicing a mutual respect for our colleagues in the field. We, as early childhood professionals, practice within the principles and guidelines outlined below as well as uphold the laws and regulations of our professional licensure standards.

The Code's purpose is to: (1) identify the key principles guiding our professional conduct; and (2) provide guidance for practice and personal dilemmas in our conduct of research and practice. The Code is intended to assist professionals in resolving conflicts as they arise in practice with children and families and with other colleagues.

The following principles and guidelines for practice include:

    I.   Professional Practice;
   II.   Professional Development and Preparation;
  III.   Responsive Family Practices; and
  IV.   Ethical and Evidence Based Practices.

I.   **PROFESSIONAL PRACTICE** encompasses the practice principles to promote and maintain high standards of conduct for the early childhood special education professional. The early childhood special education professional should base his or her behaviors on ethical reasoning surrounding practice and professional issues as well as an empathic reflection regarding interactions with others. We are committed to beneficence acts for improving the quality of lives of young children with disabilities and their families. The guidelines for practice outlined below provide a framework for everyday practice when working with children and families and with other professionals in the field of early childhood special education.

    Professional and Interpersonal Behavior

       1.   We shall demonstrate in our behavior and language respect and appreciation for the unique value and human potential of each child.

       2.   We shall demonstrate the highest standards of personal integrity, truthfulness, and honesty in all our professional activities in order to inspire the trust and confidence of the children and families and of those with whom we work.

       3.   We shall strive for the highest level of personal and professional competence by seeking and using new evidence based information to improve our practices while also responding openly to the suggestions of others.

       4.   We shall serve as advocates for children with disabilities and their families and for the professionals who serve them by supporting both policy and programmatic decisions that enhance the quality of their lives.

CODE OF ETHICS

5. We shall use individually appropriate assessment strategies including multiple sources of information such as observations, interviews with significant caregivers, formal and informal assessments to determine children's learning styles, strengths, and challenges.

6. We shall build relationships with individual children and families while individualizing the curricula and learning environments to facilitate young children's development and learning.

Professional Collaboration

1. We shall honor and respect our responsibilities to colleagues while upholding the dignity and autonomy of colleagues and maintaining collegial interprofessional and intraprofessional relationships.

2. We shall honor and respect the rights, knowledge, and skills of the multidisciplinary colleagues with whom we work recognizing their unique contributions to children, families, and the field of early childhood special education.

3. We shall honor and respect the diverse backgrounds of our colleagues including such diverse characteristics as sexual orientation, race, national origin, religious beliefs, or other affiliations.

4. We shall identify and disclose to the appropriate persons using proper communication channels errors or acts of incompetence that compromise children's and families' safety and well being when individual attempts to address concerns are unsuccessful.

II. **PROFESSIONAL DEVELOPMENT AND PREPARATION** is critical to providing the most effective services for young children with disabilities and their families. Professional development is viewed and valued as an ongoing process guided by high standards and competencies for professional performance and practice. Professionals acquire the knowledge, skills, and dispositions to work with a variety of young children with disabilities and their families within natural and inclusive environments promoting children's overall growth, development and learning, and enhancing family quality of life. Finally, professionals continually should seek and interpret evidence based information for planning and implementing individually appropriate learning environments linked to ongoing assessment and collaboration with parents and professional team members.

1. We shall engage in ongoing and systematic reflective inquiry and self-assessment for the purpose of continuous improvement of professional performance and services to young children with disabilities and their families.

2. We shall continually be aware of issues challenging the field of early childhood special education and advocate for changes in laws, regulations, and policies leading to improved outcomes and services for young children with disabilities and their families.

3. We shall be responsible for maintaining the appropriate national, state, or other credential or licensure requirements for the services we provide while maintaining our competence in practice and research by ongoing participation in professional development and education activities.

4. We shall support professionals new to the field by mentoring them in the practice of evidence and ethically based services.

III. **RESPONSIVE FAMILY CENTERED PRACTICES** ensure that families receive individualized, meaningful, and relevant services responsive to their beliefs, values, customs, languages, and culture. We are committed to enhancing the quality of children's and families' lives by promoting family well-being and participation in typical life activities. The early childhood special education professional will demonstrate respect for all families, taking into consideration and acknowledging diverse family structures, culture, language, values, and customs. Finally, families will be given equal voice in all decision making relative to their children. The following practice guidelines provide a framework for enhancing children's and families' quality of lives.

CODE OF ETHICS

Enhancement of Children's and Families' Quality of Lives

1. We shall demonstrate our respect and concern for children, families, colleagues, and others with whom we work, honoring their beliefs, values, customs, languages, and culture.

2. We shall recognize our responsibility to improve the developmental outcomes of children and to provide services and supports in a fair and equitable manner to all families and children.

3. We shall recognize and respect the dignity, diversity, and autonomy of the families and children we serve.

4. We shall advocate for equal access to high quality services and supports for all children and families to enhance their quality of lives.

Responsive Family Centered Practices

1. We shall demonstrate our respect and appreciation for all families' beliefs, values, customs, languages, and culture relative to their nurturance and support of their children toward achieving meaningful and relevant priorities and outcomes families' desire for themselves and their children.

2. We shall provide services and supports to children and families in a fair and equitable manner while respecting families' culture, race, language, socioeconomic status, marital status, and sexual orientation.

3. We shall respect, value, promote, and encourage the active participation of ALL families by engaging families in meaningful ways in the assessment and intervention processes.

4. We shall empower families with information and resources so that they are informed consumers of services for their children.

5. We shall collaborate with families and colleagues in setting meaningful and relevant goals and priorities throughout the intervention process including the full disclosure of the nature, risk, and potential outcomes of any interventions.

6. We shall respect families' rights to choose or refuse early childhood special education or related services.

7. We shall be responsible for protecting the confidentiality of the children and families we serve by protecting all forms of verbal, written, and electronic communication.

IV. **ETHICAL AND EVIDENCE BASED PRACTICES** in the field of early childhood special education relies upon sound research methodologies and research based practices to ensure high quality services for children and families. As professionals researching and practicing within the field, it is our responsibility to maintain ethical conduct in building a cadre of practices based on evidence. Establishing an evidence base not only involves critically examining available research evidence relative to our professional practices, it also involves continually engaging in research to further refine our research-based or recommended practices.

Sound and ethical research strategies always should be used including adherence to institutional review board procedures and guidelines prior to the conduct of research and use of peer-reviewed venues for published dissemination of findings. Honoring and respecting the diversity of children and families should guide all research activities.

Evidence Based Practices

1. We shall rely upon evidence based research and interventions to inform our practice with children and families in our care.

CODE OF ETHICS

2. We shall use every resource, including referral when appropriate, to ensure high quality services are accessible and are provided to children and families.

3. We shall include the diverse perspectives and experiences of children and families in the conduct of research and intervention.

Ethical Practice in Research

1. We shall use research designs and analyses in an appropriate manner by providing a clear rationale for each. We shall provide enough information about the methodologies we use so that others can replicate the work.

2. We shall maintain records of research securely; no personal information about research participants should be revealed unless required by law.

3. We shall conduct on-going research and field work that is consistent with and builds upon the available cadre of evidence based practices.

4. We shall utilize collaborative and interdisciplinary research for strengthening linkages between the research and practice communities, as well as for improving the quality of life of children with disabilities and their families.

ACKNOWLEDGEMENTS

DEC appreciates the work of DEC members who participated in the revision of the Code of Ethics: Harriet Boone (chair), Cynthia Core, Sharon Darling, Terri Patterson, Cheryl Rhodes, & Dianna Valle-Riestra.

APPROVED BY THE DEC EXECUTIVE BOARD: SEPTEMBER 1996
REAFFIRMED: APRIL 16, 1999
REAFFIRMED: DECEMBER 5, 2002
APPROVED FOR FIELD REVIEW: OCTOBER 27, 2008
APPROVED BY THE DEC EXECUTIVE BOARD: AUGUST 11, 2009

Division for Early Childhood
27 Fort Missoula Road • Missoula, MT • 59804 • Phone: 406-543-0872 • Fax: 406-543-0887
E-mail: dec@dec-sped.org • www.dec-sped.org

Permission to copy not required – distribution encouraged.

Index